ANTISEMITISM IN THE
ARAB-ISRAELI CONFLICT

Antisemitism in the Arab-Israeli Conflict

TIME TO CONFRONT THE ELEPHANT IN THE ROOM

DAVID H STONE

VALLENTINE MITCHELL
LONDON • CHICAGO

First published in 2025 by Vallentine Mitchell

Catalyst House,
720 Centennial Court,
Centennial Park, Elstree WD6 3SY, UK

814 N. Franklin Street,
Chicago, Illinois,
IL 60610 USA

www.vmbooks.com

Copyright © 2025 David Stone

British Library Cataloguing in Publication Data:
An entry can be found on request

ISBN 978 1 80371 064 8 (Hardback)
ISBN 978 1 80371 054 9 (Paperback)
ISBN 978 1 80371 055 6 (Ebook)
ISBN 978 1 80371 056 3 (Kindle)

Library of Congress Cataloging in Publication Data:
An entry can be found on request

For Harry, Sofia, Leo, Clara, Diego,
Amelie, Marla, Lavi and Ariyah.

Contents

All our aspiration is built on the assumption – proven throughout all our activity in the Land – that there is enough room in the country for ourselves and the Arabs.

David Ben-Gurion

The immoderate egoism inherent in the Jews' nature ... makes them incapable of keeping faith with anyone or of mixing with any other nation: they live, rather, as parasites among peoples, suck their blood, steal their property, pervert their morals.

Haj Amin al-Husseini

For the Jews the essential point of principle is the creation of a sovereign Jewish State. For the Arabs, the essential point of principle is to resist to the last the establishment of Jewish sovereignty in any part of Palestine.

Ernest Bevin

The primary and sustaining cause of the Arab-Israeli conflict is genocidal antisemitism; the rest is footnotes. It's as simple as that. And it's as serious as that.

Mark Pickles

Politics is nothing else but medicine on a large scale.

Rudolf Virchow

List of Images

1. Map of Middle East and North Africa.

2. Horseshoe Theory.

3. 'Israeli Apartheid' banner.

4. Zionist leader Nahum Sokolow (possibly 1922).

5. Group of young Iraqi Jews who fled to Palestine following the 1941 Farhud pogrom in Baghdad.

6. The Mufti meets Hitler Berlin 1941.

7. President Nasser in 1962.

8. Yasser Arafat addressing the UN.

9. Rabin, Clinton Arafat sign Oslo Accord on White House lawn 1993.

10. Signing of Abraham Accords 2020.

Acknowledgements

I am indebted to numerous friends, colleagues and family members who have helped me crystallise my thoughts around this complex and often distressing subject.

I cannot mention all of who have helped me in this project but particular thanks go to: Michael Dickson, Isaac Zarfati, Lana Betesh, Devora Stoll, Neil Blair, Irene Naftalin, and my many other friends at *StandWithUs* who encouraged me to undertake the work and who have been supportive throughout; Professor Michael Baum and Lord Leslie Turnberg who ceaselessly probed and challenged my central hypothesis; Toby Harris, Sue Garfield and Jenni Tinson at Vallentine Mitchell who patiently guided me through the editorial and publishing process; and an anonymous reviewer who offered advice and suggestions that greatly improved the text.

Finally, any insights I have gained in researching this topic are the result of my standing atop the shoulders of giants – Bernard Lewis, Walter Laqueur, Martin Gilbert, Lyn Julius, Robin Shepherd, Daniel Goldhagen, Matthias Küntzel, Efraim Karsh, Ben-Dror Yemini, Adi Schwartz, Einat Wilf, David Collier, Gerald Steinberg, Itamar Marcus, Hillel Neuer, Alan Johnson and many others too numerous to name. Without their revelatory work I would still be scrambling in search of the elusive key to the understanding of this most frustrating and seemingly intractable of conflicts.

Preface

During the writing of this book, a calamity struck the Jewish state of Israel. On Shabbat (Saturday) 7th October 2023, on the joyful festival of *Simchat Torah*, an antisemitic Islamist paramilitary group, Hamas, perpetrated a large-scale massacre of Israelis. In a frenzy of violence, Gaza-based Palestinian terrorists breached the border with Israel and murdered around 1,200 people, mostly civilians, raped women, killed children in front of their parents or vice versa, burned alive entire families, paraded mutilated bodies like trophies, and dragged hundreds of hostages of all ages into Gaza. The attackers posted their gruesome exploits on social media, spreading grief and terror throughout the country. Israeli commentators described it as the most terrible day in Israel's history. Its savagery evoked bitter memories of the brutal attacks on Jews in nineteenth and twentieth century Europe.

Many called it the worst pogrom since the Holocaust. In the hours following the attack – and even before Israel launched her counteroffensive on the Gazan-based terrorists – a tsunami of fear engulfed the Jewish diaspora as thousands of flag-waving activists marched through capitals chanting explicitly anti-Jewish slogans and proclaiming their solidarity not with the victims but with the murderers.

If definitive proof were needed of the lethal role in the twenty-first century of antisemitism in the unappeasable hatred of Israel, both in the Middle East and throughout the world, this was surely it. Yet the very existence of the phenomenon in the prolonged violent stand-off between Arabs and Jews has long been denied, ignored or belittled, with disastrous consequences. It was and remains the elephant in the room that has bedevilled attempts to achieve a just peace between Israel and her adversaries, including the Palestinians, for over a century. That grim reality is the necessary context for anyone wishing to understand the origins and persistence of the Arab-Israeli conflict.

Foreword

Clausewitz tells us that war is politics by other means. To any civilised person this means war is always a catastrophic failure of politics. The relevance of that looms large in this analysis of the decades-long Arab-Israeli conflict.

Why has politics failed the long-suffering people of Israel and its neighbours? Anyone with even the most cursory knowledge of the Middle East will be aware of the numerous failed attempts to forge a durable peace between the Jewish state and its enemies. That began to change with what might best be described as 'cold peace' treaties with Egypt and Jordan. In recent years some other Arab countries have also sought a warmer peace with Israel, most notably the UAE and Bahrain through the Abraham Accords, while Saudi Arabia itself now seems to be getting closer to normalising relations.

But still, the genocidal mullahs of Iran and the various Palestinian organisations remain implacably opposed to Israel's continued existence, let alone its right to live in peace and security. In contrast to the complex ramifications of the conflict that fill today's media to an obsessive degree, the underlying cause is as simple as it is disturbing: antisemitism.

Throughout the fourteen centuries since the era of Muhammad, antipathy to Jews in Muslim lands has waxed and waned according to the individual inclinations of the rulers. Jews, like Christians, were granted the status of *dhimmis* that in theory protected them from abuse but in reality consigned them to second-class citizenship.

Although the murderous hatred that characterised much antisemitism in Europe was largely absent in the Middle East and North Africa, that changed in the early twentieth century with the founding of the Muslim Brotherhood in Egypt, an extreme Sunni religious movement that gave rise to what today we call Islamism and still finds violent expression in contemporary jihadist groups as well as among populations influenced by them.

In the late 1930s, the Brothers' anti-Jewish zealots found kindred spirits in the Nazi leadership. The resultant toxic cocktail of extreme nationalist ideologies would all but guarantee that, if allowed to proliferate unchecked, Arab anti-Zionism would effectively become Nazified. Given the visceral anti-Jewish loathing that has characterised Zionism's enemies since before the establishment of modern Israel in 1948 until today, the massacre of Israelis and others on 7 October 2023 by Hamas as well as ordinary Gazan civilians was shocking but unsurprising. The immediate aftermath, which I saw for myself, was horrifically reminiscent of a bloody scene from the Nazi Holocaust. That atrocity starkly characterises the role that homicidal antisemitism still plays in sustaining the conflict.

All war is tragic but the century-long conflict between Arabs and Jews is all the more so for being avoidable. The historical record of repeated Zionist and Israeli attempts at peace-making through territorial compromise ('land for peace') has never been reciprocated by Israel's most intransigent foes. 7th October itself was the consequence of a form of 'two-state solution' between Israel and Gaza. The result is a lethal deadlock, since the demands of the Arab, Iranian and Islamist 'axis of resistance' cannot be realised without the annihilation of the world's only Jewish state. Having suffered close to two millennia of exile, persecution, pogroms and latterly genocide, the Jewish people will simply not give up their re-established sovereignty in their historical homeland no matter how hard they must fight for it.

The extraordinary rebirth of Israel against the odds was paid for in blood, both Jewish and Arab, and that painful toll will continue to be extracted unless Palestinian Arab and Iranian dreams to destroy the 'Zionist entity' are finally abandoned.

The historical origins and continuing influence of unquenchable Jew-hatred form the core of this book. Stone's diagnosis may seem pessimistic but in truth it also offers hope. Acknowledgement of the hard reality could help pave the way to successful intervention by opening the eyes of an ignorant and sometimes complicit international community. A community that includes politicians, the media, human rights groups, universities and professional 'peace processors' which has, more often than not, exacerbated rather than ameliorated the conflict. In the 2023-2024 Gaza war, for example, there is no question that the words and actions of much of this community has encouraged and strengthened Hamas terrorists and their Iranian masters, and thus extended the conflict and increased the bloodshed.

While it may be more convenient and politically correct for Westerners to blame 'both sides' at best, or, more usually the Israelis alone, such dangerous posturing must be exposed for what it is. We all need to wake up to reality and take steps to confront and neutralise the incontrovertible truth of this conflict: the Palestinian Arabs, the Iranian fanatics, and those who support them, utterly reject the existence of a Jewish state in this land whatever form it might take. Only when that is admitted will Israelis, Arabs, Iranians and others caught up in this protracted dispute stand any chance of enjoying the fruits of a peaceful future that is surely the birthright of every human being.

Richard Kemp
Former British Army Commander

Introduction

On 2 June 1967, I was a first-year medical student with minimal interest in Zionism or in the long-running conflict between Arabs and Jews in the Middle East. If anything, I was resistant to the whole notion of a Jewish state. Twenty-four hours later I was fully committed to Zionism and Israel. What changed in that short window of time? Two things. First, my belated discovery of the hair-raising threats pouring forth from the Arab world against Israel that preceded the Six Day War. I was too young to appreciate the nature of this hatred – and only much later did I discover the atavistic source that lent it nourishment. Second, an extraordinary televised press conference in which the newly appointed Israeli Defence Minister, Moshe Dayan, responded to a journalist's question about the world's passivity (and I paraphrase): 'We don't want a single American or British boy to die for Israel. We will defend ourselves.' I have since concluded, based on the evidence presented in this book, that Dayan's heart-stopping defiance, while admirable, should have been unnecessary. Dayan was right to assert Israel's self-sufficiency in her existential struggle. As I will explain in the book, I believe that the international community, in adopting its familiar and deadly bystanding posture (at best) towards the fate of Jews, was wrong then – politically, militarily, and morally – and is wrong today, more than half a century later.

At the core of this book sits a harsh diagnosis. For all its complexity, the Arab-Israeli conflict springs not from political disagreements about territory nor from competing historical narratives but from a single overpowering source: Jew-hatred. The evidence is unequivocal that the underlying cause of the frozen confrontation in which Jews and Arabs find themselves rooted is a particularly noxious brand of anti-Jewish racism – eliminationist antisemitism, a desire to remove Jews from a geographical location or, in extreme cases, from the face of the earth. Unless and until this hatred is acknowledged and neutralised, peace will be unattainable.

Islamic civilisation has enriched humanity through its contributions to philosophy, religion, literature, mathematics, science, medicine, architecture and more. That great heritage should not blind us to the long history of poor treatment experienced by minorities living under Muslim regimes, nor to Islamism, a relatively new and reactionary interpretation of Islam that has nurtured and weaponised antisemitism for its own hegemonic purposes.

With a few important exceptions, Arab and Muslim leaders and opinion formers have systematically misled their people about the nature of Jews, Zionism and Israel. In this book, I will demonstrate that the process of antisemitic conditioning has been a blight on the Middle East and North Africa (MENA) for centuries, continues to play a seminal role in the Arab-Israeli conflict, and has poisoned the wider discourse about Israel. This is not an original observation yet its significance is too often overlooked by commentators including respected journalists, academics and politicians.

When human behaviour is driven by irrational cognitive processes, it is hard to alter it through rational means. As Jonathan Swift observed, 'It is useless to attempt to reason a man out of a thing he was never reasoned into.' I hold to the conviction that most people are capable of a change of mind (and heart) if presented with sufficiently compelling evidence. Mustering that evidence has been the challenge I set myself in writing these pages. My starting point is a familiar one to all who have an even passing acquaintance with Jewish history – the *Shoah* (Holocaust), the greatest catastrophe suffered by the Jewish people in modern times. Consciously or unconsciously, it dominates almost all aspects of Jewish life, including the complex Jewish relationship with Israel. For different reasons, to which I

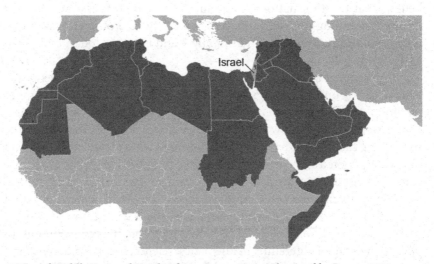

1. Map of Middle East and North Africa. Source: Original created by Ryanzy 2015

refer extensively in the book, it also permeates Arab and Muslim attitudes to Israel, and perhaps also to the peculiar way in which ostensibly uninvolved outsiders respond to the conflict.

My purpose in writing this book is twofold: firstly, to inform readers of the underreported sombre realities about the Arab and Muslim perception of Israel as 'the Jew among the nations' and the role of that perception in fanning the flames of conflict; secondly, to explain why this topic has growing relevance to us all of us regardless of nationality, ethnicity, religion or political orientation.

1

Overview – on Elephants, Red Herrings and Canaries

The Night of Broken Glass

Just before midnight on 9 November 1938, the Nazi regime launched a pogrom against the Jews of Germany, burning and destroying property including hundreds of synagogues, killing around one hundred people and injuring many more, and sending 30,000 to concentration camps. The soundscape of the whole of Germany had turned into a cacophony of breaking glass. *Kristallnacht*, that orchestrated explosion of antisemitic violence, is often marked as the start of the prolonged and savage mass atrocity that has become known to Jews as the *Shoah* (Catastrophe) and to the wider world as the Holocaust.

The writing had been on the wall for Germany's Jews for years, at least since the accession to power of Adolf Hitler in 1933. As early as 1919, he had announced that 'ultimate goal must definitely be the removal of the Jews altogether,'[1] a sentiment that surprised few Germans as it had been detectable in that country since the late Middle Ages. With hindsight, we know that the terrors of *Kristallnacht* were the inevitable consequence of a prolonged psychosocial process of extreme anti-Jewish demonisation, discrimination and humiliation, and presaged even greater horrors to come. A degree of controversy has surrounded the mechanisms of this antisemitic stereotyping and the extent to which the German people had internalised a *culturally shared cognitive model of Jews* that prepared the ground for the Holocaust.[2] What is not disputed is that antisemitism had become deeply embedded within German society by the early twentieth century and that its presence facilitated the rise to power of a fiercely antisemitic political party that succeeded in exploiting widespread anti-Jewish beliefs for genocidal purposes.

The Jews may have been the Nazis' primary targets but the collateral damage scarred the entire European continent and beyond. The attack on

Germany's Jews was soon followed by an attack on most of Europe. Almost exactly two years after *Kristallnacht*, the English city of Coventry was subjected to *Operation Moonlight Sonata* that killed 800 people and destroyed 4,000 homes. By the end of 1945, at least fifty million people were dead and much of Europe had been reduced to rubble. When the guns fell silent, the world was stunned to discover that, in addition to the ruins and carnage of war, something else had befallen the German occupied territories: around six million European Jews – two-thirds of the total Jewish population of the continent – had been murdered. The most educated, cultured and sophisticated country in Europe had perpetrated a crime of such inhumanity and on such a vast scale that the imagination froze. What had transpired was simply beyond comprehension. Yet the unfathomable disaster of the *Shoah* did not fall out of a clear blue sky; it was predictable, though few predicted it, and avoidable, though few sought to avoid it.

Since those terrible days, the familiar mantra 'Never Again' may have salved the consciences of world leaders past and present but it rings hollow in the light of post-war events. While Germany embarked on a prolonged and painful process of de-Nazification, the underlying receptivity of German society as a whole to Hitler's genocidal message has been inadequately addressed. That predisposition was not just German but European. We know that several Eastern European countries contributed directly to the mass slaughter of Jews, but this disturbing reality has yet to be acknowledged more than three-quarters of a century later.[3] That failure to deal with a painful past may explain why antisemitic tropes (including ancient and modern blood libels) refuse to disappear and continue to exert a troubling influence on European religious and secular culture.[4]

The fact is that the deep-seated moral pathology that facilitated the genocidal eruption of the world's oldest hatred in Europe has not disappeared and may be intensifying. There is ample evidence that a distorted perception of Jews (including the Jewish state of Israel) is a growing feature of the twenty-first century. This apparently immutable psychopathology has severe consequences: it enables antisemites to continue to wreak havoc throughout the world but especially in the Middle East, a strategically important region adjacent to liberal Europe but far enough away to thrust it, when expedience demands, out of sight and out of mind.

Antisemitism is not solely or even mainly about Jews but is a product of the antisemite's warped perception of Jews. And antisemitism's impact is not confined to Jews but is liable, if left unchecked, to engulf large swathes of humanity – Arabs, Muslims and Christians included – who had believed themselves to be insulated from the danger.

Zionism and Anti-Zionism

The Zionist dream of Jewish self-determination is one that anti-Zionist critics of Israel have long contended is defeatist since, they claim, it posits the continuation of never-ending antisemitism as an unchangeable reality. Unfortunately, history has had the last word on this debate. Socialist philosopher Isaac Deutscher concluded, after contemplating the catastrophe of the Holocaust, that 'If, instead of arguing against Zionism in the 1920s and 1930s, I had urged European Jews to go to Palestine, I might have helped to save some of the lives that were to be extinguished in Hitler's gas chambers.'[5]

While eastern Europe was an important culture medium for Zionist thinkers and activists, there is a common misconception that the Zionist impulse was an exclusively European phenomenon and that Arabs had unfairly paid the price for the Europe's persecution of its Jews, a view that prompted the slick but inaccurate remark (attributed to Palestinian-American intellectual Edward Said among others) that the Palestinians were 'the victims of the victims.' In the Jewish communities of the Middle East and North Africa (MENA), some of whose roots in their host countries stretched back millennia, a similar yearning for a return to the Land of Israel had simmered over the generations. For these *Mizrachi* (Eastern) Jews, a political awakening occurred in the late nineteenth century in tandem with (and influenced by) their *Ashkenazi* (eastern, central and western European) co-religionists. Since their expulsion from their homeland by the Babylonian and Roman invaders, they had sought to appease the demands of their new Muslim rulers in a quest to achieve integration into wider society. Their efforts too proved futile. For both *Ashkenazim* and *Mizrachim*, European and Arab versions of antisemitism respectively were prime drivers of their attraction to Zionism.

While the Arab-Zionist dispute has deep historical roots, it was launched in its fully violent form by Haj Amin al-Husseini, a firebrand nationalist cleric with insatiable political ambition. The British, who had driven the Turks from the Levant in 1917, appointed Husseini to the powerful position of Grand Mufti of Jerusalem in 1921 despite his having instigated anti-Jewish riots in Jerusalem in April 1920 that killed nine people (five Jews and four Arabs) and injured hundreds. The incident was timed to send two messages, the first to the San Remo Conference that was poised to enshrine Britain's 1917 pro-Zionist Balfour Declaration in international law. The second message was aimed at the Jews. For as well as being an Arab nationalist, Husseini was a vicious antisemite who would later forge an alliance with Adolf Hitler in an effort to import the Final Solution to the Middle East. That explicitly genocidal brand of antisemitism would become a consistent feature of Arab (and, in recent decades, Iranian) hostility to Israel thereafter. Husseini's legacy, openly revered by today's Palestinian leadership, was, and remains, barely acknowledged let alone challenged outside of Israel and (sections of) the Jewish world. Little wonder the hundred-year war against the Jews continues unabated given that its underlying cause is ignored.

A Strong and Secure Israel?

Many think of modern Israel as strong and secure. They are mistaken for two reasons.

First, her war of independence is not yet over. Within hours of David Ben-Gurion proclaiming Israel's statehood on 14 May 1948, the armies of five Arab states joined local militias already in the country and sought to strangle the country at birth. With the odds in their favour, given the massive imbalance of power between an embryonic and near-bankrupt new state and the assembled might of the Arab nations, they failed. Israel somehow survived, defying the predictions of the US State Department among other international observers. The Arab states tried again in 1967 and 1973 and failed again. Although Jordan and Egypt (unenthusiastically) signed peace treaties with Israel, and the Abraham Accords of 2020 promoted 'normalisation' between the Israel and the United Arab Emirates, Bahrain, Morocco and Sudan, most of the regimes adjacent to Israel's boundaries (Gaza, Palestinian Authority, Syria, Lebanon, Saudi Arabia), as well as most of the other members of the Arab League, have remained as hostile as ever. The Palestinians signed an interim peace treaty with Israel in 1993-95 but then relaunched their violent campaign against the Jewish state at the turn of the century. Today, numerous Iranian-backed terrorist organisations – notably Hamas, Hezbollah and Islamic Jihad – sustain these efforts to kill Israelis and destroy the Jewish state while the world displays indifference or calls for 'restraint on all sides.' Smaller scale wars and ceaseless terrorist attacks on Israeli civilians constituted the new normal until the pivotal moment of the Hamas invasion and killings of 7 October 2023.

Yet Israel remains a functioning, creative and increasingly prosperous democracy. This success comes at a price. The prolonged violence has exacted a tragic human and economic cost on both Israelis and Arabs. But there is no moral symmetry in this perpetual stand-off between aggressors and defenders. The Israelis' fear has a singular dimension: it is existential. They know they cannot afford to lose a single war or another major terrorist onslaught on the scale of the October disaster. This quote (originally attributed to Israeli prime minister Golda Meir) summarises the nature of the confrontation that is well into its eighth decade: 'If the Arabs put down their weapons today, there would be no more violence. If the Jews put down their weapons today, there would be no more Israel.'[6]

The second reason Israel is fearful of the future is her political rather than physical vulnerability. More than half the time of the UN is spent discussing – and censuring – Israel via hostile resolutions, commissions of inquiry and high-profile reports. In 2023, following the pattern of many previous calendar years, she was condemned by the UN General Assembly more often than all the other member states combined. She is the only country that is the subject of a permanent agenda item on the UN Human Rights Council – meaning that she is ritually denounced in that forum at every meeting regardless of what else is happening in the world. She is the only country that finds her legitimacy constantly questioned, that is denied the right to choose her capital city, that sees her independence day marked by the UN as a 'catastrophe,' that is targeted for economic and political isolation by the global BDS (Boycott, Divestment and Sanctions) movement, and that suffers predictions of her inevitable physical demise on a daily basis. In this permanently febrile and hate-filled atmosphere, it is galling (if unsurprising) to Israelis that, when bloodcurdling threats against them and their country are issued and even on occasions acted upon, the international community remains aloof, or actively joins the baying lynch mob, while simultaneously condemning Israelis as the alleged authors of their own misfortune.

We have seen this pattern of behaviour before, just a few decades ago. The difference is that this time the Jewish people have the capability to defend themselves and have shown their willingness to deploy it – out of necessity rather than choice. Well-meaning foreigners periodically attempt to broker peace by proposing mutual compromise, a strategy that is sound in principle but always disappoints in this case since one side (the Palestinians and their allies) seeks the obliteration of the other (the Jewish state within any borders).

Why Israel's Fate Concerns Everyone

History matters, not just as a repository of truths but as a contextual record that greatly enhances our understanding of the present and the risks we are likely to face in the future. Within living memory in Europe, the world looked the other way as the Third Reich geared itself up to commit what was arguably the greatest crime in history. With the Nuremburg testimonies etched on the conscience of humankind, we then witnessed the Soviet Union revive the violent antisemitic traditions of Tsarist Russia. Totalitarian empires eventually collapse under the weight of their hubristic overreach and human rights abuses but not before they have caused immeasurable human misery. The Arab League is hardly comparable to Europe's twentieth century fascist and communist regimes but it shares with these power blocs one supreme aspiration – the disempowerment of Jews. That is because most of today's Muslim-majority countries still struggle to regard Jews as anything other than *dhimmis*, a longstanding minority status in the Islamic Middle East that was abruptly upended by Israel's rebirth in 1948.

History, said Mark Twain, has a habit of rhyming rather than repeating. No society that persecutes its minorities can flourish for long. When antisemitism takes root, it corrodes the delicate structures of mutual respect and support that have been constructed, perhaps over centuries, across social, cultural, ethnic and religious divides. 'A society in which Jews are not safe will ultimately not be secure for journalists, or for freedom, or for any values of human decency,' said Warren Goldstein, Chief Rabbi of South Africa.[7]

Just as Germany's treatment of its Jews in the 1930s should have rung warning bells across the globe, today's reincarnation of antisemitism should do the same. Islamist violence, that has long drawn much of its inspiration from antisemitic (as well as anti-western and, at times, anti-communist) ideology, has already inflicted enormous suffering worldwide as well as in Israel. The 9/11 assault on the US in 2001 was its most infamous manifestation though there have been mass casualty incidents in the Middle East, Europe, Africa, Asia and the Americas. A French database of global terrorism (excluding the Arab-Israeli conflict) reported 33,769 Islamist attacks that killed at least 167,096 people between 1979 and 2019.[8]

The feeble international response to the anti-Israel Arab-Islamist campaign – backed directly by a post-revolutionary Islamist Iran and indirectly by a neo-Stalinist Russia – has had predictable consequences for all the inhabitants of all countries. When arch-terrorist and PLO chief Yasser Arafat was being feted by the UN and other international bodies in the 1970s, Israel was forced to introduce additional defensive measures to protect her citizens. Decades before travellers found themselves queuing to clear airport security everywhere, the Israelis had to do it first. Long before the West found its democratic values under attack with a vehemence unseen since the Second World War, Israel had to deal with that threat first – starting on the day she declared her independence and almost every hour of her existence ever since.

Our Moral Imperative

Calls for impartiality, balance and even-handedness are not always what they seem. Approaching the Arab-Israeli conflict as though both sides have an equal claim to understanding and support leads to a dark place where differences are blurred between democracies and dictatorships, human rights and terrorism, freedom and tyranny, life and death. In Israel's case, the choice is between peaceful coexistence and (another) Jewish genocide. Should each of these outcomes be treated as morally equivalent? Does 'balance' require the setting of the moral compass equidistantly between those two poles? How many millions of Israelis should sacrifice their lives in the name of compromise? The answers to these questions affect more than the security and future of one small nation.

The conflict between Israel and her enemies is no longer, in revisionist Zionist leader Jabotinsky's phrase of the 1930s, a matter of 'right against right.' Whatever moral symmetry might have existed in the past, in the twenty-first century the choice is clearer: a liberal democracy is seeking to hold at bay an array of authoritarian kleptocracies and terrorist groups bent on politicide and mass murder. A mid-point between those two positions amounts to complicity with terrorism – neutrality is untenable. The people of Israel have had to fight to protect their homeland since 1948 and have sacrificed tens of thousands of their brightest and best to keep their families and country safe. It is long past time for all who claim to support the values of peace, democracy and freedom to stand behind Israel in her quest for a just peace.

On Elephants, Red Herrings and Canaries

The late UK Rabbi Lord Jonathan Sacks described anti-Zionism as the new antisemitism. Years earlier, the Rev. Martin Luther King Junior offered the same diagnosis: 'When people criticise Zionists, they mean Jews. You're talking antisemitism.'[9] Both were calling out the oppressive yet near-invisible presence of Jew-hatred, the elephant in the room.

It is no coincidence that the world's only Jewish state is treated as the Jew among the nations. From the day of her birth in 1948, her neighbours have subjected her to intolerance, demonisation and violence. But it would be a mistake to consider this sublimation of age-old antisemitism into anti-Zionism and anti-Israelism a purely Jewish problem. The concerted assault on the legitimacy of Israel is symptomatic of a general intolerance of minorities that has long blighted the Middle East and North Africa (MENA) region.[10]

The phrase 'the canary in the coal mine', is a metaphor bequeathed to us from an era when the fate of that little creature literally acted as an early warning sign of subterranean danger. Just as the diaspora Jews were traditionally the canaries whose fate preceded that of other minorities, in the twenty-first century that burden has been largely thrust onto the backs of Israelis, citizens of an entity that epitomises Jewish collectivity. Israel is today's canary in the international mine. The manner in which a global lynch mob from across the political spectrum has abused that country – to the point of demanding her extinction – is predictive of the possible fate of other democratic nations, large and small, around the world.

This book presents verifiable evidence that antisemitism is not a red herring in the annals of the unremitting violence between Arab and Jew but is the elephant in the room, the root cause and sustaining driver of a conflict that has raged, more or less unabated, for over a century. Today's prime target of that age-old hatred is the Jewish state of Israel. What starts with the Jewish state will not end with the Jewish state. If a nuclear-armed Iran fulfils the genocidal promises of its leaders, the consequences will be dire for the entire Middle East and the world as a whole.

'The truth is that we are all living in Israel, it's just that some of us don't know it yet,' said Sam Harris[11] the American philosopher in 2014. The canary in the mine is transmitting its alarm call. When will we heed it?

Notes

1   US Holocaust Memorial Museum. Adolf Hitler Issues Comment on the 'Jewish Question.' https://www.ushmm.org/learn/timeline-of-events/before-1933/adolf-hitler-issues-comment-on-the-jewish-question (Last accessed 11 June 2024).

2   D. Goldhagen, *Hitler's Willing Executioners* (London: Abacus, 1997).

3   Efraim Zuroff, '5 EU countries that shouldn't be throwing stones', *Times of Israel*, 27 July 2022. https://blogs.timesofisrael.com/5-eu-countries-that-shouldnt-be-throwing-stones/ (Last accessed 11 June 2024).

4   Stephen Burgen, 'Spanish Catholic church to investigate antisemitic rituals', *Guardian*, 11 August 2022. https://www.theguardian.com/world/2022/aug/11/spanish-catholic-church-to-investigate-antisemitic-rituals?CMP=share_btn_tw (Last accessed 11 June 2024).

5   Martyn Hudson, 'Revisiting Isaac Deutscher', *Fathom*, Winter 2014. https://fathomjournal.org/revisiting-isaac-deutscher/ (Last accessed 11 June 2024)

6   The Palestinians Must Lay Down Their Arms to Achieve Peace – Editorial, *Jerusalem Post*, 11 October 2022. https://www.jpost.com/opinion/article-719355 (Last accessed 11 June 2024)

7   Warren Goldstein, 'Canary in the coal mine', *Jerusalem Post*, 15 January 2015. https://www.jpost.com/opinion/canary-in-the-coal-mine-387914 (Last accessed 11 June 2024)

8   Dominique Reynié, *An evaluation of Islamist violence in the world (1979-2019)*, Paris, Fondation pour L'innovation Politique, November 2019. https://www.fondapol.org/en/study/islamist-terrorist-attacks-in-the-world-1979-2019/ (Last accessed 11 June 2024)

9   Martin Kramer, 'In the words of Martin Luther King…', *Martin Kramer on the Middle East*, 12 March 2012. https://martinkramer.org/2012/03/12/in-the-words-of-martin-luther-king/ (Last accessed 11 June 2024)

10   L. Julius, *Uprooted* (London: Vallentine Mitchell, 2018), pp.252–3.

11   Harris S. 'Why Don't I criticize Israel?' *Tablet*, 30 July 2014. https://www.tabletmag.com/sections/news/articles/sam-harris-why-dont-i-criticize-israel (Last accessed 11 June 2024)

2

What Is Antisemitism?

'An antisemite is someone who hates Jews more than is absolutely necessary.' Historian Deborah Lipstadt, President Biden's special envoy on antisemitism, alludes to this quote attributed to the philosopher Isaiah Berlin.[1] Superficially frivolous, the quip is insightful – while there may be many reasons for hating Jews that are unrelated to ethnicity or religion, hating Jews *because they are Jews* is the essence of antisemitism.

A distinction is sometimes drawn between Judeophobia (religious antipathy to Jews) and antisemitism (racial or ethnic hatred of Jews). Semantics aside, antisemitism has become the favoured descriptor for hostility, of whatever origin or intensity, towards Jews – or, more accurately, to the antisemite's conception of Jews, individually or collectively. More important than the theoretical foundations of this hostility are its multiple injurious effects.

The International Holocaust Remembrance Alliance (IHRA) working definition of antisemitism[2] is becoming accepted worldwide. This definition is invaluable for identifying and monitoring antisemitism but it cannot explain the phenomenon – that goal will always prove elusive. The best we can hope for is to acquire as intimate an understanding of antisemitism as possible – and necessary – to mitigate its injurious effects.

This chapter explores the history, nature and types of antisemitism before setting out the IHRA definition and its implications for the Arab-Israeli conflict.

History of Antisemitism: an Overview

Antisemitism has been described as the oldest or longest hatred.[3] According to American historian Walter Laqueur (who escaped Nazi Germany as a teenager), antisemitism antedated Christianity though at that point it was just one of many national and ethnic antagonisms that were common in the ancient world.[4] Ironically, the early followers of a Jewish sect set in motion the wheels of a virulent Judeophobia based on their resentment at what they felt was the mainstream Jewish rejection of the authentic messiah, Jesus Christ. In medieval Europe, theologically based antisemitism gained momentum. Christian polemicists argued that the Jews suffered the loss of their temple and country as divine punishment for their stubbornness in defying the will of God. The matter was straightforward: Jews were responsible for deicide. They were, as a group, regarded as the literal anti-Christ. Redemption beckoned for these benighted adherents of the Old Testament (the Hebrew Bible or *Torah*) by the straightforward act of renouncing Judaism and embracing the one true Christian faith.

Over the subsequent centuries, the European Church burdened Jews with a raft of discriminatory legislation restricting their rights as citizens and their capacity to earn a living by severely limiting the professions they were permitted to enter. Jews were obliged to wear special clothing, were confined to ghettoes, and were subjected to incessant demonisation and insults as well as to physical assaults, periodic expulsions and pogroms. This extreme religious intolerance acquired racial overtones as early as the fifteenth century when Spanish Jews were compelled to choose between expulsion, death and conversion to Christianity. Although this last option was popular, a convert (*converso*) was treated with suspicion through the alleged lack of purity of blood (*limpiezo de sangre*) arising from the immutability of Jewish birth.

By the mid-nineteenth century, Jews discovered that conversion had become an uncertain escape route from discrimination and persecution. A new variant of antisemitism was emerging based on post-Darwinian eugenic racial theories that designated Jews as an alien minority who were biologically distinct from and inferior to the gentile majority. That was a harsher verdict than that of Christian theology since members of the 'Jewish race' were now condemned to a fate that was without the possibility of reprieve. By the 1930s, the redemptive religious path was fully blocked to European Jews whom the Nazis categorised as sub-human and unworthy of life.

Meanwhile, the religiously-inspired antisemitism that had long been rife throughout the Muslim world acquired an extra potency in the early twentieth century from three additional sources: European fascism, Soviet propaganda and Islamism. This toxic cocktail would play a major role in both the Arab-Israeli conflict and the Jewish *Nakba* – the forced exodus of almost 900,000 Jews from MENA countries in the mid-twentieth century.

Following the fall of the Third Reich, antisemitism was revived and re-weaponised by the Soviet Union. Its political and military backing for Arab states was accompanied by a novel brand of anti-Israel propaganda that incorporated anti-capitalism and anti-Americanism. The legacy of this Stalinist anti-Zionism is discernible today not just in the Arab world but also in the West where the progressive left that has, in a reversal of the geographical direction of the spread of early twentieth century Jew-hatred, re-imported Middle Eastern antisemitism into Europe and, more recently, North America; in both of these regions, antisemitic incidents have reached record levels and have generated growing fears among Jewish communities that had felt secure following the end of the Second World War.

The constant rebranding and recycling of antisemitic stereotypes across ideologies and continents produces strange bedfellows, such as the right-left Horseshoe Effect and the Red-Green (left-Islamist) alliance. The multiplier effects of these coalitions should not be underestimated; small groups of extremists can combine to exert an influence that would have been beyond their reach when acting separately.

The Horseshoe: How Far Right and Far Left Converge

The notion that antisemitism is exclusively or largely confined either to the far right or far left, a view often expounded in progressive and conservative quarters respectively, is not evidence-based. Significant sectors of both ideological extremes find common ground in their antipathy to Jews and Israel while agreeing on little else. Horseshoe Theory, first proposed in 2002

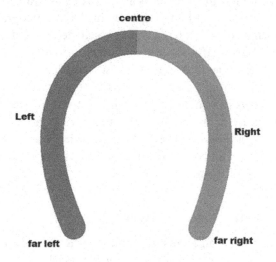

2. Horseshoe Theory. Source: Wikimedia under Creative Commons Licence

by French philosopher Jean-Pierre Faye, offers an apt image for the way in which political extremes tend to converge with regard to their antisemitic attitudes and policies. The threat posed to Jews by both political wings was summarised by Ramos: 'From the Nazi regime to the USSR, history has proven that Jews have no true refuge in the right or left, in conservative or progressive spaces.'[5]

The expression of racist views on the fringes of politics should never be lightly dismissed. If they are unchallenged, they may encroach onto the centre ground where they pose a greater threat to civilised society. When a toxic ideology is given free rein anywhere, it can wreak havoc everywhere. What starts on the extremes may not remain on the extremes. Anti-Jewish racism is a classic example: a tendency to resort to antisemitic stereotypes can be found today across the political spectrum including in mainstream political parties where it lurks beneath a thin veneer of civilised 'debate.'

The Red-Green Alliance

Nowhere is the Horseshoe Effect more evident than in the Red-Green Alliance (not to be confused with the identically-labelled, socialist-environmentalist coalitions that are popular in Europe). It represents a counterintuitive elision of far left progressive and far right Islamist ideologies that have emerged from a decades-long interaction of identity politics, intersectionality and critical race theory.[6] This process has generated a worldview in which Jews are regarded as white, privileged and oppressive, combined with a negation of Jewish peoplehood and a consequent denial of the Jewish right to self-determination – in stark contrast to the Palestinians.

This discriminatory rejection of Jewish self-identity is antisemitic in effect if not intent. Though embraced by the Western left, it resonates with the hostility to Jews displayed by ultraconservative Muslims in the MENA region and beyond. Because many Jews, especially in schools and campuses, are attracted to progressivism, the Red-Green Alliance also undermines the Jewish diaspora's connection to Israel as well as empowering extremist groups that promote antisemitic agendas.

When a Minority Turns on Itself

A disturbing aspect of all forms of prejudice is the spectacle of members of a group making common cause with the bigots who despise them. This may reflect Jewish (or Israeli) self-hatred among a minority of Jews who have internalised antisemitic tropes, or its opposite whereby self-regarding Jews wrap themselves in a comforting cloak of righteousness. Those adopting the latter course may feel vindicated when they are rewarded with exaggerated deference from their antisemitic friends because they are seen as valuable assets. These Jewish eyes blaze with the zeal of the convert. Their anti-Zionist and anti-Israel diatribes are peppered with sanctimonious 'as-a-Jew' declarations to bolster their insider-outsider credentials. This may be a form of Stockholm Syndrome – identification with the aggressor. Whatever the explanation of the malady, attempting to enter into a dialogue with its victims is unproductive as few who throw themselves into the arms of their enemies have the insight to recognise the reality of their situation.

The Enigma of Antisemitism

Antisemitism is an extraordinarily durable hatred. Why should this be? Perhaps there is a deep-seated human need to identify a scapegoat – a concept that originated in the Hebrew bible[7] whereby an animal was ritually burdened with the collective guilt of a people. Why do antisemites scapegoat Jews specifically? Theological dogma played an important role in the past. Having rejected two major religions (Christianity and Islam), Jews became prime targets. But because antisemitism may be found in both non-Christian and non-Islamic societies, other factors must also play a role. Among the most important is the cognitive disorder that projects onto Jews fictitious (and always malign) characteristics that are not only the epitome of evil but also harbour injurious consequences for non-Jews. These imagined characteristics are many and varied but a common denominator of most types of antisemitism is a belief in a Jewish conspiracy to dominate and ultimately rule the world. This trope is often ignored or minimised, according to French writer Brigitte Stora, especially by defenders of anti-Zionism:

> I wondered why so little of the antisemitic discourse is listened to. Because antisemitism is first of all a discourse, a language that many people use, sometimes without realising they do, and that is being spoken again and again almost all over the world. The idea of global Jewish conspiracy to rule the world is the central and structural theme of every antisemitism.[8]

Conscious and Unconscious Antisemitism

The contemporary view of racism and other types of cognitive bias is that it need not be a purely subjective or conscious characteristic.[9] Individuals may unwittingly behave in an antisemitic manner either through ignorance or a lack of awareness of their own deep-rooted antisemitic motivation. Their peer group (such as a nation or political 'tribe') or institution (such as a police force or NGO) may also influence them to act antisemitically. Whatever the reason, unconscious or unintentional antisemitism can occur. That insight renders void the protest that an emotion or a behaviour cannot be antisemitic unless it is accompanied by a strong sense of subjective hatred of Jews, individually or collectively, or of the Jewish state.

Antisemitism as a Cognitive Disorder

Psychologists and social scientists have attempted to locate the source of the cognitive aberration that is antisemitism with only partial success. Among the more credible theories are those that suggest the fulfilment of an emotional need in the antisemite, such as the neutralisation of guilt about the Holocaust, European colonialism or covert violent fantasies. In such cases, projection is one hypothesised mechanism whereby individuals or groups displace their self-disgust onto Jews. Antisemitism may thereby provide deep emotional satisfaction, often including a sense of moral purity, that is actually pleasurable for those who indulge in it.[10] A complex interaction of factors is likely to play a role though the contribution of each will vary according to circumstances.

Psychologists and anthropologists have developed theories of cognition that may be helpful in enhancing our understanding how large numbers of people acquire false notions about Jews. Cognitive processes are closely linked to underpinning cognitive models. A cognitive model is a pre-existing abstract or metaphorical conceptualisation of a specific phenomenon for the purposes of comprehension and prediction. People may acquire cognitive models about certain ethnic, religious or national groups by absorbing them from parents, communities, the educational system or the media – in fact any environmental source of relevant data. The precise way this works in the human brain is obscure. American psychologist Daniel Levitin emphasises the automatic and unconscious nature of cognitive processes. He draws an analogy with computer programming and the way in which digital codes translate into comprehensible information that appears on our computer screens without our awareness of the codes' existence: 'This is what the neural code is like. Millions of nerves firing at different rates and different intensities, all of it invisible to us.' [11]

Culturally Shared Cognitive Models of Jews

In his investigation into the most violent eruption of antisemitism in modern times, the Holocaust, Daniel Goldhagen argues that genocidal antisemitism was facilitated in Germany by an underlying *culturally shared cognitive model* of Jews within the population as a whole.[12] The model (that is derived from a prejudiced view of Jews) took many centuries to evolve from Christian Judeophobia to the racialist dogmas of post-Darwinian eugenicists, finally reaching its zenith in the early twentieth century at which point it provided the perfect launching pad for the Nazi Final Solution. This theory, while controversial among Holocaust historians, is potentially applicable to all of predominantly Christian Europe. It may have equal relevance to the Arab-Israeli conflict given the long history of Muslim antipathy to Jews starting with the *dhimmi* status of the weak and contemptible second-class citizen. This mutated over time, up to the Islamist-influenced modern era, into a violent and, at times, explicitly genocidal Jew-hatred. The academic debate surrounding Goldhagen's thesis should not distract attention from the serious threat posed by eliminationist antisemitism in the MENA region since it harbours the possibility of consequences as catastrophic as those suffered by European Jews.

Goldhagen's work is particularly apposite to this discussion given the introduction of Nazi stereotypes of Jews to the MENA countries in the twentieth century. A Nazified version of Islamist antisemitism was the stock-in-trade of the Muslim Brotherhood and their disciples, including the first leader of the Palestinian Arabs, Haj Amin al-Husseini, and continues to make its presence felt in the genocidal rants of contemporary Arab and Islamist figures. It was also a prominent feature of the Soviet anti-Zionism that made its greatest impact in the Middle East following Germany's defeat in 1945. Arab leaders were content to replace the antisemitic ideology of their erstwhile supporters in the Third Reich with that of their new Communist allies (though elements of both co-existed without apparent difficulty in the minds of many Israel-haters in the region and beyond – a classic example of the Horseshoe Effect). In the West, the deployment of the Nazi smear against Israelis became a favourite tactic of the New Left in the 1960s and was promoted by controversial British historian Arnold Toynbee[13] among others. It remains a popular anti-Israeli trope today.

Antisemitism in the Context of Other Racisms

Antisemitism is similar in some ways to other types of ethnoreligious bigotry and dissimilar in others. In common with most forms of racism, the antisemite identifies a group of people with attributes that are considered (from the perspective of the racist) unsavoury, undesirable or contemptible to the point that a physical and social distancing is felt important or necessary, and is often accompanied by verbal or, in extreme cases, physical violence. Where antisemitism parts company from other types of racism is its quasi-psychotic and delusional nature, including a vast range of conspiracy theories. The antisemites' perception of Jews may, like all stereotypes, occasionally contain a grain of truth but this is lost in the ether of a parallel imaginary universe constructed around the persona of the Jew (or Jewry, Zionism or Israel) that is divorced from reality. This hatred finds expression along a spectrum from vague mistrust to openly proclaimed genocidal enmity.

In modern progressive circles, there is a tendency to relegate antisemitism to somewhere near the bottom of the hierarchy of racisms.[14] In the US, the term racism is now virtually confined to prejudice against people born with black or brown skin colour. As Jews are usually (and often inaccurately) perceived as white, this implies that Jew-hatred is qualitatively different and less serious than other forms of prejudice. This enables antisemites to insist that their anti-Jewishness is somehow less reprehensible than other forms of racism.

The marginalisation of antisemitism is even odder – and more worrisome – when one considers the manner in which antisemitism has expressed itself over many centuries. For antisemitism is not only a dislike or hatred of Jews; antisemites regard Jews as a malign, cunning and menacing global threat that is not always obvious as it is cleverly concealed behind a web of lies, deception and conspiracies. While all forms of racism are irrational, antisemitism is uniquely dangerous because antisemites nurse such paranoid fantasies about Jews that they are easily persuadable to move from passive ideation to acting out. The result is that antisemites may seek to harm Jews, up to and including mass murder, and have periodically succeeded in fulfilling their ambitions. They rationalise their eliminationism as a form of 'self-defence' against Jewish plotting. Antisemites, when mobilised into well-organised religious or political movements, have threatened or claimed the lives of millions of people in Europe and the Middle East, and continue to threaten the well-being and survival of millions more.

Antisemitism and Anti-Zionism

Past attempts to offer a typology of antisemitism have listed a range of anti-Jewish beliefs and behaviours that include religious, racialist and political dimensions and motivations. These strands often overlap, are intertwined and can be mutually reinforcing.

While the explicit expression of antisemitism is rare in the West nowadays due to the post-Holocaust taboo, it lingers in unexpected quarters and its habit of mutating over time renders its identification more difficult. Overt antisemitism has traditionally emanated from well-recognised settings – the far-right, the far-left, or the mainstream ('dinner party' or 'pub' chatter) – to which a new source must now be added: anti-Zionism. Since 1948, Jew-hatred has focused increasingly on the alleged crimes of Israel and, by extension, her 'Zionist' supporters (that happen to include most Jews). This abrasive 'new antisemitism' is found mainly in far-left circles though there is evidence that it is moving into the mainstream. It is directed at Jews both as individuals and as a collective, including the ultimate embodiment of Jewish collectivity, the state of Israel. Its peculiar danger lies in the cover it offers to antisemites who seek to disguise their true nature. Most anti-Zionists, however, deny an antisemitic motivation regardless of the growing consensus to the contrary among Jews. This attitude is so widely shared among intellectual elites, notably on the progressive left, that it requires careful exploration.

Question: Is Anti-Zionism a Form of Antisemitism?

In deciding whether or not anti-Zionism is a form of antisemitism, terminological clarity is essential. Zionism is the ideology that promotes Jewish self-determination in the form of sovereign statehood in the ancestral homeland of the Jewish people. Anti-Zionism is an ideology that opposes Zionism in both principle and practice – and that usually equates to rejecting Jewish sovereignty in any circumstances and behind any borders. This is distinct from criticism of policies and actions of the state of Israel, her governments or her citizens. The waters are muddied, however, by the lazy use of the term 'anti-Zionist' to depict a critic of Israel. As most Jews and Israelis are forthcoming, to a greater or lesser extent, in their criticisms of specific Israeli government policies and actions, or of the behaviour of some Israelis, does this imply that most Jews and Israelis are anti-Zionist? Clearly not as this would lead to the logical absurdity of labelling most Jews and Israelis as anti-Zionists. As for the accusation that

Jews and Israelis seek to portray all criticism of Israel as antisemitic (the Livingstone Formulation, discussed below), that is equally absurd – readers would be hard-pressed to find a single Jew or Israeli expressing that view.

Anti-Zionists are fond of arguing that conflating anti-Zionism with antisemitism is a category error or worse. They point out that not all Jews are Zionists and that anti-Zionists cannot therefore be antisemitic. While the first part of that statement is factually correct, the second is a *non sequitur* for three reasons. First, anti-Zionist Jews, whether on the radical left or the religious right, are a small minority that are unrepresentative of today's mainstream Jewish opinion; the large majority of Jews – around 80-90 per cent – are supportive of Zionism.[15,16] Second, historically there have always been a small number of Jewish antisemites whose presence is used by activists to legitimise their hatred. Third, denying Jews the right to an already extant self-determination is viewed by most Jews as antisemitic. This last point is not an abstract one: the anti-Zionist aim of removing Jewry's last bastion of safety is increasingly recognised as a violation of the most important human right – to life.

What is remarkable is not that a minority of Jews are opposed to Zionism but the relatively small size of that group given the diversity of Jewish culture, history, geography, religion and politics. It was not always the case. When Theodor Herzl established the modern Zionism movement in the 1890s, Jewish communities varied in their enthusiasm for the idea. Assimilationists believed the future of Jewry lay in disappearing into the ambivalent embrace of the majority cultures while religious Jews, especially on the *Chasidic* or *Charedi* (Ultra-Orthodox) wing, viewed the aspiration to Jewish statehood prior to the coming of the Messiah as sacrilegious. Secular Jews generally embraced Zionism as they could see no other exit from perpetual persecution. The argument raged across all Jewry for decades before being decisively settled by one Adolf Hitler who, along with his fellow-Nazis, transformed Zionism from an ideology into a necessity.

Answer: Anti-Zionism is Antisemitism

For most Jews, anti-Zionism is just the latest manifestation of earlier forms of Jew-hatred – and equally dangerous. In both Jewish and non-Jewish circles, a consensus is emerging that denying Jewish self-determination is discriminatory, as set out in the IHRA definition of antisemitism[2] and a violation of the UN Charter.[17] Denying Jews, and only Jews, the right to self-determination may or may not be rooted in a subjectively antisemitic mode of thinking but its effect is antisemitic.

Some commentators try to draw a distinction between political and antisemitic anti-Zionism. That view is hard to sustain. Anti-Zionist rhetoric may superficially appear purely political but it contains elements of the earlier religious and racial antisemitism in which reality melds into hate-laden fantasy. British political theorist Alan Johnson describes the process vividly:

> Antisemitic anti-Zionism bends the meaning of Israel and Zionism out of shape until both become fit receptacles for the tropes, images, and ideas of classical antisemitism. In short, *that which demonological Jew once was, demonological Israel now is*: uniquely malevolent, full of blood-lust, all controlling, always acting in bad faith, the obstacle to a better, purer, more spiritual world...[18]

Johnson suggests that antisemitic anti-Zionism has three components: a programme, a discourse, and a movement. The programme is the abolition of Israel and its replacement with Palestine; the discourse is demonising – Zionism is racism, Israel is a settler-colonialist state that ethnically cleansed the Palestinians and is now committing genocide; and it is part of the BDS (Boycott, Divestment and Sanctions) movement to exclude one state – and only one state – from the economic, cultural and educational life of humanity.

3. 'Israeli Apartheid' banner. Source: Michael Coughlan under Creative Commons Licence

In an uncomfortable echo of medieval Christian Judeophobia, anti-Zionists, especially on the left, have extended a welcome to some Jews who can obtain a degree of absolution as 'good Jews' by publicly distancing themselves from Israel; the others – the 90 per cent who refuse to renounce Zionism – are subjected to continuing ostracism, insults or worse. English political historian Vernon Bogdanor has emphasised the historical continuity of anti-Zionism with its earlier incarnations: 'Nineteenth century antisemitism began by singling out Jews for the deprivation of civil rights. It climaxed with the Holocaust. Modern antisemitism begins by singling out Jews for the deprivation of the right of self-determination. Its final aim is the elimination of Israel.' [19]

Towards the Normalisation of Antisemitic Anti-Zionism and Anti-Israelism

The European Enlightenment in the late eighteenth century brought some respite to Jews but from the 1880s politicians and intellectuals resumed their attacks, this time with renewed vigour. Following the accession of Alexander III to the throne of Russia, a wave of vicious pogroms was launched throughout the Jewish Pale of Settlement (the western region of the Russian Empire in which Jews were permitted to reside) and that forced Eastern European Jews to review their limited options, of which only two offered real freedom: one was emigration, the other was Zionism.

Prior to the Second World War, the overt expression of antisemitic views – even in relatively liberal circles – was considered unremarkable. That changed following the general revulsion at the Holocaust. After a relatively brief post-war interregnum of a few decades during which most antisemites kept their heads below the parapet, the world appears dangerously amnesic. Hostility to Jews – now expressed as anti-Zionism or extreme 'criticism' of Israel – is considered acceptable or even fashionable. This obviously matters for Jews and Israelis but it also affects the non-Jewish world. British political analyst Robin Shepherd prophetically anticipated the political and geographical spread of anti-Israelism:

> The fact is that from a large proportion of contemporary Europe's opinion formers we are now experiencing a tidal wave of hysteria, deception and distortion against the Jewish state which has not only brought resurgent anti-Semitism in its wake but also risks becoming a stain on the continent's entire political culture...As important, it is vital to recognise that there is now a serious risk of anti-Israeli

contagion spreading from Europe to the United States, just as a hateful discourse has spread from the Middle East itself into Europe.[20]

Do Jews 'Play the Antisemitism Card' to Protect Israel?

Anti-Zionist and other extreme critics of Israel have a habit of protesting their opposition to all forms of racism and then deploying a racist tactic to accuse Jews of bad faith by conspiring against them to silence criticism of Israel. British social scientist David Hirsh has labelled this the Livingstone Formulation[21] named after a former mayor of London who was expelled from the Labour Party for antisemitism. What is astonishing is that Livingstone's transparent ruse, itself utilising a conspiratorial antisemitic trope, appears to have worked: anti-Zionists feel they have insulated themselves in this way from any taint of antisemitism. At an Intelligence Squared debate in 2019 in London, the motion that 'anti-Zionism is antisemitism' was defeated by a margin of four to one. Those who applaud that result will be discomfited to read Kaplan and Small's landmark 2006 study[22] of 5,000 citizens in ten European countries in which they reported a direct statistical correlation between anti-Israelism and conventional antisemitism: 'Even after controlling for numerous potentially confounding factors...anti-Israel sentiment consistently predicts the probability that an individual is antisemitic.' Those findings were replicated by a later study[23] of 4,000 adults in Great Britain.

A related accusation is that contemporary antisemitism is exaggerated and that European Jews are excessively sensitive, perhaps due to their subjective feelings of insecurity arising from their recent traumatic experience on that continent. In a chilling riposte to that view, a European Union report sets the record straight:

> When you last walked by one of Europe's many beautiful synagogues, were heavily-armed police officers standing guard at its gates? It is a jarring sight. But, over seventy years after the Holocaust, it is also all too familiar. It is not just synagogues that require protection – at countless Jewish community centres and schools, too, special security measures are in place. Jewish people also encounter vicious commentary online, in the media and in politics; endure hostile stares and gestures in their neighbourhoods; come across graffiti and other forms of vandalism; and face discrimination in social settings, at school and at work.[24]

In the UK, the opposition Labour party became riddled with antisemitism under the leadership of Jeremy Corbyn who, we were assured by his legions of supporters, 'doesn't have an antisemitic bone in his body' despite his public hailing of the genocidally antisemitic Hamas and Hezbollah terror groups as his 'friends' and other disturbing *faux pas*. This cannot be attributed to paranoia on the part of a hypersensitive Anglo-Jewish community. In 2020, the Equality and Human Rights Commission, the UK's official anti-discrimination watchdog, reported that the Labour Party had displayed 'serious failings in leadership, processes and culture in dealing with antisemitism' and found 'specific examples of unlawful harassment and unlawful indirect discrimination.'[25] That may have been symptomatic of a wider malaise: the Community Security Trust, a Jewish charity that seeks to protect British Jews from antisemitic assaults, reported the largest ever number of antisemitic incidents in the UK in 2021.[26] This trend prompted the UK government's antisemitism adviser, Lord Mann, to call for a broadening of antisemitism education in schools to include contemporary manifestations of the hatred rather than focusing exclusively on the Holocaust.[27]

Antisemitism is Resurgent Globally

Twenty-first century antisemitism is real. Antisemitic attacks are on the increase globally but are not always visible due to poor monitoring or a reluctance by official agencies to publicise them. Reflecting changing public attitudes, Western politicians of all ideological hues have flirted (or worse) with antisemitism in a manner that would have been unthinkable a generation ago.

Antisemitic activity has elbowed its way from the extremist fringe into the mainstream political and media discourse to the point where many diaspora Jews, particularly in Europe, feel anxious about their futures. In a 2018 survey of over 16,000 self-identified Jewish adults across twelve European Union countries (containing 96 per cent of the EU's Jewish population), 89 per cent of respondents felt that antisemitism was increasing and 38 per cent reported that they had considered emigrating in the previous five years.[28] A Tel Aviv university group that monitors antisemitism globally reported a dismal picture: 'The data on antisemitic incidents since 2021 from across the Jewish world is discouraging. While the fight against antisemitism was fiercer than ever on different fronts, several of the countries with the largest Jewish minorities in the world witnessed a sharp rise in anti-Jewish attacks compared to 2020.'[29] The upward trend accelerated further in the wake of the 7 October 2023 Hamas attack even before the Israeli military response wreaked havoc on the Gaza strip.

Recognising Antisemitism

Contempt for Jews is often expressed as anti-Zionism or severe and disproportionate criticism of specific Israeli policies. This is what Norman Geras has called *alibi antisemitism* whereby the perpetrators disguise their true feelings behind the fig leaf of a respectable, even humanitarian, ideology.[30] A related phenomenon that has yet to achieve widespread recognition is *fake phylosemitism* whereby antisemites disguise their racist singling out of the Jewish state behind ostensible solidarity with selected Jews or Jewish communities, usually in the diaspora, who share their views. A German official appointed to counter antisemitism in the state of Baden-Württemberg, for example, appears to have exploited his position to pursue a covert anti-Israeli and antisemitic agenda.[31]

A new variant of a familiar disease has emerged. The ancient hatred has mutated into a novel form that focuses obsessively on the epitome of Jewish collectivity, the Jewish state of Israel. Oblivious to the irony, antisemites accuse Jews of exaggerating or exploiting their experience of antisemitism for nefarious purposes, including the protection of Israel, the very institution that most Jews regard as their insurance policy against any future existential threat. For that reason alone, antisemitism is a major concern for most Jews in the early twenty-first century.

At the same time, the capacity of antisemites to inflict serious harm on Jews has changed for the better since 1948. Jews are no longer passive and powerless victims of the hatred directed against them. Firstly, the state of Israel offers a protective barrier that had been absent for two millennia – a barrier that antisemites seek to dismantle for obvious reasons. Secondly, Jewish communities around the world have worked, over a period of years, with numerous non-Jewish supporters, organisations and governments to confront the threat by means of a characteristically Jewish response. They have studied the phenomenon, reached a strong (if not universal) consensus, and forged a powerful intellectual weapon: the IHRA definition (see below).

When is Criticism of Israel Antisemitic?

Much discussion has centred on the nature of this antisemitic anti-Israelism and how it may be distinguished from normal criticism of Israeli policies and practices. The explanation for antisemitic anti-Israelism is, in a sense, self-evident – the reborn Jewish state has become a lightning conductor for antisemitism. British journalist Jake Wallis Simons has coined the term 'Israelophobia' for this form of antisemitism that fixates on the Jewish state rather than the Jewish race or religion.[32] On the other hand, many non-antisemitic Jews, Israelis and others are critics of specific Israeli policies. The confusing result is that (almost) all antisemites are harsh critics of Israel while not all harsh critics of Israel are antisemites. This poses a fundamental question: how may hostility to Israel, including criticism of her policies and practices, be distinguished from antisemitism?

A pioneering approach to differentiating antisemitism from legitimate criticism of Israel was the rule of thumb proposed by Israeli human rights activist Natan Sharansky. He offered Three Ds that should raise suspicion of antisemitic motivation or behaviour: – demonisation, double standards and delegitimisation.[33]

The International Holocaust Remembrance Alliance Definition of Antisemitism

Sharansky's ideas, in modified form, were influential in the development of a European definition of antisemitism that is recognisable today as that of the International Holocaust Remembrance Alliance (IHRA). Their consensus statement is supported by most Jewish organisations and is gaining widespread recognition by governments across the world – around forty countries and counting. The Alliance, a Berlin-based coalition of thirty-four democracies, was initiated by Swedish prime minister Persson in 1998 along with partner NGOs and expert advisors. It developed into a collaboration between the Organization for Security and Cooperation in Europe (OSCE) and the European Monitoring Centre on Racism and Xenophobia (EUMC). Persson had the foresight to recognise that antisemitism was resurgent around the world and had to be stopped. Two seminal events in 2001 injected urgency into the task: the 9/11 attacks on the US that triggered a surge in global antisemitism, and the UN-sponsored Durban antiracism conference that labelled Israel an apartheid state deserving of pariah status (see Chapter 7). After more than a decade of study, debate and consultation, the Alliance published a Working Definition in 2016: 'Antisemitism is a certain perception of Jews, which may be expressed as hatred toward Jews.'[2]

An integral part of the definition, that is a guide to identifying antisemitism and is not intended to have legal force, were eleven illustrative examples, around half of which directly related to Zionism and/or Israel. The examples describe behaviour that *could* be antisemitic depending on the context. Here are the ones largely (though not exclusively) unrelated to Israel or Zionism:

- Calling for, aiding, or justifying the killing or harming of Jews in the name of a radical ideology or an extremist view of religion.
- Making mendacious, dehumanising, demonising, or stereotypical allegations about Jews as such or the power of Jews as collective — such as the myth about a world Jewish conspiracy or of Jews controlling the media, economy, government or other societal institutions.
- Accusing Jews as a people of being responsible for real or imagined wrongdoing committed by a single Jewish person or group, or even for acts committed by non-Jews.
- Denying the fact, scope, mechanisms (e.g. gas chambers) or intentionality of the genocide of the Jewish people at the hands of National Socialist Germany and its supporters and accomplices during the Second World War.
- Accusing the Jews as a people, or Israel as a state, of inventing or exaggerating the Holocaust.

The illustrative examples that are largely (though not exclusively) related to Israel or Zionism are preceded by a statement that is the touchstone principle: 'Criticism of Israel similar to that levelled against any other country cannot be regarded as antisemitic.'

What *may* be antisemitic includes:

- Denying Jews their right to self-determination e.g. claiming that 'Israel is a racist endeavour.'
- Applying double standards by requiring of Israel behaviour not expected or demanded of any other democratic nation.
- Using the symbols and images associated with classic antisemitism (e.g. claims of Jews killing Jesus or blood libel) to characterize Israel or Israelis.
- Drawing comparisons of contemporary Israeli policy to that of the Nazis.
- Accusing Jews of dual loyalty (to Israel or Jews worldwide).
- Holding Jews collectively or individually accountable for actions of Israel.

These examples are especially crucial as so much contemporary antisemitism is channelled towards the Jewish state. And indeed critics of the definition tend to focus on the examples relating to Israel, arguing that it forbids 'legitimate criticism of Israel' and is an arbitrary 'Zionist' definition that should not be endorsed by those who value free speech. Both arguments are specious. Legitimate criticism of Israel is explicitly protected by the definition and the definition is not legally binding. Moreover, it has been approved by most Jewish organisations and institutions around the world, including Israel. If Jews are denied the right to define their own experience of prejudice, whose right is it?

A helpful light is shone upon this question by the UK's experience of anti-black racism. The Macpherson enquiry was established in 1997 to ensure that the (London) Metropolitan Police would learn lessons from the racist murder of a teenager, Stephen Lawrence, in 1994. Its report was ground-breaking in that it established two principles: institutional (or cultural) racism can exist with or without personal racism, and racism should be primarily defined by its target, rather than its perpetrator.[34] These principles effectively validate the IHRA definition and ensure that the descriptor 'Zionist' can no longer be deployed freely as a term of abuse against Jewish or non-Jewish people.

Notes

1   D. Lipstadt, *Antisemitism Here and Now* (London, Scribe Publications, 2019), p.14.
2   International Holocaust Remembrance Alliance. About the IHRA non-legally binding working definition of antisemitism. https://www.holocaustremembrance.com/resources/working-definitions-charters/working-definition-antisemitism (Last accessed 11 June 2024).
3   R. Wistrich, *Antisemitism: The Longest Hatred* (New York: Pantheon Books, 1991).
4   W. Laqueur, *The Changing Face of Antisemitism.* (New York: Oxford University Press, 2006), p.2.
5   Brooke Ramos, 'Horseshoe Theory, the Squad, and the Bipartisan Tendency Toward Antisemitism.' *Jewish on Campus,* 1 September 2021. https://medium.com/jewish-on-campus/horseshoe-theory-the-squad-and-the-bipartisan-tendency-toward-antisemitism-33705b44fa41_(Last accessed 10 June 2024).
6   Reut Group, 'The Red-Green Alliance is coming to America. The Impact of the Islamo-Leftist Coalition on US Jewry & Foreign Policy, & Israel's

National Security.' Tel Aviv, Reut Group, 10 January 2022. https://www. reutgroup.org/Publications/The-Red-Green-Alliance-is-Coming-to-America (Last accessed 11 June 2024).

7   Leviticus 16:8-10.

8   B. Stora, 'Antisemitism: an intimate domination.' London Centre for the Study of Contemporary Antisemitism https://londonantisemitism.com/ news/antisemitism-an-intimate-domination-brigitte-stora/ (Last accessed 11 June 2024).

9   B. Gawronski, W. Hofmann, C. J. Wilbur,' Are "implicit" attitudes unconscious?' *Consciousness and Cognition*, 15, 3, 2006, pp. 485-499.

10 E. Garrard, 'The Pleasures of Antisemitism,' *Fathom*, Summer 2013. https://fathomjournal.org/the-pleasures-of-antisemitism/ (Last accessed 11 June 2024.

11 D. Levitin, *This is Your Brain on Music* (London: Penguin Books, 2019), p.120.

12 D. Goldhagen, *Hitler's Willing Executioners* (London: Abacus, 1997).

13 Y. Rosenberg, 'When an Israeli Ambassador Debated a British Historian on Israel's Legitimacy—and Won,' *Tablet*, 31 January 2014. https://www. tabletmag.com/sections/news/articles/herzog-toynbee-1961 (Last accessed 11 June 2024).

14 D. Baddiel, *Jews Don't Count.* (London: TLS Books, 2021).

15 D. Graham, J. Boyd. *Committed, Concerned and Conciliatory: the Attitude of Jews in Britain Towards Israel* (London, Institute for Jewish Policy Research, 2010), p.9. https://www.jpr.org.uk/reports/committed-concerned-and-conciliatory-attitudes-jews-britain-towards-israel (Last accessed 11 June 2024).

16 F. Newport, 'American Jews, Politics and Israel.' *Polling Matters (Gallup),* 27 August 2019. https://news.gallup.com/opinion/polling-matters/265898/american-jews-politics-israel.aspx (Last accessed 11 June 2024).

17 United Nations Charter (Full Text), Preamble, Article 1(2). Geneva, United Nations, 1945. https://www.un.org/en/about-us/un-charter/full-text (Last accessed 30 December 2023).

18 A. Johnson, 'The Left and the Jews: Time for a Rethink.' *Fathom*, Autumn 2015. https://fathomjournal.org/the-left-and-the-jews-time-for-a-rethink/ (Last accessed 11 June 2024).

19 Vernon Bogdanor, 'Singling out Israel is a very modern antisemitism.' *Jewish Chronicle*, 6 May 206.

20 R. Shepherd, *A State Beyond the Pale.* (London: Orion Books, 2009), p.37.

21 D. Hirsh, 'How Raising the Issue of Antisemitism Puts You Outside the Community of the Progressive: The Livingstone Formulation.' In E. Pollack (ed.) *From Antisemitism to Anti-Zionism: The Past & Present of a Lethal*

Ideology (Boston, USA: Academic Studies Press, 2017), pp. 2-28. https://doi.org/10.1515/9781618115669-002 (Last accessed 11 June 2024).

22 E.H Kaplan, C. A Small, 'Anti-Israel Sentiment Predicts Anti-Semitism in Europe', *Journal of Conflict Resolution*, 50,4 (August 2006), pp. 548-561.

23 D. Graham, J. Boyd, 'The Apartheid Contention and Calls for a Boycott: Examining Hostility Towards Israel in Great Britain', *JPR Analysis*, 29 January 2019. https://archive.jpr.org.uk/object-uk509. (Last accessed (Last accessed 11 June 2024).

24 European Union Agency for Fundamental Rights, *Experiences and perceptions of antisemitism: Second survey on discrimination and hate crime against Jews in the EU*, FRA 2019, p.1. https://fra.europa.eu/sites/default/files/fra_uploads/fra-2018-experiences-and-perceptions-of-antisemitism-survey-summary_en.pdf (Last accessed 11 June 2024).

25 Equality and Human Rights Commission: Investigation into Antisemitism in the Labour Party, Report, October 2020, p.6. https://www.equalityhumanrights.com/sites/default/files/investigation-into-antisemitism-in-the-labour-party.pdf (Last accessed 11 June 2024).

26 Community Security Trust, 'Antisemitic Incidents Report.' (London: CST, 2021), p.4. https://cst.org.uk/data/file/f/f/Incidents per cent20Report per cent202021.1644318940.pdf (Last accessed 11 June 2024).

27 Lord John Mann, 'Anti-Jewish Hatred: Tackling Antisemitism in the UK 2023: Renewing the Commitment,' HM Government's Independent Adviser on Antisemitism. https://antisemitism.org.uk/wp-content/uploads/2022/12/PDF-Antisemitism-Report-2023.pdf (Last accessed 11 June 2024).

28 European Union Agency for Fundamental Rights, Experiences and perceptions of antisemitism: Second survey on discrimination and hate crime against Jews in the EU. FRA 2019, p.3. https://fra.europa.eu/sites/default/files/fra_uploads/fra-2018-experiences-and-perceptions-of-antisemitism-survey-summary_en.pdf (Last accessed 11 June 2024).

29 The Center for the Study of Contemporary European Jewry, 'Antisemitism Worldwide Report 2021.' https://cst.tau.ac.il/wp-content/uploads/2022/04/Antisemitism-Worldwide-2021.pdf (Last accessed 11 June 2024).

30 N. Geras, 'Alibi Antisemitism', *Fathom*, Spring 2013. https://fathomjournal.org/alibi-antisemitism/ (Last accessed 11 June 2024).

31 Benjamin Weinthal, 'Israeli General Slams "Antisemitic" German Official for Defaming Israeli Hero,' *Jerusalem Post*, 12 August 2022. https://www.jpost.com/diaspora /antisemitism/article-714601 (Last accessed 11 June 2024).

32 J. W. Simons, *Israelophobia: The Newest Version of the Oldest Hatred and What To Do About It* (London: Constable, 2023).

33 N. Sharansky, '3D Test of AntiSemitism: Demonization, Double Standards, Delegitimization', *Jewish Political Studies Review*, 16, (Fall 2004), pp.3-4.
34 W. Macpherson, *The Stephen Lawrence Inquiry* (London: Home Office, Cm 4262-I, 1999).

3

What is Zionism?

Zionism is the most misrepresented political ideology in history. Its meaning has been distorted to conceal a fundamental if inconvenient truth: there is nothing remarkable or sinister about Zionism. Antisemites have redefined it to fit with a preconceived, malign and fictional reality.

Definitions of Zionism

Nathan Birnbaum, an Austrian-Jewish writer who would later be elected Secretary General of the Zionist Organisation, coined the term in 1890 though the ideas it encapsulated were already being discussed by that date. Of the various definitions, perhaps the most widely accepted one in the Jewish world is this: *Zionism is the national movement for the return of the Jewish people to their homeland and the resumption of Jewish sovereignty in the Land of Israel.*[1] A more succinct alternative version (that should appeal to progressives) is that *Zionism is the national liberation movement of the Jewish people.*

Initially, the aim of Zionism was to fulfil for Jews the universal right to self-determination through the re-establishment of a Jewish state. When that was achieved in 1948, Zionism's role became uncertain but there is a near-consensus in Israel and the Jewish diaspora that it remains relevant. Today the meaning of Zionism is sometimes expanded to include efforts to develop and defend the state of Israel.

Beginnings

The state of Israel is in its eighth decade. Because the Zionist movement antedated the establishment of the state by about another half-century, the modern Zionist project is around 125 years old in total. That statement may be factually correct yet it is also misleading. For the roots of Zionism stretch far back in time and have long been firmly embedded in the collective Jewish psyche. Without the intimate historical Jewish connection to the homeland, Zionism would make little sense to Jews (or anyone else).

The Kingdom of Israel is thought to have been established in 1050 BCE (Before the Christian Era) before splitting into two parts 120 years later. Its capital Jerusalem, or Zion, is mentioned at least 150 times in the *Tanach*, the Jewish scriptures (and, as a point of comparison, not at all in the Koran). Its focal point was the First Temple, built by King Solomon in the tenth century BCE. Archaeologists argue over the veracity of much of the biblical narrative but most scholars agree that extra-scriptural sources leave no doubt as to the existence in that time and place of an Israelite, Hebrew-speaking civilisation.

The Jewish aspiration to return home can be traced to 733 BCE after Assyrian king Tiglath-Pileser III had invaded and annexed large parts of the northern kingdom (Israel) and deported masses of its inhabitants. At the start of the sixth century BCE, following the Babylonian conquest of the southern kingdom (Judea), a further deportation of thousands of Judeans (Jews) occurred,[2] and Solomon's Temple was destroyed in 586 BCE. Fifty years of Jewish exile ensued before a return to the homeland was permitted by the Persian king Cyrus, who had overthrown the Babylonians. Judea was then ruled by the Persians, the Seleucids (Greeks) and, after about a century of restored Jewish sovereignty, the Romans, who occupied the Jewish state in 63 BCE.

Rome instituted direct rule on Judea in the year 6 CE; this was accompanied by increasing repression that led to a series of Jewish uprisings in the second century.[3] Having destroyed Jerusalem along with its Second Temple in 70 CE, the Romans ruthlessly crushed the remnants of the revolt, massacred or expelled most of the remaining Jews, and in the year 135 renamed Jerusalem *Aelia Capitolina* and Judea *Syria Palaestina*[4] though the Jews referred to it as *Eretz Israel*, the Land of Israel.

In 636, the Arab conquest of the region brought mixed fortunes for the exiled Jews who were initially allowed back to Jerusalem but later again prohibited from entering. The Muslim rulers built the *Al Aqsa* Mosque and the *Qubbat aş-Şakhra* (Dome of the Rock) on the Temple Mount (*Haram al-Sharif*), the site of the destroyed Jewish Temple. In 1211, around 300 Jews from England and France managed to reach Jerusalem but most were killed by the Crusaders in 1219 while the few who survived were expelled and found refuge in Akko (Acre). Over subsequent centuries, some Jews succeeded, despite major obstacles, in returning to their homeland while others who had never left somehow survived and avoided deportation; both groups tenaciously ensured a continuous, indigenous Jewish presence in *Eretz Israel*, albeit as an impoverished and persecuted minority.

Of necessity, most Jews were confined to the diaspora where they preserved a sense of nationhood via the writings and customs of Judaism that is replete with texts, songs, festivals, customs and prayers referencing the homeland and its Holy City. The heartfelt yearning to return, as encapsulated in the phrase 'the ingathering of the exiles,' is manifested ritually in, for example, facing towards Jerusalem in daily prayers, calling for the rebuilding of the city during blessings after meals, and ending the annual Passover *Seder* (festive meal) ceremony with the entreaty 'Next year in Jerusalem!'

Among the many conquerors of the Land of Israel from antiquity to the present were Assyrians, Babylonians, Persians, Seleucids, Romans, Byzantines, Sassanids, Arabs, Umayyads, Abbasids, Fatimids, Seljuks, Crusaders, Ayyubids, Mamluks, Ottomans and finally the British. All were seen off eventually and Jewish sovereignty re-established. In the light of this chronology, it is a reasonable assumption that Israel today would be over 3,000 years old had it not been for foreign invasion, conquest and expulsion. Moreover, Zionism must be regarded as the most (ultimately) successful anti-imperialist movement in history. That the Jews never abandoned their attachment to their homeland is the cultural-religious context out of which modern political Zionism emerged. It explains the widespread and passionate support throughout the Jewish world that the early Zionist leaders were able to garner in their quest for a restored Jewish nation state.

From Praying to Pioneering: the Jews Cleave to their Homeland

In the Middle Ages, Jewish communities are known to have existed in the four holy cities of Jerusalem, Hebron, Tzfat (Safed) and Tiberias as well as in Akko (Acre), Yaffo (Jaffa), Ashkelon, Beer Sheva, Gaza, Rafah, Jericho, Caesarea and elsewhere. Waves of Jewish immigration arrived from Spain following their expulsion from that country in 1492. Small numbers of Jewish immigrants from the diaspora were permitted to join their indigenous compatriots in *Eretz Israel* but faced great obstacles in reaching their homeland, and were frequently subjected to religiously inspired pogroms when they arrived, particularly when Syria (of which 'Palestine' was a district) was ruled by the Ottoman Empire from the early sixteenth century onwards. By the start of Ottoman rule, around 10,000 Jews lived in the Galilee region alone. The community was boosted by a steady trickle of Jews arriving from Eastern Europe in the late eighteenth century, and from Yemen a century later.

In the mid-nineteenth century, the Turkish-administered territory that would later become British Mandatory Palestine – roughly today's Israel, West Bank (Judea and Samaria), and Jordan – was still a barren, malaria-ridden and barely habitable wasteland. It was home to around 300,000 people drawn from a diversity of ethnic groups, including the aboriginal Jews (comprising at this point probably less than ten per cent of the total population), Circassians, Arabs, Druze, Kurds and Europeans. Many of the Arabs were nomadic Bedouin or immigrants from Algeria, Egypt, Syria, Libya and elsewhere. Poverty and disease were rife and economic activity minimal.

The opening of the Suez Canal in 1868 stimulated the construction of basic infrastructure such as roads, mail and telegraph services, and in 1892 the railway between Jaffa and Jerusalem was inaugurated. But the Ottoman Empire was already showing signs of fracturing and would finally be dismantled as a result of its rulers choosing the losing side in the Great War.

The *Yishuv*

Throughout the second half of the nineteenth century, the Jewish population – the *Yishuv* – of *Eretz Israel*, though still a minority for the reasons explained, had begun to grow, especially in the port city of Jaffa and above all in Jerusalem where Jews had become the majority around 1850 and have remained so to this day. During this period, nationalist ideology was spreading throughout Europe and the Middle East and the dream of a reborn Jewish state in the homeland, an idea which had begun to surface in the late nineteenth century, no longer seemed an unattainable possibility.

The first significant surge of self-consciously 'national' Jewish immigration from Europe (the *First Aliyah*) is usually traced to the early 1880s. By 1917, following the transformation of Zionism into a serious political movement, the Jewish population of the *Yishuv* had increased to between 90,000 and 100,000 or one sixth of the total of the Palestine district. Most of these Jews had been refugees fleeing pogroms, discrimination and poverty in Russia and Eastern Europe, particularly in the decade prior to the First World War (the *Second Aliyah*); the remainder were living in established Jewish communities that were mainly located in the four holy cities.

A *de facto* Jewish national home already existed in the Jewish ancestral homeland by the time of the Balfour Declaration in 1917. This chronology is important. The revitalisation of that homeland and the development of an elaborate communal infrastructure had been achieved through the extraordinary dedication, hard work and sacrifice of Zionist pioneers without any help or support from colonial powers. What was now needed was international recognition of that reality to assure its further development and long-term survival. The opportunity arose during the latter stages of the First World War when Great Britain started the process of planning the fate of the vast territories that had been held for four hundred years by the Ottoman Empire.

Modern Political Zionism

The range of options available to most Jews at the end of the nineteenth century was limited. After trying all the other paths to emancipation on offer – integration, assimilation, the Enlightenment – and encountering immoveable obstacles, it seemed to many Jews that only Zionism remained. Some, particularly in Europe, felt that demanding equal rights was worth one last throw of the dice and held out hope that they would finally be accepted by the non-Jewish societies in which they resided. They were tragically mistaken.

Critics of Zionism fail to appreciate that its appeal to Jews lies less in its ideological or political content as in its practical necessity. For Zionism is first and foremost a Jewish survival mechanism. The notion that Jews 'chose' Zionism from a range of enticing alternatives is false. Other gates to freedom had all been slammed shut. For the Jews confined to the Tsarist Pale of Settlement and other ghettoes throughout eastern Europe, the turning point was the assassination in 1881 of Alexander the Second for which the Jews – all Jews – were blamed (though the killer was a non-Jew).

The pogroms that followed plumbed such unprecedented depths of cruelty that they propelled the Jews of Russia in three radical directions – into flight (mainly to other parts of Europe and the USA), into the ranks of the communist and anarchist revolutionaries, and towards Zionism, a somewhat nebulous notion at the time. Moses Hess, a socialist colleague of Karl Marx, was an early advocate of Jewish statehood in his 1862 *Rome and Jerusalem: The Last National Question*. In 1882, Leon Pinsker, a middle-aged Russian-Jewish physician, had the prescience to grasp that only sovereignty ('auto-emancipation') offered a realistic hope of Jewish survival:

> We must reconcile ourselves, once and for all, to the idea that the other nations, by nature of their eternal, natural antagonism, will

forever reject us. We may not shut our eyes to this natural force, which works like every other elemental force; we must take it into account… We must use all means which human intellect and human experience have devised, in order that the sacred work of national regeneration may not be left to blind chance.[5]

Fourteen years later, a young and highly assimilated Austro-Hungarian Jewish journalist, Theodor Herzl, reached the same conclusion and in doing so issued a clarion call to his fellow Jews to join him in establishing the modern Zionist movement: 'Let the sovereignty be granted us over a portion of the globe large enough to satisfy the rightful requirements of a nation; the rest we shall manage for ourselves.'[6]

That message struck a chord with Jews across the world. That 'portion of the globe' was *Eretz Israel*, the ancestral homeland from which Jews had been ejected repeatedly – and as often as not refused re-entry – but with which they had maintained a strong connection, both physical and spiritual. Because Zion was the biblical synonym for Jerusalem, the capital of ancient Israel, the site of Solomon's Temple and the focus of Jewish prayer and yearning for over two millennia, the emotional attraction of Zionism to Jews was instant and profound. Herzl's message was also a product of its time when a widespread clamour was arising from nations around the world, especially in Europe, that had been the subjects of foreign colonial powers. Inspired by freedom fighters such as Garibaldi, national liberation movements were sparking the imaginations of idealistic young people everywhere. But Herzl's real genius lay in a key insight: words alone would be insufficient, they needed to be backed by practical action. He summoned the First Zionist Congress in Basel in 1897 and announced this unambiguous goal: 'Zionism seeks for the Jewish people a publicly recognised legally secured homeland in Palestine.' That sentence became the manifesto for the first generation of Zionist political activists.

When Herzl arrived on the scene, the global Jewish community, both western (*Ashkenazi*) and eastern (*Mizrachi*) Jews, had greeted him as a secular messiah. His premature death at the age of 44 dealt a severe blow to his followers who had to await the entrance into the Jewish revivalist drama of a new generation of Zionist leaders led by the charismatic Russian-born activist Chaim Weizmann. A distinguished Manchester-based chemist by profession, Weizmann recognised that the only way to fulfil the Zionist dream of Jewish statehood was to persuade the Great Powers of the day of the justice of the Zionist cause. Where better to start than with the most powerful empire the world had ever seen?

The Balfour Declaration: Myth and Reality

Weizmann's lobbying of the British government bore fruit with spectacular success. On 2 November 1917, the British War Cabinet issued a statement in the form of a letter from Lord Arthur James Balfour, the Foreign Secretary, to Lord Lionel Walter Rothschild, an Anglo-Jewish dignitary, for transmission to the Zionist Federation of Great Britain and Ireland. The letter stated that:

> His Majesty's government view with favour the establishment in Palestine of a national home for the Jewish people, and will use their best endeavours to facilitate the achievement of this object, it being clearly understood that nothing shall be done which may prejudice the civil and religious rights of existing non-Jewish communities in Palestine, or the rights and political status enjoyed by Jews in any other country. [7]

The Balfour Declaration, as this document became known, was a ground-breaking British government statement that recognised the unbroken historical, religious and cultural connection of the Jewish people to the land from which they had been largely expelled, and destroyed as a sovereign nation, by the Romans some 2,000 years earlier. The Declaration obligated the British government to use its 'best endeavours' – meaning that they would implement all reasonable measures rather than merely offer support in principle – to achieve the objective of the establishment of a 'national home for the Jewish people' in Palestine. That was not a land transfer nor even a policy statement but rather an expression of sympathy with the aspirations of the Zionist movement.

The motivation driving the Declaration's authors is somewhat opaque. It may have comprised a curious mixture of idealism, military geopolitics and phylosemitism. It may even have been driven, paradoxically, by more than a tinge of antisemitism; British ministers were convinced that expressing sympathy for Zionism would be welcomed by the majority of Jews around the world who would mobilise international Jewish 'influence' to persuade both Russia and America to maintain their alliance with Britain in their confrontation with the Germans and the Turks.

The Declaration has acquired iconic status in Zionist history as it was the first public expression of Great Power endorsement of the Zionist aspiration to re-establish sovereignty in the historical Jewish homeland. It was incorporated into international law via the San Remo Resolution of

1920 and the League of Nations Mandate for Palestine in 1922. But a closer look at the historical record reveals a hidden truth: the Balfour Declaration was not the first expression of Great Power support for Zionism. At the end of the First World War there was widespread international sympathy for Zionism as for other national liberation movements. The specifically British role in promoting Zionism via the Balfour Declaration was important but should not be overrated. London would not have adopted such a far-reaching policy without taking account of the likely response of its allies.[8] How did Lloyd George and Arthur Balfour know that it would be so well received?

Weizmann, president of the British Zionist Federation, along with a small number of gifted colleagues, had virtually guaranteed a warm reception for the Declaration through their tireless negotiations with senior officials around the world. They knew that Britain was far from an outlier.

4. Zionist leader Nahum Sokolow (possibly 1922). Source: George Grantham Bain Collection United States Library of Congress Prints and Photographs Division under digital ID ggbain.33385

Because of the growing consensus around US President Wilson's advocacy of the universal right to self-determination, most governments correctly sensed that support for Zionism was growing. Weizmann set about capitalising on that trend by seeking public endorsement from as many important powers as he could, including Italy, Turkey, Japan and, as has recently been revealed, China's new post-imperial leadership.[9] Even the German Kaiser, struggling to cope with multiple setbacks in the latter stages of the First World War, was showing interest in the Zionist cause, a development that undoubtedly focused British minds. While their main target was the British government, the Zionist leadership spotted another possible ally hiding in the shadows.

The French Connection

If the British affirmation of Jewish rights in 1917 proved a turning point for the international community's attitude to the Jewish people, it was not the first endorsement Zionist aims by a powerful state. That accolade goes to France, one of the least phylosemitic countries in Europe. It was secured, with the knowledge and approval of the French prime minister Alexandre Ribot, by the Zionist activist Nahum Sokolow.

Sokolow is generally regarded as an historical footnote in Israel's history. This is unjust. He was a brilliant polyglot writer and the first to translate Herzl's iconic novel *Altneuland* into Hebrew, giving it the title *Tel Aviv* (literally, 'An Ancient Hill of Spring') that in 1909 was adopted as the name of the first modern Hebrew-speaking city. Sokolow's talents were recognised by Weizmann, who charged him with the task of drumming up support around the world for the aims of the Zionist movement. Counter-intuitively, Sokolow's initial interest lay less in the British, despite their importance as the world's foremost colonial power, than in their eternal rivals, the French. Zionism's game-changing diplomatic breakthrough, engineered by Sokolow, antedated the Balfour letter by six months. On 3 June 1917, a dramatic new policy was announced by Jules Cambon, head of the political section of the French foreign ministry, and one of the most celebrated diplomats of the time. Here is the key section of Cambon's letter that was addressed to Sokolow:

> It would be a deed of justice and of reparation to assist, by the protection of the Allied Powers, in the renaissance of the Jewish nationality in that Land from which the people of Israel were exiled so many centuries ago. The French government, which entered this

present war to defend a people wrongly attacked, and which continues the struggle to assure the victory of right over might, can but feel sympathy for your cause, the triumph of which is bound up with that of the Allies. I am happy to give you herewith such assurance.[8]

This French statement of sympathy for Zionism became known as the Cambon Declaration, the progenitor of its more illustrious British version. Why did the French government support Zionism in the early twentieth century? Perhaps they saw it as a vehicle for implementing the secret Anglo-French Sykes-Picot agreement pertaining to the post-war configuration of the region; if they did, they were wrong. More likely, they were moved by the persuasive powers of the Zionist leaders, and Sokolow in particular, combined with an awareness of President Wilson's assertion of self-determination as a universal human right as the war was drawing to a close.

Another critical factor may have been Sokolow's *coup*, just weeks before his meeting with Cambon, in persuading Pope Benedict XV to reverse the Catholic church's previous anti-Zionism that had been predicated on the belief that the Jewish people's dispersion was punishment for their refusal to recognise Jesus as the Messiah. The return of the Jews to Palestine, opined the Pontiff (according to Sokolow), was 'providential: God has willed it.' (It took, however, close to another half a century before the Vatican formally sought to lay its anti-Jewish demons to rest when a large majority of the Second Vatican Ecumenical Council approved the *Nostra Aetate* document in the face of determined Arab opposition[10]).

France was an unlikely ally of the Jewish people and their Zionist ambitions. The upper echelons of French society had been ambivalent about Jews for centuries. In 1789, the Jews of Metz asked for protection against the threat of anti-Jewish mob violence of which there had been outbursts in Alsace. Stanislas de Clermont-Tonnerre, a liberal nobleman from Paris, asserted that, while the Jews suffered oppression, the state could not recognise their collective rights since there could not be 'a nation within a nation' though they could be granted everything as individuals.[11] This principle was incorporated into Napoleonic law.

The role of the Dreyfus trial in 1894 in persuading Herzl of the need for restored Jewish sovereignty is well documented if somewhat mythologised. What is not at issue is the degree to which deep-seated antisemitism had long infected French politics, the army, the arts and academia. Both the colonisation and decolonisation of the Maghreb worsened the plight of Jews in that region. Few today realise that many

North African Jews were sent to concentration camps during the Second World War by the Vichy administration that implemented Nazi policies in its North African colonies as well as in mainland France.

Balfour's Impact on Jews

Unsurprisingly, the Balfour Declaration was greeted joyously in Jewish communities around the world. Jewish support for Zionism grew rapidly and was soon transformed into a grass-roots mass movement especially in Russia and Eastern Europe where radical socialist ideas permeated Zionist thinking. Although Zionism was neither created by the Declaration nor granted any special legal status by it, it was a political statement of great importance as it was the first time a major power had publicly offered unequivocal support for the reconstitution of the Jewish national home. That gave the Zionist movement an enormous psychological and diplomatic boost and paved the way for its subsequent political recognition by the international community.

Balfour's Impact on Arabs

The Arab reaction to news of the Balfour Declaration was unenthusiastic but by no means universally hostile. Within Palestine, the influential Nashashibi family, unlike their rivals the Husseinis, were generally sympathetic as were many other Arab dynasties. Emir Faisal, son of the Hashemite Sharif Hussein Bin Ali of Mecca and brother of Abdullah (whom the British would later appoint the first ruler of Transjordan), reached an agreement with Weizmann in January 1919 that appeared to place relations between the two communities on a peaceful and cooperative footing. This was followed by an effusively positive letter ('We will wish the Jews a most hearty welcome home') from Faisal to US Supreme Court Justice Felix Frankfurter of the Zionist Organisation.[12]

Faisal, perhaps under pressure from radicals, quickly withdrew his support for the agreement. Had he not done so, the entire Arab-Jewish conflict with its consequent toll of death and suffering might have been avoided since two national homes – a small Jewish state and a much larger Arab one – could have been quickly established. The former might have provided a safe haven for many of the nearly 200,000 Jews that were massacred by White Russians and Ukrainian nationalists in the year 1919 alone along with their children and grandchildren who, along with countless other European Jews, would later perish in the Holocaust.[13] Little wonder that Arab rejectionism, pioneered by Faisal, generated such bitterness in the Jewish world as opportunity after opportunity to reach an equitable agreement was contemptuously cast aside by successive Arab leaders. More than seven decades after the establishment of the modern state of Israel, Arab spokespeople, in their determination to cast the Palestinians as the sole victims of a conflict initiated and sustained by their own leaders, continue to ignore the necessity of sovereignty for one of the most persecuted nations in history.

Wider Impact of the Balfour Declaration

The Declaration has been blamed for creating the so-called 'Palestine triangle' – Britain, the *Yishuv*, and the Arabs – between the points of which much tension, antagonism and violence ensued. Both Jews and Arabs later denounced British behaviour as a betrayal of earlier promises regarding their national sovereignty. Historians are divided on the significance of the Declaration as a decisive factor in triggering the ensuing tumultuous course of events in the Middle East; some have argued that nationalist sentiment of all types may have been a more important factor than any specific Western policy change.

Anti-Zionists accuse Balfour of an unwarranted colonialist disposition of foreign (i.e. 'Arab' or 'Palestinian') territory. A stronger case can be made for the opposite assertion – that the Declaration marked a great stride forward for decolonisation. The Declaration in no way precluded the establishment of Arab sovereignty, to which the British government had already committed itself in the McMahon-Hussein correspondence of 1915-16 (see Chapter 4). By openly throwing their weight behind the cause of Jewish as well as Arab self-determination, the British government gave notice to the world that a new era was dawning whereby even the most marginalised and ill-treated peoples on earth could look forward to throwing off the yoke of imperialism and asserting control over their own destinies in their homelands. The Declaration thus had a geopolitical significance far beyond the specific aspirations of the Jewish people.

Incorporation of the Balfour Declaration into the Palestine Mandate

Following the end of the First World War, a prolonged diplomatic process began in January 1919 with the Paris peace conference that led to the Treaties of Versailles (1919), Sèvres (1920) and Lausanne (1923). In the course of this complicated series of negotiations, the victorious powers set about disposing of the conquered territories including those that had long been ruled by Germany and the Ottoman Empire.

In January 1920, the Paris conference created the League of Nations and its associated Covenant, Article 22 of which established the Mandates System. The Balfour Declaration was incorporated – with the help of the Zionist Organisation – into a Palestine Mandate that was conferred on Great Britain by the Principal Allied Powers at the San Remo Conference in April 1920. The San Remo Resolution, which included and elaborated upon the Balfour Declaration, was inserted into the Preamble of the Mandate, which became legally binding on all fifty-one states of the League. It was ratified by the Treaty of Sèvres and confirmed in its final version (after consultation with the United States) by the Council of the League of Nations in 1922. The Mandate is regarded by most Jews as their Magna Carta and the foundational source of the State of Israel's international legitimacy.

The Palestine Mandate, rather than the Balfour Declaration, was thus the key breakthrough for Zionism though the two were intimately connected through the San Remo Resolution. The Declaration had paved the way for the Mandate – a legally binding international obligation to ensure that the Jewish national home would be duly established in close cooperation with the Jewish people via an 'appropriate Jewish agency' (the Zionist Organisation). The aim of Zionism, as formulated at the First Zionist Congress in 1897, was now well on its way to being finally 'secured by public law.'

Inter-War Antisemitism Threatens Jewish Self-Determination

When the Great War ended, the world had changed beyond recognition. President Wilson's Fourteen Points were gaining traction and, since a prominent one of these was the pursuit of self-determination in the context of decolonisation, global sympathy for Zionism surged. Since a multitude of fledgling nations were champing at the bit to achieve imminent sovereignty in Europe, Africa and the Middle East, it appeared only a matter of time before the Jews would do the same. And indeed they did but not before two cruel twists of fate, one in Europe and the other in the Middle East, inflicted devastating and near-terminal blows to their prospects of survival – as individuals, families, communities and a revived nation.

One blow was delivered by Adolf Hitler, the other by Muhammad Amin al-Husseini. These odious politicians both rose to political power around the same critical period of history, and both leveraged the basest of human instincts to bolster their popularity. Above all, they shared a world-view that would determine almost all of their subsequent decision-making and found expression in a single overriding emotion: an unbridled loathing of Jews. An alliance between these two standard bearers of eliminationist antisemitism became virtually inevitable. This ominous and under-appreciated connection between National Socialism and Islamist anti-Zionism set the scene for the unfolding of a series of subsequent tragedies in Europe, the MENA region and around the globe.

Why Zionism Still Matters to Jews

The phenomenon of eliminationist antisemitism is not just a matter of history. Today we are witnessing a frightening global uptick in antisemitism that too often costs lives. It is a disturbing fact that many antisemitic individuals, groups and countries, whether in the Middle East or elsewhere, are not just antipathetic to Jews – they aim to bring about the annihilation of the Jewish people and their state. For that reason alone, the survival of Israel as a haven of last resort for all Jews, is non-negotiable. As Israeli legal scholar Amnon Rubinstein reflected in 2002, Zionism remains an existential necessity for Jews: 'The truth of the matter is that from the extinguished crater – from the apparent volcano of antisemitism – a stream of searing lava occasionally erupts…Just as the Jews of Russia in 1881 and the Jews of Iraq in 1941 felt they had no choice, now too, there is ultimately no gate to salvation open other than the Zionist gate.'[14]

As long as Israel exists, that gate will remain open to Jews wherever they live in the world. The continuing relevance of Zionism and Jewish sovereignty in the twenty-first century is emphasised in this statement by the educational NGO *StandWithUs* that links the state of Israel with Jewish history, identity, freedom and safety across three millennia:

> Israel is the birthplace of Jewish ethnic identity, language, culture, and religion, and Jews have maintained a constant presence there for over 3,000 years. Zionism represents the Jewish people's unbreakable bond and age-old desire to be free in their ancestral home. On a political level, Zionism is a liberation movement supporting Jewish self-determination in the land of Israel. Jews endured over 1,900 years of oppression and violence across Europe and the Middle East

and still live in a world plagued by antisemitism. In this context, Israel's existence and wellbeing is vital to the Jewish people's safety, survival, and human rights.[15]

Persistent Arab and Iranian anti-Zionism reinforces the conviction of most Israeli and diaspora Jews that the Zionist path, embodied in the Jewish state of Israel, is the only one that remains open to them. Because antisemitic anti-Zionism is the principal underlying cause of the conflict between Israel and her neighbours, it is unlikely to end until Arab and Muslim leaders lay to rest their societies' anti-Jewish demons. There are indications that this may be possible: Israel signed peace treaties with Egypt and Jordan (and transiently the Palestinians) in the twentieth century and, via the US-sponsored Abraham Accords, with several Arab states in the twenty-first. Unfortunately there have been many false dawns in the past. Israelis receive bitter reminders of this reality on a regular basis, most dramatically on 7 October 2023.

Zionism Through the Retrospectoscope: a Nationalism of No-Choice

Over the past 140 years, first the *Yishuv* and then Israel provided refuge to countless Jews fleeing discrimination, persecution and murder. The precise number is impossible to calculate but it runs to well over a million – and perhaps many millions if you include their descendants. Yet that remarkable record, that more than vindicates the Zionist vision, could have been so much better. Had Britain implemented the terms of the League of Nations Mandate for Palestine, millions more innocent lives might have been saved. By the mid-twentieth century, this was the key lesson most Jews – secular and religious, *Ashkenazim* and *Mizrachim* – had learned from their long and anguished history: full self-determination was their only cast-iron guarantee of physical, cultural and religious survival. The goal of Zionism had been to establish a Jewish state that would provide a safe haven for Jews and grant the Jewish people the universal human right to live in freedom and determine their own destiny. That was achieved, in theory, in 1948. Is Zionism therefore now redundant?

To answer that question, we need to review the position of Jews worldwide in the twenty-first century. The focus of eliminationist antisemitism is no longer Europe but the Middle East where Israel has faced unremitting hostility since the first day of her independence on 15 May 1948. Terrorism is a daily fact of Israeli life. Multiple well-armed extremist groups maintain their posture of 'resistance against the occupation'–meaning violence against Israelis, both military and civilian – in their dogged quest to 'liberate Palestine from the River to the Sea.' In this they are encouraged, armed and financed by an Islamist Iran that declares its intention to destroy the state of Israel either directly or via its multiple proxy militias (including Hamas, Hezbollah, Palestinian Islamic Jihad and the Houthis) throughout the Middle East. Extraordinarily, all these Israel-haters are supported in their politicidal and genocidal aims by many member states and officials of the United Nations. Because of these unremitting threats to her security, the Jewish state has to maintain compulsory military service and remain in a permanent state of the highest vigilance. That distracts attention from other national priorities and imposes a huge toll of physical, emotional and economic stress on her population.

Alan Johnson puts it well:

> Anti-Zionism meant one thing in the early twentieth century: an argument among Jews, mostly, about how best to meet the threat of antisemitism. Anti-Zionism has come to mean something entirely different after the Holocaust and after the creation of the State of Israel in 1948: it has come to mean a programme of comprehensive hostility to all but a sliver of world Jewry, a programme for the eradication of actually existing Jewish self-determination.[16]

Israel has accomplished much in her short existence as a modern state but she could achieve far more, domestically and internationally, were the conflicts with her neighbours to cease and permit the redirection of scarce resources currently devoted to defence into medical, educational, scientific, social and environmental programmes that desperately need them. The work of Zionism remains unfinished business.

Notes

1   Jewish Virtual Library. 'A Definition of Zionism.' https://www.jewishvirtuallibrary.org/a-definition-of-zionism (Last accessed 31 December 2023).
2   The term 'Jew' is identical with 'Judean' in Hebrew and most other languages.
3   Josephus, *The Jewish War* (London: Penguin Books, 1981).
4   D. Gordis, *Israel: A Concise History of a Nation Reborn* (New York: HarperCollins, 2016), pp. 3-4.

5   L. Pinsker, *Auto-Emancipation* (New York: The Maccabean Publishing Company, 1906), p.9.

6   T. Herzl, *The Jewish State* (London, Penguin Book, 2010), p.26.

7   L. Turnberg, *Beyond the Balfour Declaration* (London: Biteback Publishing Ltd, 2017), p.25.

8   M. Kramer, 'The Forgotten Truth about the Balfour Declaration, '*Mosaic*, 5 June 2017. https://scholar.harvard.edu/files/martinkramer/files/forgotten_truth_balfour_declaration.pdf (Last accessed 11 June 2024).

9   Z. Rothbart Z, 'Lost Letter on Zionism from "Father of the Chinese Nation" Surfaces, *The Librarians*, 10 February 2021. https://blog.nli.org.il/en/sun-yat-sen (Last accessed 11 June 2024.

10   F. Cartus, 'Vatican II and the Jews,' *Commentary*, January 1965. https://www.commentary.org/articles/fe-cartus/vatican-ii-the-jews/ (Last accessed 11 June 2024).

11   A. Shapira, *Israel: A History* (London: Weidenfeld & Nicolson, 2015), p.7.

12   W. Laqueur, B. Rubin (eds.), *The Israel-Arab Reader* (London: Penguin Books, 2008), p.19.

13   W. Laqueur, *The Changing Face of Antisemitism.* (New York: Oxford University Press, 2006), p.104.

14   A. Rubinstein, 'Only the Zionist gate remains open,' *Haaretz*, 13 March 2002. https://www.haaretz.com/2002-03-13/ty-article/only-the-zionist-gate-remains-open/0000017f-f415-d487-abff-f7ff82650000 (Last accessed 31 December 2023).

15   *StandWithUs*, Israel's Story and Zionism. https://www.standwithus.com/israels-story-and-zionism (Last accessed 11 June 2024).

16   A. Johnson, 'The Left and the Jews: Time for a Rethink,' *Fathom*, Autumn 2015. https://fathomjournal.org/the-left-and-the-jews-time-for-a-rethink/ (Last accessed 11 October 2022). (Last accessed 11 June 2024).

4

The Arab-Israeli Conflict –
Who Is To Blame?

The Arab-Israeli conflict has aways attracted more than its fair share of moralistic preaching. With the passage of time, the finger of blame has been increasingly pointed at Israel. This chapter will try to establish whether that condemnatory posture is justified and the next will explore its primary motivation.

Evidence matters

A key concept is central to any discussion of the responsibility for this (or any) international dispute: the primacy of facts. An evidence-based approach is not the sole prerogative of academic historians or lawyers. That seems an uncontentious condition. Why, then, do so many of the harshest critics of Israel ignore almost all the evidence?

To clarify: evidence is not a synonym for 'arguments that support my point of view' since that will produce an endless reiteration of preconceived prejudices. Evidence is derived from objectively demonstrable facts cited in context. There is no room here for the post-modernist concept of 'competing narratives' in which there are multiple versions of the truth, all of which should be regarded as equally valid. Either something happened or it did not. Establishing the truth requires a careful and systematic review of sources paying particular attention to their integrity and credibility, and seeking to subject controversial assertions to close scrutiny and corroboration.

Evidence comprises more than a series of statements of the bald facts: it also involves a process of critical analysis including the ordering of those facts in a sequence indicating their relative importance or priority. This step is where problems and controversies are most likely to arise as it requires the exercise of subjective judgment. Daniel Kahneman, Nobel prizewinning Israeli-American psychologist and economist, describes two types of human thinking in his 2011 book *Thinking, Fast and Slow*.[1] Type 1 is instant, affective, largely irrational and often wrong. Type 2 is slow, reflective, analytical and more insightful but harder to undertake and is underused due to our innate intellectual laziness. In relation to the Arab-Israeli conflict, type 1 thinking tends to dominate the discourse, following well-trodden paths that lead to numerous false premises. This reflexive reaction should be easily discredited due to its reliance on fantasy rather than reality. For reasons we shall explore, this has not happened – to the detriment of peace-making.

The Arab War Against the Jews: a Bird's Eye View

The start of the conflict between Jews and Arabs antedated the State of Israel by more than a generation. Some point to the 1917 Balfour Declaration, that expressed British support for a Jewish national home, as the starting gun of the dispute.[2] But the serious violence was instigated in 1920 by a rising star of the Palestinian Arab elite, Haj Amin al-Husseini, just as the League of Nations was about to hand a Mandate to Britain to implement the Declaration with the full force of international law.

Husseini is widely regarded today as the first leader of the Palestinian Arabs but he was a supporter of Syrian hegemony over the Mandatory territory rather than an advocate for a specifically Palestinian nationalism that had not yet emerged by that date. His political views evolved over time but his overriding credo was antisemitism, both religious and racial. Along with his coterie of violent henchmen, he ensured that all opportunities for Jewish-Arab coexistence were snuffed out. His obsessive hatred of Jews set the pattern for the total Arab rejection of any Jewish sovereignty in the Middle East – a prospect that he reviled as being contrary to Islamic law – and the legacy of that intransigence guaranteed bloody Arab clashes with first Zionists and then Israelis over the next century.

The incorporation of the Balfour Declaration into international law through the San Remo Resolution and the League of Nations Mandate could have led to peace between two embryonic states, one Jewish and the other Arab, with the precise configurations determined by negotiation. Sadly, the Arab leaders – Husseini foremost among them – were so consumed by visceral Jew-hatred that they rejected any Jewish sovereignty anywhere in the Middle East, ever. That was a recipe for conflict unless the Jews capitulated. They declined to do so.

On 30 November 1947, the day after the passing of the UN partition resolution (181), Arab paramilitaries, supported from abroad, launched an all-out civil war against the *Yishuv*. The conflict was fully internationalised when five Arab armies (plus a further two expeditionary forces) attacked the new state following the Declaration of Israeli Independence on 14 May 1948. Thereafter, Israel was subjected to several wars, incessant terrorism, and economic boycotts by most of her neighbours. Having nowhere else to go, the Jews – driven to the edge of extinction in Europe by their Nazi persecutors and ethnically cleansed from the MENA countries – refused to surrender.

Israeli leaders were never triumphalist and always extended the hand of peace that was eventually partially accepted. Israel signed 'cold peace' treaties with Egypt in 1978 and Jordan in 1994, followed by warmer normalisation treaties with the United Arab Emirates, Bahrain and Morocco in 2020. But the underlying Arab-Muslim antipathy to Jews, nurtured over almost a millennium and a half, persisted. The void left by the exit of a handful of Arab states from active confrontation with Israel was more than filled by an increasingly bellicose Islamic Republic of Iran and its proxies, all of whom were motivated by a single overriding goal – to rid their region (and, if possible, the world) of the intolerable blemish on the purity of Islam: the evil, usurping Zionists.

Innumerable attempts to resolve the conflict through territorial compromise – in which Israel offered to withdraw from up to 98 per cent of the disputed territories to enable the creation of a Palestinian state – have floundered on the rock of repeated Arab rejectionism. It is this posture, not Israeli opposition, that has frustrated the Palestinian desire for statehood and has led a number of Arab leaders to break ranks and express impatience with the Palestinians.

Since 1979, the hegemonic ambitions of Iran, along with her terrorist proxies, have expanded the dimensions of the Arab-Israeli conflict just as the rest of the world took comfort from the illusion that it had contracted to a less worrisome Israeli-Palestinian one. The radical mullahs, angered by signs of Arab rapprochement with Israel, have assumed the leadership of the rejectionist front. Iran has openly vowed to destroy Israel by 2040, a goal it has not rescinded throughout the years of negotiations with the major global powers over its 'peaceful' nuclear programme. Former head of Israeli military intelligence, Amos Yadlin, is one of many senior defence figures to have sounded the alarm about Iran's regional aggression and Israel's limited options in halting it.[3] He identified Iran as Israel's primary strategic threat closely followed by Syria and the radical terrorist militias of Hezbollah and Hamas, both of which are financed, armed and trained by the fanatical Islamic Revolutionary Guards Corps that Iran's first Supreme Leader, Ayatollah Khomeini, founded shortly after seizing power in 1979.

To Begin at the Beginning: Blaming Balfour

In the extensive demonology of anti-Zionism, the name of Lord Arthur Balfour occupies a pivotal position as the godfather of the Zionist movement. Anti-Zionists claim that the Balfour Declaration, issued in 1917, was an illegal, unjust and morally reprehensible act that lies at the root of the Arab-Israel conflict and for which the UK should apologise.[4] They further assert that the Declaration effectively handed Palestine to its Jewish minority at the expense of the previously promised sovereignty – via the McMahon letter and other undertakings – to its Arab majority. They point to Balfour's letter as proof of the colonialist nature of Zionism and modern Israel, an artificial entity that would not have been created had it not been for the arbitrary gifting of Palestinian territory, without consulting the local inhabitants (most of whom were non-Jews), to alien European Jewish settlers by a remote colonial power. What is the evidence for these claims?

As outlined in Chapter 3, the Balfour Declaration committed the British government to using its 'best endeavours' – meaning that they would implement all reasonable measures rather than just offer support in principle – to achieve the objective of the establishment of a 'national home for the Jewish people' in Palestine. The Declaration was later incorporated, virtually word for word, in two major international agreements in 1920 – the San Remo Resolution of the Principal Allied Powers and the League of Nations Mandate for Palestine – that elevated the status of the Declaration into a legally binding commitment. The League handed the Mandate to the British Government with the explicit, unambiguous purpose of implementing the Declaration. Though the British, under severe Arab pressure, later reneged on their obligations, the Mandate eventually led, through a devious and blood-drenched route, to the establishment of the modern State of Israel in 1948.

Many commentators have suggested that the terms of the Balfour Declaration were only partially fulfilled in that Jewish aspirations were met while those of the Arab population of Palestine and the Middle East were ignored. Superficially, this is a plausible argument but it is fallacious. The Declaration is a short document comprising three key principles. The first was the establishment of the Jewish national home; this was technically realised in 1948 in the form of Jewish sovereignty when Israel declared her independence, but it remains work in progress as many of Israel's neighbours – with the collusion of external parties – sought (and continue to seek) her destruction. Without a strong army and the expenditure of huge resources on defence, Israel could not have survived. Those who today reject Israel's legitimacy and threaten her with annihilation, violate both the spirit and the letter of the Declaration, a commitment that was incorporated, via the League of Nations Palestine Mandate and the UN charter, into international law.

The Declaration's second element – the protection of the civil and religious rights of the non-Jewish population of Palestine – has been meticulously respected through Israel's Declaration of Independence and the related Basic Laws. All Israeli citizens have guaranteed civil and religious rights: participation in democratic elections, free speech, peaceful protest, individual and collective worship, access to public services, and legal redress in the event of complaint. Specific legislation protects the rights of women, children, LGBTQIA+ people and other minorities. This impressive list compares favourably with other Western liberal democracies and stands in marked contrast to the position of Jews and other minorities in Arab states. Even Israel's bitterest critics acknowledge that she is the only MENA country where Arabs can freely criticise their government and vote to oust it from office.

Although the Declaration did not address Arab national ambitions, those too were granted expression in the form of the twenty-two Arab States subsequently created in the wake of the San Remo convention that was held less than three years later. One of these was Transjordan that was brought into being by the British in 1921-22 under Article 25 of the Mandate in an attempt to appease Arab objections to Zionism as well as to reward the Hejaz-based Hashemite dynasty for their support of the British war effort against the Turks. Transjordan's territory comprised the larger portion of the original Mandatory Palestine over a quarter of a century before Israel achieved her independence. The majority of the citizens of Jordan, as that country is now called, self-identify as Palestinians, and is effectively the sovereign state of the Arabs of Mandatory Palestine – though its rulers self-define it as the Hashemite Kingdom of Jordan.

The Declaration's third part – the protection of the status of existing Jewish communities in the diaspora – was violated throughout the Arab world. Arab governments turned on their Jewish citizens as a collective punishment for Israel's establishment and actively promoted the exodus, including expulsion, of close to 900,000 Jews from countries across the MENA region. To this day, none of these countries has accepted responsibility for this Jewish *Nakba* – the large-scale ethnic cleansing, including the theft of property and other assets, of Jews that had lived in Arab countries for millennia – let alone provided even minimal recompense to the victims.

The historical record is unequivocal: of the three main elements of the Balfour Declaration only the second part – the protection of Arab rights within Israel – has been fully realised. The first and third – those relating to the national and individual rights of the Jewish people respectively – have yet to be accepted by most of Israel's neighbours and by much of the international community. This is the inverse of the evidence-defying narrative that portrays the Balfour Declaration as a betrayal of the Arabs, a shameful stain on British foreign policy, and the root cause of the Arab-Israeli conflict.

Jewish Hopes for the Mandate

While welcoming the Balfour Declaration in principle, *Yishuv* leader David Ben-Gurion was circumspect, firmly rejecting any notion that the Jews had benefitted from colonial munificence. The League of Nations Mandate was another matter. Although the Declaration carried a degree of moral authority, its incorporation into the Mandate in 1920 transformed it into a legally binding agreement to help reconstitute a Jewish national home in Palestine in a manner that promised international and regional recognition.

Nothing in the terms of the Mandate impeded an equitable realisation of the legitimate aspirations of both Jews and Arabs. That has always been the stated position of both the Zionist leaders and Israeli governments in contrast to the consistent and hypocritical rejection of the right of the Jews to sovereignty by most of the Arab states and the Palestinians. In the complex international negotiations during the immediate post-war period, the issue of Jewish self-determination (along with that for other national groups) was more or less permanently on the table. That was a source of pride and hope for the Jewish people. A new chapter on the road to Jewish security and freedom had opened and was a cause for celebration in both the *Yishuv* and diaspora. Their euphoria was short-lived.

Arab Sabotage of the Mandate

After Prince Faisal's short-lived support for the Balfour Declaration, Arab opposition grew rapidly. Initially, it took three main forms: objection to the treatment of Western Palestine as separate from Syria of which the district of Palestine was widely regarded as an integral part; hostility to Zionism as an allegedly European colonialist initiative that appeared to favour a minority of the residents of Palestine at the expense of the majority and might threaten the ambitions of the pan-Arab nationalist movement, out of which a specifically Palestinian Arab nationalism would later emerge; and a fear of betrayal of previous British promises that Arab leaders had extracted as the price of their support for the British army's campaign against the Turks during the First World War.

This last point was a bone of contention that may have arisen from a straightforward misunderstanding. Both Arabs and Jews had been incensed by a secret plan, the 1915 Sykes-Picot agreement, to divide the post-war Middle East between France and Britain. To offset it, both Arabs and Jews managed to extract separate British promises – the McMahon-Hussein correspondence and the Balfour Declaration respectively. The former was a 1915-16 exchange of letters between Sir Henry McMahon, British High Commissioner in Cairo, and Sharif Hussein of Mecca (father of Faisal and Abdullah) in which the British agreed to support Arab self-determination in the Hejaz (modern Saudi Arabia) and elsewhere. Arab politicians insisted that McMahon's promise also applied to Palestine despite repeated British claims that Palestine had been explicitly excluded from McMahon's undertaking.

All of these concerns might have been successfully allayed had it not been for a further factor that was poised to enter the drama in spectacular and destructive fashion. That factor was naked Jew-hatred.

The Tragic History of the Mandate – and British Abandonment of the Jews

The real tragedy of the Palestine Mandate (1922-1948) lies not in its conception but in its execution. It was marred by a steady British retreat from its moral and legal obligations – even in the face of the growing horror of the Holocaust – to both the Jewish people and the international community. In an attempt to appease anti-Jewish violence orchestrated by the pro-Nazi Grand Mufti of Jerusalem, Haj Amin Al Husseini, the government increasingly distanced itself, in two successive white papers authored by Colonial Secretaries Winston Churchill and Lord Passfield (Sidney Webb) in 1922 and 1929 respectively, from the Mandate's Article 6 that required the facilitation of Jewish immigration and settlement.

That was followed by a further anti-Zionist hardening of British policy throughout the 1930s that was diametrically opposed to the intentions of both the Balfour Declaration and the Mandate. On the recommendation of the Woodhead Commission, the British government repudiated its own Peel Commission's 1937 partition plan – accepted with reservations by Palestine's Jews but rejected outright by its Arabs – that would have brought about an early version of the 'two-state solution' in Western Palestine. Just as the entire world (with a few honourable exceptions such as the Dominican Republic and the limited British *Kindertransport* programme) was closing its doors on Jews trying to escape the Nazi threat, Britain's Colonial Secretary Malcolm MacDonald issued the infamous 1939 white paper that drastically restricted Jewish immigration to Palestine to 15,000 per year for five years after which it was to cease entirely. No such restrictions were placed on Arab immigration. British adherence to Article 6 of the Mandate was now hanging by a thread.

At the start of the Second World War, Britain abandoned any pretence to facilitate Jewish immigration. The decade from 1938 saw the British navy intercepting dozens of rescue ships (organised by the clandestine Jewish army, the *Haganah*) seeking to dock in Palestine. These vessels, many of which were barely seaworthy, were laden with Jewish refugees who were either refused entry to Palestine or were interned behind barbed wire in detention camps (mainly in Cyprus). Some of the ships had no alternative but to head back to ports in Axis-occupied countries. British physician Leslie (Lord) Turnberg recounts the bitter Jewish reaction to this betrayal: 'It is difficult to overestimate the revulsion in which the British were held by the Jews in Palestine as they saw them condemning so many of their brothers and sisters to certain death in the camps of Europe.'[5] Even after Germany's surrender, British callousness resulted in many Holocaust survivors either being interned or, *in extremis*, being forced to return to the scene of their trauma.

As the war ended and the horrors of the Holocaust were revealed, the surviving Jews of Europe – and worldwide – felt an understandable sense of relief. In the MENA region, the growing popularity of Zionism among Jews acted as an optimistic counterweight to the waves of pogroms that had swept across the Arab world in the wake of the Allied victories. The euphoria would be short-lived. Antisemitism lingered dangerously almost everywhere. British historian Martin Gilbert contrasts the attitudes of Jews and Arabs to the imminent prospect of a Jewish national home: 'Jews would no longer have to put up with being second-class citizens, but that was how the Muslims among whom they lived considered them: the eternal, born *dhimmis*, subject to one form or other of the Covenant of Omar.'[6]

The formation in Cairo of the Arab League in March 1945 exacerbated the already precarious position of Jews in the Arab world. The League's first act was to declare all Jews 'supporters of Zionism' and to restrict Muslim contact with them. When the Grand Mufti arrived in Egypt after fleeing France (where he had been declared a war criminal), he further inflamed anti-Jewish sentiment. Jews were again subjected to arson attacks on their property, physical assaults and orchestrated rioting across the MENA region including Mandatory Palestine.

In the course of Israel's War of Independence that erupted following the UN partition resolution of November 1947, the Mandatory administrators – under instruction from Whitehall – adopted an increasingly pro-Arab position, handing much military hardware to Transjordan's Arab Legion (led by a British officer, Sir John Glubb) with a view to ensuring a complete Arab takeover of Palestine following the British withdrawal. All of this was in breach of both the spirit and the letter of the Mandate.

If there is any cause for British shame, it is to be found in the near-total abandonment of Britain's solemnly undertaken commitments, first encapsulated in the Balfour Declaration and then in the Mandate, to the beleaguered Jewish people in its hour of greatest need.

The 'Arab-Israeli' Conflict Begins

Although a Palestinian Arab state (Transjordan, later Jordan), that the British had carved out of the original Mandate territory had existed since 1922, the Zionist leadership, in its eagerness to secure peace, twice more accepted proposals for what amounted to a second Palestinian Arab state – first in 1937 (the aforementioned Peel Commission) and again in 1947 (the UN partition plan). In both cases, the Arab leadership rejected any Jewish sovereignty while the Zionist leaders, despite their reservations, accepted the principle of 'two states for two peoples' decades earlier than anyone else in the Middle East. For the enemies of Zionism, the so-called 'two-state solution' was never enough – and therefore was not a solution – unless it comprised two Arab states.

When the British handed the Mandate back to the League of Nations and Arab armies attacked the newly-declared State of Israel in 1948, the 'two states' formula was dealt a near-fatal blow. The Arab-Israeli conflict had begun.

Key Milestones in the Arab-Israeli conflict

Historians view the British Mandate for Palestine as the crucible within which the conflict between the Zionists and their neighbours was brewed. In their struggle to recreate their national home, as the world had assured them was their right, the Jews found themselves waging a trilateral war against both the Arabs and the British.

The British decision in January 1947 to relinquish the Mandate led to the UN partition resolution later that year and to Israel's declaration of independence in May 1948. Jewish rejoicing was short-lived as their reborn state was confronted by a powerful array of Arab firepower bent on reversing the tide of history. Israel's war of independence (1947-49) cost her dearly in human treasure that she could ill afford but her primary aim – survival – was achieved. The initial attack on the emergent state by domestic militias (led by Husseini's Arab Higher Committee) and then by seven Arab armies generated conflict, chaos and panic that prompted a mass exodus of Arabs. The Rhodes Armistice Agreement of 1949 was supposed to lead to peace but the Arab states, smarting from defeat at the hands of the ragtag Jewish forces, had other ideas; they regarded the ceasefire as a means of buying time while they prepared for their promised and decisive 'second round.'

The 1956 Sinai Campaign (*Operation Kadesh*) – known as the Suez Crisis in the West, for whom it was a last-gasp projection of fading imperial power – was Israel's response to escalating Egyptian aggression, mainly in the form of *fedayeen* (terrorist) attacks on Israeli civilians.[7] Israel was the only one of the three partner countries that had a legitimate claim to self-defence, while Britain and France were protecting a colonial-era asset, the Suez Canal. Israel's actions were legally justified on three grounds – Nasser's repeated declarations of his intent to destroy the Jewish state (with the help, hardly coincidentally, of former Nazi scientists and engineers), his support for murderous cross-border raids on Israel, and his closure of both the Suez Canal and the Straits of Tiran (at the entrance to the Gulf of Eilat) to Israeli shipping.

The 1967 Six Day War was provoked by Nasser again closing the Straits of Tiran to Israeli shipping and expelling the UN peacekeeping force from Sinai. The Arab media were filled with gleeful predictions of the impending destruction of the loathsome 'Zionist entity' and the massacre of its Jewish inhabitants.[8] When Israel launched a pre-emptive strike against Egyptian and Syrian air bases, Jordan's King Hussein joined the fray by shelling Israeli civilian areas despite Israel's frantic pleas that he should desist.

Commentators identify the Six Day War as the crucial milestone in the conflict that entrenched the opposing parties in their current irreconcilable positions. Following her spectacular victory, Israel's euphoria soon morphed into disappointment at the complete lack of Arab interest in peace negotiations followed by a degree of complacency (the *Conceptzia*) that Egypt exploited in launching two further wars. The War of Attrition of 1969-70, initiated by Nasser as a campaign to wear down Israeli morale, comprised a series of extremely violent but largely pointless border clashes with accompanying high casualty rates on both sides. Then in 1973, the new Egyptian president, Anwar Sadat, attacked Israel on *Yom Kippur* (the Day of Atonement), the holiest day in the Jewish calendar. Some historians claim that the Egyptians were merely attempting to reclaim territory lost in 1967 but the Israelis viewed it as another existential struggle comparable to the Six Day War – except that this time they were on the back foot. In the days before the shooting started, the US warned Israel not to repeat a pre-emptive attack of the kind she had employed in 1967. Israel obliged, was nearly overrun by the enemy, and sustained heavy casualties for her pains.

Probably the most controversial episode in Israel's military history was the 1982 Peace for Galilee campaign that turned into the nightmarish First Lebanon War. Israel's prime minister, Menachem Begin, acknowledged that it was a 'war of choice' though Israel had suffered years of Katyusha rocket attacks from Lebanon and gruesome terrorist atrocities perpetrated by the Palestine Liberation Organisation (PLO). Again Israel prevailed and the PLO was expelled from Southern Lebanon providing Israel with temporary respite.

Despairing of ever defeating Israel militarily, PLO chief Arafat and his allies then focused their efforts almost exclusively on upscaled terrorist campaigns. The two '*intifadas*' (uprisings) of 1987-94 and 2000-2005 exacted a dreadful price on both sides, achieving nothing other than publicity for the PLO. That did not deter the Iranian proxy militia Hezbollah from mounting renewed attacks on northern Israel in 2006 thereby triggering the Second Lebanon War. When that assault on Israel failed to achieve any significant gains for the terrorist group, the Iranians gave the green light to another jihadist organisation, Hamas (Gaza's totalitarian rulers since 2007), to test Israel's southern flank by adopting the Hezbollah tactic of launching waves of rocket attacks aimed indiscriminately at civilians. By now, a default response had been established in the court of international opinion: whenever Israel responded militarily, as any country would, the UN, backed by a like-minded network of 'human rights' NGOs, condemned her for trying to protect her citizens.

The Double Exodus

Two refugee tragedies occurred in the wake of that first Arab-Israeli conflagration yet only one has been granted proper recognition.[9] By the end of the War of Independence in 1949, a conflict that had been forced on Israel by the combined assault of Husseini's militias in 1947 and the invading Arab armies in 1948, it became clear that around 740,000 Arabs had been displaced (see Chapter 8) and were being housed in refugee camps across the region. That tragic outcome has been extensively documented and publicised. Almost erased from history (and global consciousness) was a second exodus during which almost 900,000 Jews endured a similar fate; over a period of several decades – of which the years around the time of Israel's rebirth were the most dangerous – they too fled or were expelled, though not from a war zone but because they were Jews (all of whom had been branded 'Zionists' by the Arab League). Most (650,000) reached Israel where they were accommodated in temporary shanty towns (*ma'abarot*) that had been established to absorb and rehabilitate them. These MENA refugees and their descendants today form a majority of Israel's Jewish population.

Consigned for centuries to second-class citizenship under the discriminatory *dhimmitude* system, the Jews of the Arab world had experienced periodic upsurges of antisemitism that became increasingly oppressive, prompting the *Aliyah* (immigration to the Land of Israel) of hundreds of Yemenite Jews in the late nineteenth century, a precursor of the exodus of hundreds of thousands of Jews from across the MENA region a few decades later. In 1941, Iraqi Nazi sympathisers, egged on by Husseini and his supporters, unleashed a savage pogrom in Baghdad where Jews constituted around one third of the population. Over 180 Jews were killed and thousands injured. Homes and businesses were looted, and further violence threatened. The Baghdad *Farhud* ('violent dispossession') was far from unique but for the Jews of Iraq and elsewhere in the Muslim world it was a seminal moment, a confirmation of their suspicion that their presence in the region was precarious – tolerated at best and terminal at worst. That gloomy prognosis thrust Middle Eastern and European Jews together to make common cause – the attempted revival of Jewish sovereignty in the homeland. Both realised that Zionism was the only sure means of acquiring a safe and welcoming long-term haven.

Can Blame for the Conflict be Assigned – and Does it Matter?

Attributing blame for any conflict may appear an unproductive exercise but understanding the past is a critical first step in identifying and removing ongoing underlying causes. Which key moments in the conflict that might have changed history in the direction of peace?

The prospects for ending the conflict may have improved had any of the following actions been more peace-oriented, starting with Israel's (relatively few) missed opportunities:

1949:   If Israel had been more flexible on the Arab refugees at the Lausanne conference.

1967-73: If Israel had abandoned her *Conceptzia* (complacency) after the Six Day War.

1971:   If Israel had been more receptive to Sadat's offer of an interim agreement.

1982:   If Israel had agreed to explore the Reagan plan for Palestinian autonomy.

1987:   If Israel had endorsed the Peres-Hussein London Agreement that might have paved the way for a Jordanian-led territorial compromise between Israel and the PLO.

2002:   If Israel had accepted the Arab (originally Saudi) Peace Initiative as a basis for negotiations.

These 'opportunities' were flimsy at best: at Lausanne, the Arab delegation refused to sit in the same room as the Israelis; after the Six Day War, the Arab world declared their infamous Three Nos – no peace, no recognition, no negotiations; the Sadat peace offer demanded a non-existent 'right of return' of the Arab refugees; Reagan's Palestinian autonomy plan was rejected by the PLO as well as Israel; the 'Jordanian option' was a virtual non-starter given the antipathy between King Hussein and the PLO, and prime minister Shamir's mistrust (subsequently vindicated) of Arafat's intentions; and the Arab (Saudi-initiated) peace initiative, like Sadat's offer three decades earlier, required the return of the Arab refugees and their descendants to Israel.

As for Israel's Arab adversaries, the list of missed opportunities is far longer and starts just after the First World War. The prospects for avoiding or reducing conflict would have been greatly improved had any of these opportunities been seized:

1919:   If Prince Faisal had respected rather than reneged on his agreement with Chaim Weizmann and accepted Jewish as well as Arab sovereignty in the region.

1921:   If Haj Amin al-Husseini had used his appointment to Grand Mufti by the British to nurture co-existence with rather than incite violence against the *Yishuv*.

1922:   If the effective Britain' partition of Mandatory Palestine into an eastern Arab state (Transjordan) and a western Jewish national home had satisfied Arab leaders.

1922-47: If Arab leaders had accepted the Mandate immigration provisions thereby saving countless numbers of Europe's Jews from oblivion.

1937:   If Arab leaders had, like the Jews, accepted the partition proposal of the British Peel Commission.

1947:   If Arab leaders had, like the Jews, accepted the partition proposal of the UN Special Committee on Palestine.

1948-67: If the Jordanian and Egyptian leaders had established a Palestinian state during their occupation of the West Bank, East Jerusalem and Gaza Strip.

1949:   If Arab leaders had honoured their commitment at the Rhodes conference to negotiate peace with Israel.

1949:   If Arab leaders had withdrawn their insistence that the return of any refugees was conditional on (or a first step towards) the dissolution of Israel.

1964:   If Arab leaders had rejected rather than supported the newly formed Palestine Liberation Organisation's declared aim of destroying Israel.

1967:   If Arab leaders had, like Israel, accepted UN Security Council Resolution 242 instead of issuing the Khartoum Declaration: no peace, no recognition, no negotiations.

1973:   If Arab leaders had, like Israel, accepted UN Security Council Resolution 338 (that reiterated Resolution 242).

1978:   If Yasser Arafat had accepted the US-Israeli proposal at Camp David for a five-year period of Palestinian autonomy to be followed by a final settlement.

1989:   If Arab leaders had accepted the Shamir peace plan for a transitional period of Palestinian self-rule in the West Bank and Gaza followed by permanent status negotiations (i.e. a foreshadowing of the later Oslo Accords).

1993-95: If the PLO had fulfilled their commitments under the Oslo Accords to make peace with Israel rather than re-igniting their campaign of terrorism.

2000-1:   If Arafat had accepted Israel's offer (at Camp David and Taba) of Palestinian statehood in over 92 per cent of the disputed territories.

2002-3:	If Arafat had, like Israel, accepted the Bush Roadmap to the two-state solution rather than sabotaging it with terrorism and demanding the return of the Arab refugees.
2007-8:	If Mahmoud Abbas had accepted the Olmert offer (at Annapolis) of Palestinian statehood in around 94 per cent (plus land swaps) of the disputed territories.
2014:	If Abbas had, like Israel, accepted the Kerry-Allen framework for territorial compromise designed to lead to 'two states for two peoples'.
2016:	If Abbas had, like Israel, accepted the Biden peace initiative to revive negotiations with Israel.
2020:	If Abbas had, like Israel, accepted the Trump Peace to Prosperity Plan (that included 'two states for two peoples') as a basis for negotiations.
2022:	If Abbas had accepted the invitation to join the Negev (Abraham Accords) Summit and help revive the Israeli-Palestinian peace process.
1948–now:	If Arab leaders had accepted responsibility for the Jewish *Nakba* rather than demanding a return of the Arab refugees as part of a demographic strategy to destroy Israel.

That is a partial list of missed Arab opportunities – a comprehensive one would require a book in itself. Reflecting on this miserable history is a salutary experience. While it is undeniable that both sides bear a degree of responsibility for the failure of peace-making, the historical record is clear: the vast majority of lost opportunities were caused by repeated Arab rejectionism. While it is always tempting – in the interests of 'balance' – to blame all sides for the failure of peace efforts, in this case it would be not be an evidence-based judgement.

Israeli hesitancy was never based on opposition to Arab or Palestinian rights in the context of peace negotiations undertaken in good faith, as the negotiations with Egypt and Jordan demonstrated. Too often, peace talks with neighbouring regimes – including Syria and the Palestinians – failed for two reasons: successive Arab leaders never unambiguously accepted Israel's right to exist as the sovereign state of the Jewish people, nor did they relinquish their demand for the alleged (though legally non-existent) 'right of return' of the Palestinian refugees and their descendants. The purpose of that latter demand was never a secret – to extinguish Israel's Jewish character demographically thereby fulfilling the antisemitic objective of politicide.

This is the essence of the conflict. The removal of the Jewish state in its entirety is and always has been the core goal of Palestinian leaders and most of Israel's opponents. In 1947, the implacably anti-Zionist British Foreign Secretary, Ernest Bevin, diagnosed the problem as the irreconcilable clash of two principles – the Jewish goal to establish a state and the Arab determination to thwart it.[10] Even Egypt and Jordan, two Arab countries that signed peace treaties with Israel after decades of war, only granted diplomatic recognition to Israel but did not explicitly recognise Israel's right to exist as the sovereign state of the Jewish people. In both cases, public opinion lagged far behind their governments, and in both cases the fruits of peace have – from an Israeli perspective – turned out to be meagre.

The US-brokered Abraham Accords of 2020 between Israel, the United Arab Emirates, Bahrain, Morocco (and possibly Sudan), were hailed by Israelis and the US as a major breakthrough as it shattered the taboo that a wider peace agreement between Israel and the Arab world depended on a prior resolution of the Israeli-Palestinian conflict. These four Arab League states may have finally decided that the Palestinians could no longer wield a veto over peace moves. Other Arab states may hold a similar view and join the Accords in the coming years. Unfortunately, Israelis have learned from experience that formal peace agreements are no guarantee of full acceptance of Jewish sovereign rights without which the conflict is sure to continue in one form or another.

A fundamental obstacle to peace-making in the Israeli-Palestinian arena (as in the Arab world generally) is the nature of the respective governments. Like all countries, Israel has its flaws but it has remained a liberal democracy since May 1948; occasional threats to that status from illiberal politicians have prompted vocal outrage and mass street demonstrations (such as those of 2023) that have compelled Israeli governments to retreat from the implementation of extremist policies. By contrast, the Palestinian Authority has been, since its formation in 1995, a kleptocratic, anti-democratic and authoritarian regime whose leaders have ceaselessly promoted antisemitism, incited violence and glorified terrorism. The international community has incentivised this corrupt and violent ethos by showering the PA and related bodies with hundreds of millions of dollars of aid each year while simultaneously turning a blind eye to the perennial terrorist threat – realised with depressing regularity – posed by Hamas and similar extremist militias to Israeli civilians. Adding insult to injury, they misguidedly berate Israel and Israel alone for the lack of progress towards a resolution of the century-long conflict that has been motivated almost solely by a desire by Israel's enemies to commit politicide and even genocide. The Hamas pogrom on Israel on 7 October 2023 was an extreme manifestation of this destructive impulse that the terrorist group promised was a dress rehearsal for the main performance.

The conclusion is clear: while Israel cannot evade the charge of having missed some opportunities to end the conflict, the overwhelming responsibility for the impasse lies with her adversaries. Those who seek to place the blame exclusively or mainly on Israel must explain how their analysis aligns with historical reality.

Looking to the future, the persistent antisemitic and frequently violent denial of the Jewish right to self-determination will have to be overcome if there is any hope of ushering in an era of long-term peaceful co-existence.

Notes

1   D. Kahneman, *Thinking, Fast and Slow* (New York: Farrar, Straus and Giroux, 2013).

2   J. Schneer, *The Balfour Declaration: The Origins of the Arab-Israeli Conflict* (London: Bloomsbury, 2010).

3   A. Yadlin, 'Four strategic threats on Israel's radar,' *Fathom*, January 2019. https://fathomjournal.org/four-strategic-threats-on-israels-radar-a-special-briefing-by-former-idf-intelligence-head-amos-yadlin/ (Last accessed 11 June 2024).

4   I. Black, 'The contested centenary of Britain's 'calamitous promise,' *Guardian*, 17 October 2017. https://www.theguardian.com/news/2017/oct/17/centenary-britains-calamitous-promise-balfour-declaration-israel-palestine (Last accessed 11 June 2024).

5   L. Turnberg, *Beyond the Balfour Declaration* (London: Biteback Publishing Ltd, 2017), p.47.

6   M. Gilbert, *In Ishmael's House: A History of Jews in Muslim Lands* (Toronto: Yale University Press, 2011), p.205.

7   A. Shapira, *Israel: A History* (London: Weidenfeld & Nicolson, 2015), pp.274-5.

8   N. Comay, *Arabs Speak Freely* (Wiltshire: Cromwell Press, 2005), pp.27-8.

9   L. Julius, *Uprooted* (London: Vallentine Mitchell, 2018), pp.252–3.

10 A Schwartz, E Wilf, *The War of Return: How Western Indulgence of the Palestinian Dream has Obstructed the Path to Peace* (New York: All Points Books, 2020), p.2.

5

The Hamas Pogrom of 7 October 2023

On Saturday 7 October 2023, Israel – and the world – changed. The country was plunged into arguably the greatest crisis in her history. The trauma her citizens suffered on (and since) that date defies the imagination.

After a few days (in some cases hours) of sympathy, the international community – with few exceptions – reverted to type and either remained indifferent or turned against her. A global rise in antisemitism was fuelled by biased and distorted media reporting of the hideous war Hamas started with their orgy of violence.

I will not elaborate here the unspeakable horrors[1] that struck Israel with a force more than 13 times (proportionately) that of the 11 September 2001 attacks on the USA. Nor will I or try to fathom the psychopathology underpinning the obscene promise by the perpetrators to conduct similar massacres *again and again*.[2] What I suggest is that we should consider, as best we can, the implications of that event, particularly for the people, mainly Israelis and Palestinians, directly involved.

The impact of the massacre and the misery it caused in both Israel and Gaza will take time to assess. What follows is a provisional analysis based on the information available at the time of writing. It will require continuous updating in the light of further developments.

As soon as the enormous scale of the tragedy became clear, Israelis (with the exception of the extremist fringes) showed that they were more united than ever. Jews and Arabs, secular and religious, left and right, joined forces in an impressive display of mutual support. Voluntary organisations across multiple sectors came together to provide care and services for the range of pressing needs that state-run agencies seemed incapable of recognising let alone meeting. That failure of national institutions became acutely obvious to the hundreds of thousands of citizens involuntarily displaced from their homes near the southern and northern borders as a result of near-daily rocket fire from both Gaza and Lebanon. A sense of deep insecurity spread rapidly from the border-adjacent communities throughout the country.

As the protracted war rumbled on, major recriminations were directed at senior officials in the defence and political establishment that were perceived to have been negligent. In its early months of office, the hard-right government of Benjamin Netanyahu had sought to pass a series of controversial judicial reforms but was frustrated by furious public opposition manifested by vast weekly street demonstrations. This divisive issue remained high on the agenda of an unpopular government but for most of the electorate a more urgent matter was at hand – the continued viability of the Jewish state.

Beyond Israel's immediate horizon, moderate Arab countries declined to mobilise their forces to defend Hamas nor did they seek to unravel the 2020 Abraham accords. The truth is that most Arab leaders loathed Hamas and were praying for Israel to achieve its elimination. One reason for this was the threat that Islamism poses to their own regimes. A second was an overriding fear of Iran, the most powerful military force in the Middle East. The Islamic Republic's mischief-making was a major factor in the aggression on Israel unleashed by their two most powerful proxies, Hamas and Hezbollah, and was responsible for the expansion of the war into several additional fronts, including Syria and Yemen, where Tehran held considerable sway.

The wider Jewish world was also shaken to the core by the events of 7 October and its aftermath. Many diaspora Jews had become exasperated with Israel in 2023, especially after an unscrupulous Likud party sought to shore up its power base by allying itself with small ultra-nationalist parties. In the wake of the massacre, however, liberal Jews watched with dismay as their progressive friends made common cause with Islamo-fascists who were quick to disseminate antisemitic incitement via compliant mainstream and social media platforms.[3] This perceived betrayal compelled a growing number of formerly Israel-sceptic Jews to reflect on their ideological allegiances and to seek to reconnect with their national roots. And a number of mainstream Jewish organisations (particularly on the left), that had until then shown tolerance towards 'anti-Zionists-not-antisemites' in their midst, took steps to distance themselves from hatemongers seeking shelter in 'the Jewish tent'.[4]

While Jewish support for Israel remained (with a few exceptions) steadfast or even strengthened, non-Jewish empathy was patchy. Within hours of news breaking of the massacre, and before the IDF had launched its counter-offensive in Gaza, thousands of activists took to the streets of the world's cities to demonstrate their support – for the terrorists. Over the ensuing weeks, the scale of these marches grew and became vehicles for jihadist chants calling to 'globalise the intifada' and liberate Palestine 'from the river to the sea.' While the marchers claimed to be demanding peace, they issued no condemnations of the Hamas massacre, no calls to release the abducted hostages, and no demands on Hamas to cease launching rockets at Israeli civilians. Noisy pro-Palestine, pro-peace activism was revealed as fraudulent, an alibi for those who were firmly on the side of those who would attack and murder Jews. The mask had slipped. This time, most Jews got the message.

As Israel stepped up its military reaction and declared its determination to destroy the Hamas regime and its infrastructure in Gaza, the window of global sympathy for the 7 October victims slammed shut (though to his credit President Biden maintained his support for longer than most). The stinging criticism of Israel's deployment of its armed forces to defend her people seemed to confirm Dara Horn's hypothesis – people love dead Jews[5]. Women's rights groups, always quick to protest every misogynistic micro-aggression, took weeks (if they bothered at all) to condemn the prolonged and sadistic sexual violence to which Israeli women and girls had been subjected during the Hamas pogrom. UNICEF[6], ostensibly tasked to promote assistance 'for every child,' had little or nothing to say about the butchering of Israeli children or of the years of indoctrination and abuse to which Hamas had subjected Gazan youngsters. International Red Cross officials maintained their dismal historical record towards Jews by shrugging their shoulders in response to the pleas of the hostages' families. The NGO superpowers of the human rights community, including Amnesty and Human Rights Watch, appeared more interested in highlighting the 'context' of the savage crimes committed by the killers than the plight of their victims and their families.

Israeli spokespeople reminded the world that their country was justified, both morally and legally, in seeking to repel and neutralise the attackers. Yet when the IDF struck back at Hamas targets embedded deep within Gazan civilian areas, causing unavoidable collateral damage, the reflex double standard kicked in and the finger-wagging resumed, with the familiar charges of 'war crimes,' 'collective punishment,' 'massacres' and even 'genocide' hurled at Israeli commanders. Israeli attempts to remind everyone that Hamas had initiated the conflagration on 7 October fell on deaf ears. Nevertheless, despite the great lengths to which the IDF went to protect non-combatants,[7] often at the expense of her own soldiers' lives, the suffering of the Gazan people in the 2023-24 war was undeniable.

It was also far from unique. UN officials solemnly intoned that the humanitarian disaster unfolding in Gaza – for which they placed the blame almost exclusively on Israel rather than Hamas – was unprecedented in scale and severity. Their selective memories had conveniently erased the millions of lives lost in the Balkans, Syria, Yemen, Iraq, Ethiopia, the Congo, Nigeria, Sierra Leone and Ukraine as well as the genocides of Rwanda and Darfur. Also forgotten in the rush to judgement of the IDF campaign were the huge casualty tolls that accompanied Western democracies' assaults on Al Qaeda, the Taliban and ISIS just a few years earlier.

The UN, it turned out, not only failed to live up to its own lofty principles of fairness and impartiality in their obsessive berating of Israel; it was complicit in the slaughter of the innocents of 7 October. Its role in facilitating the empowerment of a plethora of terrorist groups over many decades has been established beyond dispute. It achieved this extraordinary feat through its relentless and demonising one-sided condemnations of Israel in the General Assembly, the Human Rights Council, UNESCO and even the World Health Organization. Above all, it fanned the flames of conflict between Arabs and Jews via its Palestinian refugee agency UNRWA (United Nations Relief and Works Agency for Palestine Refugees), a number of whose employees appeared to have participated in the massacre. It was an open secret (always officially denied) that the UNRWA educational system employed teachers who preached antisemitic and anti-Israeli violence and hatred that poisoned generations of young Gazan minds.

But the rot ran deeper. Israeli intelligence had long suspected that Hamas could not have constructed the vast network of terrorist tunnels running under homes, schools, hospitals, mosques and other civilian structures without the knowledge and cooperation of UNRWA. Those fears were confirmed by powerful evidence unearthed by the IDF during their operations in Gaza. It transpired that the body established as a temporary facility to promote the peaceful rehabilitation of refugees had been doing the opposite for decades – funded to the tune of billions of dollars by US, UK, EU and other taxpayers. Is it conceivable that the donors were unaware of the nature of the monster they were rearing?

Implications for the Jewish World's Response to the Conflict

The Jewish world will learn important lessons from this agonising ordeal. As the dust of the war slowly settled, the nation of Israel, including the entire global Jewish community, remained traumatised. But Israelis across the political spectrum were unrepentant. They argued that they had no choice other than to crush, as far as practicable, Hamas and their jihadist allies in the Gaza Strip. Israel's efforts to defeat her most vicious terrorist enemy were conducted at immense cost to both Israelis and Palestinians, for all of which Hamas is culpable. Once the dead are buried and displaced people on both sides of the border are able to return to their homes, a full reckoning will begin.

When that happens, there can be no return to business as usual for the global Jewish community. The seismic shock of the 7 October attack (and the disgraceful behaviour of the legions of apologists who rushed, like the UN secretary-general, to explain that 'it didn't happen in a vacuum') will take time to process. It has been a rude but necessary awakening. Jews have been forced to (re)learn a key lesson: Israel's continued existence and security are more vital than ever, not just for the Jewish and Israeli people but for the Palestinians, the Middle East and humanity.

Although the physical wounds will heal over time, the emotional damage will not. The searing images of that autumn day will be indelibly woven into the fabric of the collective Jewish psyche. In the process, a new realisation will dawn – that Jews remain a fragile, vulnerable minority despite their political self-determination and formidable army. Both were found wanting in 2023. Israeli leaders will be forced to recognise that that they must restore the IDF's defensive deterrence to enable their country to serve her foundational mission as the ultimate safe haven for all Jews everywhere. The post-Holocaust certainty that Never Again was more than a slogan has evaporated in the light of the discovery that Israel's neighbours – and many more besides – seem unable or unwilling to shed their most violent antisemitic fantasies.

None of this will be easy but neither was the rebirth of Israel in 1948. Jews may lack a contemporary Theodor Herzl but they can draw inspiration from his words: *if you will it, it is no dream*. Backed by the Jewish diaspora and well-wishers of all backgrounds, Israelis are more than capable of converting that dream of a secure and self-confident Jewish state into reality in the twenty-first century just as they did in the twentieth.

The bottom line is stark: a rebooting of Zionism is required to render it fit for our dangerous new world. This is non-optional. It must happen to avert Hamas's publicly expressed vow to repeat the bloodbath of 7 October 'again and again' until not a single Israeli – or Jew – remains alive.

Implications for the International Community's Response to the Conflict

What lessons does this devastating event hold for all seeking a better understanding of the century-long Arab-Israeli conflict and how it might be ended?

First, the so-called civilised world must acknowledge that it has failed Israelis, Jews and all of humanity by misdiagnosing the conflict. All of us must internalise the unambiguous message that Hamas has delivered: the conventional wisdom, both in Israel and abroad, about the essence of the conflict was wrong. All the usual excuses for the failure of peace-making – occupation, land, settlements, refugees, Jerusalem – pale into insignificance next to the primary root cause, the genocidal opposition to Jewish sovereignty anywhere in the MENA region. In the dying days of the Mandate, British foreign secretary Ernest Bevin, who was no friend of the Jewish people, grasped the truth when he explained with admirable concision the nature of the problem: the Jews' determination to establish a state clashed with the Arabs' determination to stop them.[8] Little has changed since then. Viewed in this light, what happened on 7 October 2023 was a logical, predictable and inevitable outcome of a persistent politicidal mindset.

Second, Hamas and their allies have left us in no doubt that an annihilationist ambition remains undimmed in many quarters and that 'all means necessary' – including genocide – continues to be an acceptable tactic to promote it. A visceral hatred of Jews has been drummed into successive generations of Arab children with the tragic results that found expression (though not for the first time) on 7 October 2023. This grim process of indoctrination over decades was always there in plain sight but was too depressing or demoralising (or, in the case of the UN, too embarrassing) to contemplate. Periodic attempts by Israel and her supporters to alert the international community to this deliberate exploitation of humanitarian aid to groom vulnerable children in the craft of killing innocent human beings were steadfastly ignored and the rivers of dollars continued to flow, with minimal due diligence, into the coffers of the terrorist plotters in Gaza and the West Bank. Those responsible in the UN, NGOs, the media, academia, churches and elsewhere for actively or passively facilitating this outrage must be held accountable.

Third, with the help of moderate Arab states – especially Israel's Abraham Accords partners – we must redouble efforts to thwart Iran's oft-repeated goal of destroying Israel, either directly or through its numerous terrorist proxies across the Middle East. These threats must be taken at face value. That will involve international cooperation to confront and disable those proxies, to interrupt the capacity of Iran to fund, train and arm them, and to take stronger action to halt Iran's advance towards the acquisition of nuclear weapons. While Israelis need no reminding that the authoritarian leadership of that country have never been shy in proclaiming their number one foreign policy goal – the destruction of the state of Israel – it seems that the rest of the world clings to a failed policy of appeasement.

Fourth, we must ensure that UNRWA is either radically reformed or, better still, scrapped altogether so that it can no longer nourish the aspiration to fulfil the non-existent 'right of return.' Merely tinkering with its school textbooks will be insufficient. Above all, we must rid Arab (including Palestinian) society of its culturally ingrained intergenerational Jew-hatred that antedates the establishment of Israel by at least a millennium. The world's complicity with the haters since 1948 – through indifference, denialism and outright collusion – was not only an obstacle to peace but a stain on humanity; after 7 October it must be deemed unacceptable and removed. Now that the catastrophic effects of this chronic large-scale brainwashing have been publicly exposed, the international community has a responsibility to rectify its negligence and fast-track the development of a comprehensive programme to counter it – the denazification of post-war Germany might serve as a useful model.[9]

Only when the world has absorbed and acted upon these lessons can real peace-building can begin. That will benefit Israelis, Palestinians and the wider region. And the incalculable suffering of all the people caught up in the cataclysm of 7 October and its sequelae will not have been in vain.

Notes

1   S. Quitaz, 'I had never witnessed such barbarism before': Major F and battle of Holit, *Fathom*, December 2023. https://fathomjournal.org/i-had-never-witnessed-such-barbarism-before-major-f-and-the-battle-of-holit/ (Last accessed 11 June 2024).

2   Hamas official threatens to repeat 7th October. https://youtu.be/BJNccv NJtGk (Last accessed 11 June 2024).

3   Muhammad Smiry on X: https://twitter.com/MuhammadSmiry/status/1736810861740929134/photo/1 (Last accessed 11 June 2024).

4   J.K. Greenberg Jewish Voices for Hate, *Tablet*, 18 December 2023. https://www.tabletmag.com/sections/community/articles/jewish-voices-hate (Last accessed 11 June 2024).

5   D. Horn, *People Love Dead Jews: Reports from a Haunted Present* (London, Norton & Co, 2021).

6   Shurat Hadin on X: https://x.com/ShuratHaDin/status/1736837774748 110886?s=20 (Last accessed 11 June 2024).

7   Colonel Richard Kemp on X: https://x.com/COLRICHARDKEMP/status/1732779663313801339?s=20 (11 June 2024).

8   A. Schwartz, E. Wilf, *The War of Return: How Western Indulgence of the Palestinian Dream has Obstructed the Path to Peace* (New York, All Points Books, 2020), p.2.

9   Denazification, Jewish Virtual Library. https://www.jewishvirtuallibrary. org/denazification-2 (Last accessed 28 November 2023). (Last accessed 11 June 2024).

6

Antisemitic Ideation and the Conflict

Balfour, you vile person, what did you do to our people?
    Is your conscience quiet?
    Go in your grave toward the blazing fire
    You are the one that expelled us, do not ask for help
    You drank our blood from a goblet, and brought this fate down
upon us...
    You brought to our people those who orphaned small children
    You have turned the best of our people into Martyrs and prisoners
    Why did you bring the Jews to us, who defile Jerusalem and its
great mosque?

Poem by a Palestinian girl on Palestinian Authority TV, 15 December 2017

Though there is much cross-fertilisation, antisemitism is both intrinsic and extrinsic to the century-long Arab-Israeli conflict. This chapter is primarily focused on the first while the next will explore the second.

Millions of words have been printed in an attempt to explain the longevity of the Arab-Israeli conflict. But two critical questions are rarely posed: why is the conflict still raging, albeit in a mutating form, despite innumerable attempts to halt it? And what motivates people or their leaders to pursue a course of proven futility that destroys lives and condemns generation after generation to violence and misery? The usual mantras – 'mistakes on all sides,' 'byzantine complexities,' 'incompetent leadership,' 'great power rivalry,' 'tribal nationalism,' 'the cycle of violence,' – are inadequate explanations even if each contains a grain of truth. If we review the evidence dispassionately, it provides us with a clear if uncomfortable answer – relentless, vicious and unappeasable antisemitism.

Antisemitism in the Middle East and North Africa: a Chronological Taxonomy

Antisemitism in the MENA region may be categorised in relation to three historical eras: before Zionism, antipathy to Jews was mainly religious in nature; in the Zionist era, political antisemitism came to the fore; and following Israel's declaration of independence, anti-Israel hatred emerged. These three antisemitic phenomena – Judeophobia, anti-Zionism and anti-Israelism – are not mutually exclusive. Furthermore, in all three periods, external geopolitical factors played key roles in the conflict.

Antisemitism in the Arab and Muslim world should be understood for what it is – a dynamic, continuous and widely shared *cognitive pathology* that evolved over time, starting with a contempt for the *dhimmi* (protected) minority, to a suspicion-laden hostility to Zionist intentions, and ultimately to an uncompromising, eliminationist hatred of Israel.

Anti-Israel propagandists, seeking to deflect blame from the tormentors to the victims, insist that it was the establishment of Israel in the mid-twentieth century that caused the destructive dynamic of Arab and Muslim antisemitism and anti-Zionism. The facts indicate otherwise. Hostility to Jews and Israelis in Arab and Muslim lands did not arise in a vacuum but developed as a result of a process of psychosocial conditioning that occurred over many centuries. With responsible Arab leadership, the rebirth of Israel could have been welcomed as an exciting addition to the family of MENA nations that would bestow enormous cultural, scientific and economic benefits to all. Instead it was cynically exploited to turbocharge the latent anti-Jewish sentiment that was already prevalent across the region. Waxing and waning unpredictably across time, it had festered unchecked at all levels of Arab and Muslim society. The result was that Israel's declaration of independence on 14 May 1948 was the spark that ignited a pre-existing time bomb – a detestation of all things Jewish – resulting in an explosion of violence against the Jewish state and Jews across the MENA region.

Evolution of Arab-Muslim Antisemitic Ideation

Phase 1: Antisemitic Judeophobia: from Romans to Ottomans (70 CE to 1896)

How did the pan-Arab anti-Jewish animus arise? This question is seldom explored by analysts of the conflict – for too many, they 'know' intuitively that the answer must be 'Zionism' and are disinclined to investigate the subject further. To discover the truth, we have to delve into the history of the origins of Islam, the Jewish communities of the MENA, the rise of Islamism, and the importation of European antisemitism in the nineteenth century.

Although early Muslim authorities rarely subjected their Jewish minorities to the theological denunciations that were commonplace throughout Christendom, they viewed their Jewish subjects with disdain and imposed legal and financial penalties on them that severely restricted their rights. Like other non-Muslims, Jews in MENA countries were second-class citizens throughout most of the fourteen centuries of uneasy co-existence with their Muslim neighbours. In the eighth century, the Umayyad Caliph, Omar Abd al-Azziz, proclaimed rules (the Covenant of Omar) for separating Muslims from non-Muslims. Some of the latter were formally categorised as *ahl al-dhimma* – the People of the Pact. This *dhimmi* status was a promise to protect Jews and Christians from threats to life and property in exchange for their acceptance of their inferior status and the payment of a special *jizya* tax to the local ruler.[1]

Apologists for the Muslim treatment of Jews have argued that it compares favourably with the cruel manner in which European Christian officials behaved towards their Jewish minorities. After all, the Church authorities, unlike their Muslim counterparts, held Jews responsible for the crime of deicide. From that original, unforgiveable sin (according to traditional Christian teaching) flowed many of the worst anti-Jewish excesses including revenge attacks in the wake of alleged murders of Christian children for ritual purposes (the blood libel). Perhaps because Jews were never accused of murdering the founder of Islam, they were treated better in Muslim countries. But the Jews rejected Mohammed's teachings and were said to have sought his death – for example, in the great battle of Khaybar in 628 between the Prophet and the three Jewish tribes of Mecca. Up to 900 Jews were killed, a massacre that is recalled today in the anti-Israeli genocidal taunt of '*Khaybar Khaybar, Ya Yahud, Jaish Muhammad, Sa Yahud*,' ('Jews, remember Khaybar, the army of Muhammad is returning.')

While it is unarguable that Muslim antisemitic atrocities were of milder severity than the European versions, the position of Jews in the Muslim world was seldom comfortable. Anglo-American authority on Islam, Bernard Lewis, writes of the Jews in Muslim lands that:

> they were never free from discrimination, but only rarely subject to persecution; that their situation was never as bad as in Christendom at its worst, nor ever as good as Christendom at its best. There is nothing in Islamic history to parallel the Spanish expulsion and Inquisition, the Russian pogroms, or the Nazi Holocaust; there is also nothing to compare with the progressive emancipation and

acceptance accorded to Jews in the democratic West during the last three centuries.[2]

While Lewis stresses that throughout most of early Islamic history (roughly from the seventh to fifteenth centuries) Jews were treated well and sometimes generously, they were always judged as inferior due to their rejection of Islam – this was the era of *Judeophobic antisemitism*. At this time, Jews were not generally accused of hatching global conspiracies, or of spreading disease or of deliberately killing Muslim children. Those paranoid fantasies would appear later after the Ottomans expanded their empire into Christian Europe where they encountered blood libels and other extreme anti-Jewish notions that they then brought back to the MENA region.

Gilbert describes the relatively benign impact on Jews of the first few centuries of Islam, especially in North Africa and Spain, although he stresses that the threat of discrimination and persecution was ever-present.[3] Laqueur is less sanguine about the Jewish experience under Muslim rule: 'In Baghdad and elsewhere, Jews had to wear a yellow badge or headgear to distinguish them. There were major pogroms in Granada (1056) and Fez (1465) in which thousands were killed, and these were not the only attacks. Some North African Jewish communities were forcibly converted; in Yemen and Baghdad at various times many synagogues were destroyed.'[4] In eleventh century Spain, a relatively tranquil scenario ended with the fall of the Granada caliphate. Gilbert writes that this event terminated the 'Golden Age' of Jewish-Muslim coexistence in Muslim Spain.[5] The position of Jews in the Middle East was equally precarious. In Jerusalem, where some Jews had remained despite successive occupations, massacres and expulsions, they were impoverished and wholly dependent on the tolerance shown to them by their rulers, and on the good (or ill) will of their Muslim neighbours.

A near-forgotten humiliation in the history of *Mizrachi* Jews was their enforced return to slavery, a practice that persisted into the late nineteenth century and, in modified form, the early twentieth century. Jewish women and girls, who were often spared execution following Muslim victories over rebellious Jewish tribes in the early years of Islam, were especially vulnerable to this fate. French historian Georges Bensousson, cited by British writer Lyn Julius, described the Jews living under Muslim rule as victims of a quasi-colonial submissive culture: 'the Muslim submits to Allah, the Muslim woman submits to her husband, the non-Muslim dhimmi submits to the Muslim, and at the very bottom of the pile is the slave.'[6] Jews were feminised in the Muslim imagination and thus seen as weak, or were compared to dogs, apes and pigs – an example, in the words of the radical political theorist Franz Fanon, of 'the animalisation of the internally colonised.' Jews were not merely viewed with contempt in the Muslim world but as cunning and treacherous. They were regularly accused of seeking to seduce Muslim women, a behaviour that earned brutal punishments. Jews were associated with such evil that religious pilgrims went to great lengths to avoid seeing Jews before travelling to Mecca.

As the Enlightenment swept Christian Europe in the late eighteenth century, the Jews of that continent drew hope from their improving situation, though it proved illusory. In the Islamic MENA region, no comparable reforms were contemplated. If anything, matters took a turn for the worse as the conservative ideologies Wahhabism and Salafism took hold in the eighteenth and nineteenth centuries; they called for the removal of corrupt influences that contaminated the purity of Islam, eventually spawning numerous jihadist movements including the intensely antisemitic Muslim Brotherhood from which several twenty-first century jihadist groups would later draw inspiration.[7]

Among the many toxic legacies of European colonialism in the Middle East, the importation of malign Jewish stereotypes from the nineteenth century onwards was especially damaging to Muslim-Jewish relations. In 1840, the Damascus blood libel was introduced to Syrian society by Christian Arabs and was a turning point for the worse. When a Capuchin monk disappeared, his fellow monks falsely accused local Jews of ritual murder, many of whom were arrested, tortured and died. Similar incidents occurred across the Ottoman Empire throughout the nineteenth century,

5. Group of young Iraqi Jews who fled to Palestine following the 1941 Farhud pogrom in Baghdad. Source: Beit Hatfutsot, the Oster Visual Documentation Center, courtesy of Moshe Baruch

mainly instigated by Catholic or Orthodox Christian clerics supported by local foreign officials. European antisemitic texts – such as August Rohling's *The Talmud Jew* – began to be translated into Arabic.

Around this time, long-forgotten antisemitic Islamic scriptural sources were resurrected, including the al-Bukhari *hadith* (account) from the ninth century that readers familiar with the Hamas founding Covenant of 1988 will recognise: 'The Day of Judgement will not come about until the Muslims fight the Jews, when the Jew will hide behind stones and trees. The stones and trees will say O Muslims, O Abdullah, there is a Jew behind me, come and kill him.'[8]

Phase 2: Antisemitic Anti-Zionism: from Herzl to Partition (1897-1947)

Jewish immigration to the homeland of *Eretz Israel* long antedated modern Zionism. Though the number of migrants was initially small, by the mid-nineteenth century Jews constituted a majority in Jerusalem. By 1890, there were around 50,000 Jews living in western Palestine (the area between the River Jordan and the Mediterranean Sea) among a population of more than half a million Arabs. The Jewish immigrants were mainly refugees from Tsarist Russia along with several thousand from Yemen and other Middle Eastern countries. Together with the indigenous Jewish inhabitants, these newly-arrived Jews founded the *Yishuv*, the Jewish community of Palestine, that organised and developed commerce, agriculture, education, health services and other necessities. Arab reaction was mixed, with some Arabs welcoming the employment opportunities presented by the newcomers and others expressing resentment. This latter group were soon in the ascendancy and increasingly turning to violence though it should be noted that Jewish life throughout the disintegrating Ottoman Empire and in the Islamic world generally was becoming hazardous – for reasons often unconnected with Zionism – after a period of relative tranquillity.

What was the source of the intensified anti-Jewish hostility in the early twentieth century? Over time, the Judeophobic version of Muslim antisemitism had mutated into a more explicitly ethnically-focused brand of hatred that mirrored European far-right notions of inherent Jewish deceit, untrustworthiness and danger. A novel demonological view of Jews was forming in Arab-Muslim society ('the Arab street'). That cluster of negative perceptions of Jews – akin to a *culturally shared cognitive model* in Goldhagen's phrase – had been slowly nurtured over many centuries.[9] When allied with a racially-based Christian antisemitism, imported from

Europe to the Middle East in the nineteenth and early twentieth centuries, this novel conceptualisation of Jews, reinforced by a combination of hostility to European colonialism and a rise in Arab nationalism, had lethal consequences: in 1912, in Fez, Morocco, the Jewish Quarter was attacked in a pogrom coinciding with the start of French colonial rule. More than sixty Jews were killed – a higher death toll than in the far more widely publicised Kishinev pogrom of 1903 – and thousands left homeless.

Ottoman suspicion of Zionism became more widespread as the twentieth century progressed. The Turkish intelligentsia, both religious and secular, were set on an inevitable collision course with the Jewish programme to revive Jewish sovereignty in *Eretz Israel*. Lewis highlights an inflammatory 1909 article entitled 'Down with Zionism, always and forever.'[10] It was published in Istanbul by the influential Turkish journalist Yunus Nadi who was one of the first to invoke the notion of Zionism's expansionist designs on huge swathes of Muslim territory, a dream that was said to be backed by both Germany and 'the strongest power in the world – that of money.' Lewis notes that the theory that Zionism aimed not at a Jewish national home but at a sprawling Jewish Empire was often repeated by later polemicists, and that 'the argument that Zionism and the Jewish national home were puppets or agents of one or other imperial power also became commonplace, though the accusation varied according to the purposes of the accuser. At first it was France or Germany, later Britain or the Soviet Union, and at the present time, the United States.' (This puppetry metaphor was reversed by a later generation of antisemites who claimed that a powerful Israel lobby controlled the governments of the US and other countries).

In the early decades of the twentieth century, Arab anti-Zionist sentiment steadily intensified and coincided with the rise of a variant of Arab nationalism that sought to retain Palestine within Greater Syria. The opposition to the Jews was frequently laced with classic antisemitic tropes. Gilbert quotes as an example a poem entitled 'The Zionist Danger' published in 1913 in a Jaffa Arab newspaper. The middle stanza reads:

> *The Jews, the weakest of all peoples and the least of them,*
> *Are haggling us for our land.*
> *How can we slumber on?*
> *We know what they want*
> *And they have the money, all of it.*[11]

Hostility to Zionism was far from universal and there were numerous sympathet.ic Arab voices in the early twentieth century but these were quickly drowned out by a wave of extremism and intimidation unleashed by the nationalist and Islamist leadership. The Ottoman rulers of Palestine offered little comfort to their Jewish subjects. Citing research by Yuval Ben-Bassat of Haifa University, journalist Nir Hasson wrote that the Turkish authorities, having expelled the Jews of Jaffa in April 1917, threatened them with genocide:

> Numerous historical sources in Hebrew recall the speech made by the Turkish governor. He threatened to do to the Jews what was done to the Armenians (the Armenian genocide was at its zenith at the time.) A telegraph recently uncovered in the Turkish prime ministerial archive reinforces these accounts. Sent by the Turkish interior minister, Nazar Talaat, to the governor of Beirut, who also oversaw Zichron Yaakov, the telegraph read: "In the village of Zamrin (Zichron Yaakov,) in the Haifa district, the Kamikam (governor) told the people that if they do not hand over the spy Lishansky, their fate will be like the Armenians, as I am involved in the deaths of the Armenians."[12]

In the post-Ottoman period, a strongly negative Jewish stereotype was promoted by the Muslim Brotherhood, a militantly fundamentalist Islamic (i.e. Islamist) group founded in Egypt in 1928 by Hassan al-Banna as a reaction against modernising trends in Islam. Jews were cast as supreme 'others' who plotted to overthrow Islam and take over the world and would succeed unless neutralised. The leading ideologue of the Brotherhood, Sayyid Qutb, shared al-Banna's anti-liberalism, anti-Zionism and antisemitism: 'Allah punished them and brought upon them humiliation and expulsion more than once. ... Hitler was his last servant, but they returned to evil-doing in the form of Israel, and they will be meeting their punishment again.'[13]

German historian Matthias Küntzel has demonstrated how Nazi-style tropes were incorporated into the Brotherhood's world view in which Jews were depicted as the source of all evil.[14] It is hardly surprising that the Muslim Brothers would later become close allies of German National Socialism (from whom they drew inspiration) and would play a crucial role in the growth of violent antisemitic anti-Zionism over the succeeding decades.

The most important manipulator of Arab opinion, Islamist or otherwise, was Haj Amin al-Husseini. Inspired by the success of Turkish nationalists in driving the Greeks out of Turkey, he mustered support for a violent response to Zionism as early as 1919, when he established *fedayeen* suicide squads. The following year, in anticipation of the San Remo Resolution that would create the Palestine Mandate, he instigated anti-Jewish rioting in Galilee and Jerusalem (to coincide with the Passover festival) that led to multiple Jewish and Arab deaths. By 1921, the violence had spread to Jaffa where forty-seven Jews were killed and from where many others fled to neighbouring Tel Aviv and elsewhere. The British administration sentenced Husseini to ten years jail *in absentia* but then appointed him Grand Mufti of Jerusalem from which powerful position, that he formally held throughout the Mandate (from which he fled in 1939), he spread further mayhem as the *de facto* leader of the Arabs of Palestine.

Husseini was a rabid antisemite who never hesitated to whip up hatred and brutal violence against Jews wherever they were. He turned to more extreme Islamist incitement as the decade progressed, insisting that opposition to Zionism was the religious duty of all Muslims. He pioneered the accusation (still widely repeated today by Palestinian leaders) that the Jews threatened to destroy the Muslim holy places of Jerusalem, especially the *Al Aqsa* mosque (the third holiest site in Islam) located on the Temple Mount (the holiest site in Judaism). The resultant tension culminated in the Jerusalem, Hebron and Tzfat massacres of 1929, along with isolated rioting elsewhere. These pogroms in Judaism's most sacred cities cost 133 lives. Many of the victims were devoutly religious Jews who were either disinterested in Zionism or opposed in principle to it. The Shaw Commission blamed the violence on Arab antisemitism yet recommended restricted Jewish immigration – a continuation of the policy of appeasement of Husseini embarked on by the British following the 1920-21 riots and elaborated in the Churchill White Paper of 1922 that had signalled London's partial retreat from the Jewish national home concept. The British government amplified Shaw's demand in the 1929 Passfield White Paper that further tightened the screws on Jewish entry and land purchase in Palestine, in clear violation of Article 6 of the Mandate.

Husseini's campaign against the Jews of the *Yishuv* in the 1920s was just the beginning of his project to bring about a *judenrein* Middle East. The Nazi-supported Arab revolt against the British authorities in 1936 offered the opportunity for the Mufti and the Brotherhood to join forces and form a three-way alliance with the German leadership who were more than willing to offer financial and propaganda support. One major barrier had to be removed first: the Nazis viewed the Arabs with almost as much disdain as the Jews. That did not seem to trouble Husseini who persuaded Hitler to reclassify Arabs – among whom there was strong popular support for the Nazis – as 'honorary Aryans' who would make common cause in the war against the Jews. When the British banished the Mufti from Palestine to Iraq in 1939, he helped engineer a short-lived pro-Nazi coup in Baghdad and was instrumental in organising the *Farhud*, the pogrom of 1941, that claimed the lives of 180 Iraqi Jewish victims, inflicted large numbers of injuries, destroyed properties and generated an atmosphere of terror in the Jewish community. Julius maintains that the *Farhud* was a Holocaust-related event caused by Nazi incitement.[15]

Despite Husseini's post-war denial, compelling evidence has come to light that the *Farhud* was almost certainly a prelude to his plans to extend the Final Solution to the Middle East. After relocating to Berlin in 1941, Husseini met with Hitler, Eichmann and Himmler, visited at least one death camp, and broadcast antisemitic propaganda in Arabic throughout the MENA region until the end of the war. He asked the German government to publish a declaration in support of Arab aims. In one of the drafts submitted by the Arab Higher Committee in June 1940, the following passage (cited by Lewis) is especially significant: 'Germany and Italy recognise the right of the Arab countries to solve the question of the Jewish elements which exist in Palestine and in other Arab countries as required by the national and ethnic interests of the Arabs and *as the Jewish question was solved in Germany and Italy*'[16] [emphasis added]. A revised version was submitted in 1941 but the commitment remained to deal with the Jews 'in the same way as the Jewish question in the Axis lands is being solved.' There is little room for textual exegesis here – the desire to emulate Hitler's annihilationist Jewish policy in Europe, about which Husseini had learned at first hand from his Nazi friends, was unmistakeable.

Husseini found in Hitler a receptive listener. This chilling paragraph from the Mufti's memoirs, quoted by British blogger Mark Pickles, is disarmingly direct:

> Our fundamental condition for cooperating with Germany was a free hand to eradicate every last Jew from Palestine and the Arab world. I asked Hitler for an explicit undertaking to allow us to solve the Jewish problem in a manner befitting our national and racial aspirations and according to the scientific methods innovated by Germany in the handling of its Jews. The answer I got was: 'The Jews are yours.'[17]

At his meeting with the Mufti in Berlin in November 1941, Hitler emphasised his 'active opposition to the Jewish national home in Palestine' and that when the German army eventually reached the Middle East 'Germany's objective would then be solely the destruction of the Jewish element residing in the Arab sphere under the protection of British power.'[18]

These were not abstract fantasies that had no possibility of realisation. Husseini was a man of action. Historian Martin Gilbert was in little doubt about his intentions: 'The most horrific of the Mufti's influences was the creation of an SS task force intended to kill the half million Jews in Palestine. At least 300,000 of those Jews were pre-war refugees from Germany and Austria.'[19]

Julius writes:

> The Mufti was indirectly responsible for the deaths of thousands of European Jews whom he prevented from leaving for Palestine during the Second World War. The Bosnian and Albanian Muslim SS divisions he set up were responsible for unspeakable crimes in Yugoslavia. In spite of all this, the Allies failed to put the Mufti on trial as a war criminal. He was indicted, judged and convicted, however, by Yugoslavia for crimes against humanity, arising from his pivotal role in establishing the Handschar and Skandeberg SS divisions which, among other crimes, deported Balkan Jews from Kosovo, Macedonia and Thrace.[20]

That wartime legacy of Nazi-inspired Arab antisemitism, so cynically weaponised by the Mufti against the Jews of Palestine and the wider Middle East, has reverberated through the years to our own time. Yet it has never been fully acknowledged nor addressed: not by the Western democracies, not by the organs of the international community, not by the Muslim countries, and certainly not by the Arab leadership.

It would be wrong to cast Husseini as the sole villain of the piece. The racist Nazi poison was allowed to spread and infiltrate every aspect of the Arab attitude to Zionism and Jews throughout the MENA region. Inevitably, at the war's end it spilled over into the next phase of the dysfunctional Arab-Jewish relationship with predictable consequences. The Arab and Muslim enmity towards the Jews was about to identify a new and conveniently prominent target for assault – the Jewish state of Israel.

Even before the UN's partition resolution 181 of November 1947 had been passed, the Arab League had drawn up plans to dispossess and expel their Jews. The Egyptian delegate to the UN warned that the passage of the resolution would result in a massacre of Jews. Similar threats were issued by the Syrian and Iraqi delegates. When the General Assembly voted in

6. The Mufti meets Hitler Berlin 1941. Source: German Federal Archives

favour of partition, the Arab reaction was swift, furious and violent. Rioting broke out in Aden, Syria and the Gulf. A draft Arab League law proposed that all Jews resident in Arab countries would be considered members of the Jewish 'minority of the state of Palestine', their assets frozen, property confiscated, freedom of movement curtailed and their legal rights as citizens suspended. This was a mass violation of Jewish human rights; the Arab League plan of 1947, writes Julius, 'became a blueprint, in country after country, for the actions that devastated the Jewish communities in Arab lands; and for the forced exodus that was to follow. Some 90 per cent of Jews had fled the Arab world by 1972.'[21]

Phase 3. Antisemitic Anti-Israelism: from Reborn Israel to the Jew Among the Nations (1948 – present)

The previous sections have catalogued some of the grossest manifestations of antisemitic Judeophobia and antisemitic anti-Zionism in the Arab-Muslim world since the seventh century. This hostility laid the foundation for the violent Arab rejection of Jewish sovereignty behind any borders. David Ben-Gurion's historic announcement in 1948 that a Jewish state had arisen after an absence of almost two millennia was not the cause of Arab hostility to Jews; it merely reinvigorated a pre-existing, if sometimes dormant, hatred that had been festering for over a millennium. Blaming the subsequent mass expulsion of hundreds of thousands of Jews from Arab countries on this single event on 14th May 1948 is a wilful distortion of history for propagandistic purposes and is itself an expression of antisemitism. On the very day of her rebirth, Israel offered a hand of peace to her Arab neighbours – and her neighbours spat in her face.

The Arab-Israeli conflict is one of the most prolonged and intractable in human history. Its key milestones were set out in Chapter 4 and some of these provide pointers to the way antisemitic anti-Israelism makes its presence felt. Throughout the few decades of Israel's existence, many Arab (and lately Iranian) leaders have openly and repeatedly expounded their politicidal and genocidal intentions in language uncannily reminiscent of German National Socialism. Was this coincidence, or a reflection of the Arab governments' close links to wartime Germany? The evidence is strongly suggestive of the latter. Many Nazis who faced arrest for war crimes sought and found refuge in the Arab world where they assisted authoritarian regimes (such as the Egyptian dictatorship) with their anti-Israeli and anti-Jewish propaganda. But Arab leaders went far beyond imitating the demonising antisemitic imagery of Goebbels and Streicher; they were equally eager to assume the mantle of the exterminationist Nazi policy towards the Jews.

After the German defeat in 1945, the Allies' programme of de-Nazification ensured that genocidal threats against Jews were silenced. No such efforts were undertaken in the Middle East and Arab leaders continued their annihilationist anti-Jewish rhetoric with undiminished enthusiasm. Azzam Pasha, the first Secretary General of the Arab League, warned in 1948: 'This will be a war of extermination and momentous massacre which will be spoken of like the Tartar Massacre or the Crusader wars.'[22] In the same year, Hassan al-Banna, Founder of Muslim Brotherhood, announced that 'If the Jewish state becomes a fact, and this is realized by the Arab peoples, they will drive the Jews who live in their midst into the sea.'[23] The coordinator of Arab forces, General Ismail Safwat (cited by Schwartz and Wilf), clarified that the war's objective was 'to eliminate the Jews of Palestine, and to completely cleanse the country of them.'[24] Three days before the 1967 Six Day War, the first chairman of the Palestine Liberation Organization, Ahmad Shukeiri, predicted that 'those who will survive [among the Jews] will remain in Palestine but I don't think any of them will stay alive.'[25] These apocalyptic predictions were powerful motivators of Jewish resolve.

How was it possible for Arab leaders to use such language at a time when the appalling scale of the German assault on the Jews was still being uncovered? That question is seldom posed, perhaps because the answer is disturbing. The long history of Arab and Muslim Judeophobia and anti-Zionism had created fertile territory for the absorption of European anti-Jewish hatred in the MENA countries where it played a significant role in the Arab-Israeli arena. Webman emphasises that contemporary Arab antisemitism comprises an amalgam of historical Islamic anti-Judaic themes and imported European versions of Christian-influenced Jew-hatred; it is thus both a continuation of the past and a new phenomenon.[26] When tiny Israel succeeded against the odds in resisting the onslaught of no less than seven Arab armies in 1948, she sent shock waves across the region – the insult to Arab and Muslim pride was almost too much to bear. Their only choice, as Arab leaders saw it, was to prepare for a 'second round' that would right the wrong and remove the stain on Arab honour by obliterating the despised Jewish state and throwing its Jewish inhabitants into the sea, in accordance with their longstanding expulsionist mindset.[27]

The Long Shadow of the Mufti: Antisemitism and Anti-Israelism in the MENA Region Post-1948

In Western anti-Israeli circles, it is almost axiomatic that anti-Zionism is not synonymous with antisemitism. In the Arab world, such a distinction is deemed irrelevant. The terms Jew, Israeli and Zionist are used interchangeably and freely, except when sophisticated spokespeople wish to project an image of moderation to foreign media. While Western apologists for anti-Israelism are keen to emphasise the political nature of the conflict, Arab and Muslim leaders have seldom been shy about their distaste for Jews and all things Jewish even when they are unrelated to Israel. Three examples illustrate the point.

Gamal Abdel Nasser (1918-1970)

Egypt's President Nasser is one of the most revered figures in Arab history. For the Western left, he is a romanticised and heroic figure who stood up to British imperialism by nationalising the Suez canal in 1956. Progressive admirers would prefer to forget that early in his career he joined the pro-Nazi Young Egypt Society and during the Second World War held meetings with another staunchly pro-Nazi group, the Muslim Brotherhood, and provided them with military training in preparation for war with the Zionists. When the Free Officers Group overthrew the Egyptian monarchy in 1952, they appointed the pro-German Ali Mahir as prime minister, a move that enabled Egypt, according to German historian Matthias Küntzel, to become 'the El Dorado of former Nazis war criminals and antisemites.'[28] When Moscow refused to deliver intermediate-range rockets to Egypt in

1959, Nasser invited more than 300 German engineers and scientists who had formerly worked for the Nazi government to develop such missiles for the Egyptian army.

Nasser denied he was an antisemite yet he was fond of quoting from the *Protocols of the Elders of Zion* and was a Holocaust minimiser. He accused Zionism of imperialism and expansionism and to the end of his life was never reconciled to Israel's existence. Are these attitudes consistent with a non-antisemitic personality? Küntzel believes not: 'It was neither Israel nor Zionism that provoked the 1967 war but the latent anti-Zionism and antisemitism in the Arab world. Nasser was at one with this mood: he was gripped by the same destructive sentiments that he whipped up in the masses.'

7. President Nasser in 1962. Source: Stevan Kragujević courtesy of his daughter Tanja

Yasser Arafat

Not long after the founding of the PLO in 1964, Arab propagandists, realising that the Western left was largely sympathetic to Israel and also perhaps under pressure from the PLO's Soviet backers, shifted their rhetoric from accusing Zionists of supporting Bolshevism to portraying them as the heirs of Nazism. It was a crude but astute tactic. Suddenly the Palestinians were viewed not as reactionary anti-Communist Islamists but as progressive bearers of the global anti-imperialist and anti-colonialist (i.e. anti-American) torch.

After becoming head of the *Fatah* terrorist movement in 1959 and the PLO in 1969, Egyptian-born Yasser Arafat quickly became the poster-boy for radical left-wing supporters of liberation movements. When he died in 2004, it was discovered that he had secretly syphoned off foreign aid intended for the Palestinian people and had accumulated a vast fortune. His toxic legacy of hatred and violence against Israelis, including gruesome terrorism targeting Jewish civilians, is seldom acknowledged – except by Israelis, who had to pay the price of his shameless betrayal of the Oslo peace accords that he signed with premier Yitzhak Rabin in 1993. But was he an antisemite?

Putting to one side his lifelong refusal to recognise Jewish nationhood and Israel's right to exist, and his responsibility as leader of the PLO for murdering large numbers of Jewish Israelis (including at a time when he was legally obliged to nurture peaceful coexistence with Israel), there is ample evidence of his antisemitic mindset. 'I was one of his troops' he said

8. Yasser Arafat addressing the UN. Source: Licensed under the Creative Commons Attribution-Share Alike 4.0 International

of the Hitler-supporting Grand Mufti Husseini, whom he greatly admired and claimed as a relative. In a 1996 Arabic address in Sweden – shortly after he had signed the Oslo Accords in which he committed himself to a lasting peace with Israel – he was reported to have announced, 'You understand that we plan to eliminate the State of Israel, and establish a purely Palestinian state,' and, in case of doubt, 'I have no use for Jews; they are and remain, Jews.'[29]

Mahmoud Abbas

Before succeeding Arafat as chairman of the PLO in 2004 and being elected, as Western media profiles insisted, the 'moderate' President of the Palestinian Authority in 2005, Mahmoud Abbas was a fundraiser for *Fatah* and directly or indirectly involved on many of their operations including the massacre of Israeli athletes at the Munich Olympics in 1972. Long rumoured to have been a KGB agent, he studied at the People's Friendship University of Russia where, in 1982, he gained a PhD with his historically illiterate thesis *The Other Side: the Secret Relationship Between Nazism and Zionism*.[30]

As well as promoting the antisemitic canard of Nazi-Zionist collaboration, Abbas was a consistent Holocaust minimiser and regularly accused the Israelis of pursuing a policy of genocide against the Palestinians, alleging on a 2022 visit to Germany (in the presence of the Chancellor) that Israel had perpetrated 'fifty Holocausts' against his people. He had a habit of inflaming Arab emotions by reviving the Grand Mufti's most incendiary Islamist techniques. In 2015, he inveighed against Israelis visiting Judaism's holiest site, the Temple Mount, for desecrating the site 'with their filthy feet.'[31] In 2016 he informed the European Parliament that 'Rabbis are telling the Israeli government to poison our wells.'[32] During his seemingly endless term of office, he acquiesced in the incitement of terrorism against Jews and rewarded convicted murderers serving prison sentences in Israel with salaries for life via the PA's 'Martyrs' Fund' ('pay-for-slay' policy).[33] Like Arafat, he appeared open to peace negotiations but rejected multiple offers of statehood on the grounds that they failed to permit the (non-existent) 'right of return' of millions of Palestinian refugees to Israel rather than to the proposed Palestinian state. This intransigence should surprise no-one: in 2014, he declared that the Palestinians would never recognize Israel as a Jewish state.

Yet Abbas, like his predecessor, was always treated respectfully and even deferentially by global leaders. European legislators greeted his well-poisoning speech with a standing ovation (just as they had endorsed Yasser Arafat and his murderous PLO in Venice in 1980). This is not an unusual phenomenon. The list of antisemitic figures with whom Israel is implausibly expected to find common diplomatic ground is a lengthy one. It includes most of the officials representing the Arab League (twenty-two countries with 420 million inhabitants) and the Islamic Conference (fifty-seven countries with 1.4 billion inhabitants).

Antisemitic Anti-Israelism – a New Product of an Old Cognitive Pathology

The steady drumbeat of Arab and Muslim antisemitism accompanying the seven decades of Israel's existence has become louder rather than softer over time. At first sight, that seems paradoxical for three reasons. First, the Holocaust-era generation of Hitler-admiring Arab rabble-rousers, epitomised by the Mufti, gradually died out and were replaced by Western-educated leaders more concerned with dealing with the pragmatic military and political complexities of what was almost universally regarded as a territorial rather than religious or inter-ethnic dispute. Second, two Arab states, including the mighty Egypt, signed peace treaties with Israel and others, plus the PLO, were drawn into the frame of what has been optimistically called a peace process. They have been joined by at least three countries that have signed the Abraham Accords with Israel. Third, by the end of the twentieth century most of the Arab world had rid itself of nearly all of its Jews thereby removing the antisemites' targets from view.

In such circumstances, antisemitism in the region should have dissolved into the mists of time to be replaced by normal international relations, whether friendly or strained. That this did not happen is attributable to several factors including an inability or unwillingness of Arab leaders to discard long-established anti-Jewish stereotypes, the infusion of Soviet-style antisemitism and anti-imperialism into the conflict (reframed as 'Israel-Palestine'), and the depiction of Israel's strongest ally as the puppet of 'the American Jewish lobby.' The near-absence of Jews in the MENA region today is no guarantee of the absence of antisemitism, as the European post-war experience showed; paradoxically, antisemitic fantasies tend to thrive in the absence of the corrective influence of real Jews rather than the imaginary objects of the antisemites' derision.

Soviet-era antisemitism was a decisive factor not only in energising a pre-existing Arab hatred of Israel but in shaping the growing Western (especially leftist) disaffection with Israel following the Six Day War of 1967.

That event dealt an insufferable blow to the prestige Soviet Union that had watched helplessly as the Arab armies it had equipped proved incapable of defeating the puny young Jewish state. Moreover, the war had awakened the collective identity of over two million Soviet Jews many of whom began to agitate for the right to emigrate to Israel. To explain these 'reactionary' phenomena, Soviet ideologues resurrected old antisemitic tropes in the guise of anti-imperialism and antifascism.[34] By the 1980s, Zionism was depicted as an international conspiracy, and the arch-obstacle to the universal triumph of socialism, echoing the earlier Christian accusation that Jews' rejection of Christ was sabotaging the dawning of the messianic era to the detriment of mankind.

The attitude of Palestinians to Israelis and Jews has remained hostile despite the Oslo Accords of 1993-95 that were supposed to promote peaceful co-existence through Palestinian self-government in areas in which no Israelis reside and Israel Defence Forces (IDF) personnel have been withdrawn. Israeli academic Daniel Polisar has tracked Palestinian public opinion surveys within the PA over more than two decades. His findings are discouraging as they reveal an adherence to stereotypically delusional views that cross several red lines into antisemitism: 'In sum, when the Palestinians look at Israel, they see a country of enormous power and influence that has done great harm to them, that seeks to displace them entirely from historical Palestine, and whose people are deficient as individuals and also lacking any collective rights to the land in general or to Jerusalem in particular.'[35]

Polisar's findings should surprise no-one with a knowledge of Palestinian affairs. In a 2019 report, *UN Watch*[36] detailed the methods that the PA employs to operationalise antisemitism: criminalising the sale of land to Jews as a capital offence; providing financial rewards to Palestinian terrorists who kill or attempt to kill Israelis; incitement of antisemitic racial hatred by Palestinian officials, including the President; routine antisemitic demonisation of Israel and incitement to terrorism by Palestinian state-sponsored media; an educational curriculum that denies Jewish rights in Israel, glorifies terrorists and preaches hatred against Jews and Israelis; and failing to ensure protection for Israelis (including worshippers at holy sites) who enter Palestinian-controlled territories. The international community's collective response to this calamitous scenario has been one of apathy.

In his classic historical analysis of the long and unhappy relationship between Arabs and Jews, Lewis offers an interesting explanation of the underlying psychological mechanism whereby the confrontation with Israel elevated Arab antisemitic ideation to new heights. He illustrates this by means of a question posed by an Egyptian literary critic after the national humiliation of the Six Day War. Commenting on the cliché-ridden caricatures of corrupt and cowardly Jews in Arab fiction, the critic asked: 'If the Israelis were really like that, how could they have inflicted a defeat on us?' The answer that emerged was a dark one and drew on European stereotypes of Jewish malevolent power whereby the feeble weaklings of traditional Arab accounts were transformed into the sons of Satan, exercising demonic power. Lewis concludes that this re-imagining of the Jewish foe as an ultra-powerful adversary fulfilled a dual Arab need – to explain the inexplicable defeats of the past and reinvigorate resistance in the future. 'The struggle against such an adversary gives cosmic stature to those who engage in it, and lends some dignity even to those who suffer a defeat, which, they firmly believe, can only be temporary.'[37]

The Muslim Brotherhood has continued to exert its baleful influence on Arab and Muslim attitudes to Jews throughout the long years of struggle against the hated Jewish state. The sense of shame that Arabs felt about their repeated defeats at the hands of a people they had considered their inferiors for centuries was vividly expressed by the militant but influential Sunni Muslim cleric Yusuf Al-Qaradawi:

> This is one of the peculiarities of our times. The nation upon which abasement and humiliation was inflicted, and which drew the wrath of Allah – the people most covetous of life – we have become their victims. The cowards have grown bold in their attitude towards us, the weak and humiliated have grown strong in their dealings with us. The small birds in our land have turned into eagles, and the sheep have turned into wolves that devour us. What has befallen our nation?![38]

Qaradawi foresaw a grim fate for the Jews: 'But Allah lies in wait for them, and He will not forsake this nation. He will not allow these people to continue to spread corruption in the land. We wait for the revenge of Allah to descend upon them, and, Allah willing, it will be by our own hands.'

These notions cannot be attributed to the 'normal' antagonism that might be expected to arise from inter-ethnic or inter-state conflict. Recent research makes clear that antisemitic anti-Zionism was far from an epiphenomenon but central to the Arab conceptualisation of the Jews, Zionism and Israel. American historian Jeffrey Herf explains how an extraordinary late burst of American, British, German and Israeli scholarship, delving into official government (including Arabic) texts, has revealed the strength and depth of the Nazi-Islamist alliance and the way it infused attitudes to Zionism and Israel.[39] This specifically Arab-Muslim anti-Jewish hostility is comparable to that developed in German society from the early nineteenth century onwards.[9] Whereas Christian Judeophobia evolved into racial antisemitism that perceived the Jew as a threat to German national life, the Muslim view of Jews evolved from that of the feeble *dhimmi* Jewish stereotype into its polar opposite – the all-powerful, wealthy Zionist Jew that posed a mortal threat to the Arab nation and Islam and thus had to be stopped by all means necessary. In both the German and Arab-Muslim cases, the longstanding dormant antisemitism of these societies was stimulated to pursue a course of eliminationist violence by circumstances – the arrival of two new genocidal political ideologies, Nazism and Islamism respectively. When Husseini understood the explosive synergy that combining the two could achieve, Islamo-fascism became his tactical assault weapon of choice in his confrontation with the Jews of Palestine.

There are other parallels between the experience of Germans and Arabs. The roles of religion and politics have been commented upon. Equally potent was the impact of literature – and here the similarities are striking. Prominent in the antisemitic propagandist's toolkit are Canon Rohling's *The Talmud Jew*, Henry Ford's *The International Jew*, the Tsarist forgery *The Protocols of the Elders of Zion*, and, of course, Hitler's *Mein Kampf*. All peddle absurd conspiracy theories and all have been translated multiple times into Arabic. The *Protocols* especially seems to resonate strongly with the Arab public and still appear regularly on the best-seller lists of Beirut, Cairo, Damascus and Ramallah. Jews observe with irony the extent to which such poisonous material, once heavily promoted by Joseph Goebbels to facilitate the Holocaust, is eschewed in the countries that spawned them while remaining popular in societies held by many Western progressives to be on the front line in the contemporary struggle against Zionism and global fascism.

Given the Manichean nature of this still rarely acknowledged antisemitic anti-Zionism and anti-Israelism that continue to grip the Arab imagination, it is hardly surprising that attempts at peace-making have proved so frustrating. Because the all-pervasive demonic antisemitism in Arab-Muslim culture has never been adequately recognised and confronted, it has persisted. The consequences for all the stakeholders in the conflict have been tragic since the only acceptable outcome, in the minds of influential Arab leaders and thinkers up to the present day, is the total elimination of Zionism (Israel), at a minimum, and of the Jews themselves, if that is required. Since the Jewish state will never contemplate either national suicide or the placing of most of its citizens at risk of genocide, the gap between the two sides is of necessity irreconcilable unless Arab attitudes change. (Note how this evidence-based analysis contrasts with the conventional but flawed conjectural explanations – especially 'the occupation,' 'illegal Jewish settlements' and the absence of the 'two-state-solution' – for the stalemate between the protagonists).

How can we explain this wilful blindness? How is it possible that the international community has tolerated the revival of genocidal Jew-hatred in the twenty-first century? The explanation is not difficult to discover. When the conflict was subjected to a Soviet rewriting of history in the 1960s, in which the PLO was portrayed as an anti-imperialist progressive movement, the crucial missing link between Nazism and Islamism was erased from view to the point where most commentators, especially on the left, became blind to it. Herf contends that the ideas of al-Banna and Husseini were lost from view, were never known in the first place, or were dismissed as musty historical details:

> Yet al-Banna's statement that Husseini would 'continue the struggle' that Hitler had waged against the Jews and Zionism proved correct. As leader of the Arab Higher Committee in Palestine, Husseini did 'continue the struggle' against the Jews by insisting on war in 1947 and 1948 in order to prevent Israel's establishment, and by fuelling the fusion of Islamism and Palestinian nationalism that would make rejecting the fact of Israel's existence a core principle of Arab politics for the next half-century.[39]

Since 1948, the Middle East has witnessed enormous changes including the accumulation of vast oil-generated wealth, revolutions and counter-revolutions, wars, terrorism and the prospect of a nuclear-armed Islamist Iran seeking to extend its hegemony across the region. With relatively few (though important) exceptions – notably the two Arab-Israeli peace treaties (with Egypt and Jordan) in the twentieth century and the Abraham Accords (with Bahrain, United Arab Emirates, Morocco and perhaps Sudan) in the twenty-first – none of these momentous events has yet succeeded in dislodging the obsessive enmity towards Jews and Israel within Arab (or Iranian) political elites or in wider Arab or Muslim culture. A collective perception of Jews that has been forged over centuries cannot be dismantled in decades – especially when its existence is denied despite a mountain of evidence derived from multiple sources including history, politics, literature, religion, the media, propaganda and research.

The Anti-Defamation League (ADL) is an American Jewish organisation that conducts periodic sample surveys, using robust methodology, of global antisemitism. The most recent comprehensive survey[40] was conducted in 2013-14. Overall, antisemitism has been rising but there are marked variations between regions in negative attitudes to Jews: in the USA, one in ten adults harbour antisemitic views, while in Europe, the figure is one in four. In the MENA region, the figure rises to three in four, the highest in the world. The populations with the highest percentages within the Middle East are those of the West Bank (Arab population) and Gaza (93 per cent).

These figures cannot be dismissed as the consequence of conflict. As has been described, antisemitism in the Palestinian population antedates the conflict with Israel by several decades. The ADL survey, moreover, focuses on attitudes to Jews not Israelis, and solicits opinions about the influence of Jews in, for example, politics, finance and the mass media. Iraq, a country that is neither located on Israel's borders nor is usually in direct conflict with Israel, has a high antisemitism prevalence of 92 per cent for reasons that are obscure. Furthermore, Iran – locked in a prolonged stand-off with Israel over its nuclear programme and support for Palestinian terror groups that are in perpetual confrontation with Israel – has a relatively low rate (60 per cent) by MENA standards. That is no cause for complacency given the antisemitic nature of the Islamist regime's leaders who, unusually for the region, outstrip public opinion in the fervency of their hostility to Jews and their state, but it does suggest that the toppling of Iran's Islamist government could conceivably moderate the antisemitic rhetoric and behaviour emanating from that country.

Iran – Israel's Genocidal Nemesis

The Islamic Republic of Iran openly admits to antisemitism including the belief that Jews spread pornography and homosexuality.[41] Here is an example from the government's website: 'The Zionist regime is one of the promoters of homosexuality in the world and is the organizer of promotional events like homosexual marches in various cities. Tel Aviv is the homosexuals' favourite town in the world.' Sheina Vojoudi, an Iranian dissident who lives in Germany, points to antisemitism as one of the central factors of the Iranian regime's domestic and foreign policy and they use it to distract Iranians from the pressing bread-and-butter problems: 'The Islamic Republic has destroyed Iran to save its enmity with Israel and the Jewish people. Israel is the only word that you can hear from the Mullahs and the Islamic Republic's officials for all the problems that we've been facing in Iran, from the economic problems to the environmental problems, from the social issues to the political issues.'[42]

Iran's antisemitism has been internalised into its prime foreign policy objective – politicide (that often elides into genocide). In 2002, former President of Iran Ali Akbar Hashemi Rafsanjani of Iran – at the time hailed as a moderate in the West – discussed the 'Islamic bomb' as a means of annihilating Israel. 'The Jews should in truth be expecting the day on which this superfluous limb [Israel] will be torn away from the body of the Muslim region and Muslim world, and all the people assembled in Israel [that is, the Jews] will once again be scattered all over the world and become refugees.'[43] 'Israel is a cancerous tumour,' proclaimed Ali Hosseini Khamenei, Iranian Supreme Leader in 2010. 'So what do you do with a cancerous tumour? What can be done to treat a tumour other than removing it?'[44] He repeated his clinically precise message in 2018, adding 'it is possible and it will happen.'[45]

In 2015, the Islamic Republic set a target date of 2040 for the destruction of Israel. At an Al Quds Day rally in central Tehran in 2017, the regime unveiled a clock counting down the days until the Jewish state's predicted doom. This bizarre theatricality should not be viewed with equanimity but as a manifestation of something far more disturbing. Here is the sombre verdict of an Israeli report:

> Iranian antisemitism is state-sponsored, institutional, and an instrument of the regime as part of its official and declared policy to destroy the State of Israel… One can say that the Iranian strategy towards Israel consists of three primary components: the development of nuclear weapons; support for terrorism; antisemitism and denial of the Holocaust. The three are interlinked and provide support for each other. The antisemitic component and the denial of the Holocaust in the Iranian policy provide it with ideological-religious justification for the uncompromising struggle against Israel.[46]

According to the US State Department (not known for its warmth towards Israel), Iran's regime is the leading international state sponsor of antisemitism. It finances, arms and trains several militias – notably Hamas, Hezbollah and Islamic Jihad – that have been designated as terrorist groups by the major democracies. All are actively involved in violent activities directed at Israel and her citizens and at least one (Hezbollah) has perpetrated acts of terror against Jews abroad such as the bombing of a Jewish community centre in Buenos Aries in 1994 killing eighty-five people and injuring hundreds. Sustained coverage of the antisemitic and homicidal activities of these groups is almost absent from the mainstream global media (see Chapter 7).

Hassan Nasrallah, leader of Iranian proxy militia Hezbollah, has never hidden his antisemitism: 'If we search the entire globe for a more cowardly, lowly, weak, and frail individual in his spirit, mind, ideology, and religion, we will never find anyone like the Jew — and I am not saying the Israeli,'[47] and 'If they (Jews) all gather in Israel, it will save us the trouble of going after them worldwide.'[48] Hamas, the Iranian-backed rulers of Gaza, are equally forthcoming: 'The Jews will not live in peace and comfort under our rule. Treachery will keep being their nature throughout history. The day will come when the whole world will rid itself of the Jews.'[49] At the onset of the First *Intifada*' (in 1987) they announced: 'Here are the Jews, the brothers of apes, the murderers of the prophets, the blood suckers, the war agitators—murdering you, depriving you of your life after they have stolen the Motherland and your home. Only Islam can break the Jews and destroy their dream.'

This book could be filled with similar repellent quotes emanating from Israel's most intractable enemies in whom their allies and sympathisers see 'only anti-Zionism' or 'legitimate criticism of Israel.' But we know that these Islamist extremists should be believed for they have regularly turned their words into actions, most terrifyingly in southern Israel on 7 October 2023.

Notes

1   M. Gilbert, *In Ishmael's House: A History of Jews in Muslim Lands* (Toronto: Yale University Press, 2011), p.131.

2   B. Lewis, *Semites and Anti-Semites: An Inquiry into Conflict and Prejudice* (New York: WW Norton & Company, 1999), p.121.

3   See Gilbert, *In Ishmael's House,* p.53.

4   W. Laqueur, *The Changing Face of Antisemitism.* (New York: Oxford University Press, 2006), p.193.

5   See Gilbert, *In Ishmael's House,* p.49.

6   L. Julius, *Uprooted* (London: Vallentine Mitchell, 2018), p.74.

7   M. Zografos, 'Genocidal Antisemitism: A Core Ideology of the Muslim Brotherhood,' Institute For The Study Of Global Antisemitism and Policy, Occasional Paper Series no. 4/2021. https://isgap.org/wp-content/uploads/2021/06/GenocidalAntisemitism-Markos-Zografos.pdf pp.1-4. (Last accessed 11 June 2024).

8   Yale Law school, the Avalon Project. https://avalon.law.yale.edu/20th_
    century/hamas.asp (Last accessed 11 June 2024).
9   D. Goldhagen, *Hitler's Willing Executioners* (London: Abacus, 1997), p.33.
10 See Lewis, *Semites and Anti-Semites*, pp.171-2.
11 See Gilbert, *In Ishmael's House*, pp.141-2.
12 Nir Hasson, 'Constantinople's Little-known Rift With Its Reps in Ottoman
    Palestine', *Haaretz*, 27 June 2014.
13 See Zografos, 'Genocidal Antisemitism', p 16.
14 M. Küntzel, *Jihad and Jew Hatred: Islamism, Nazism and the Roots of 9/11*
    (Candor NY: Telos Press, 2007).
15 See Julius, *Uprooted*, p.89.
16 See Lewis, *Semites and Anti-Semites*, p.157.
17 M. Pickles, 'The Arab-Israeli Conflict Made Simple.' 1 August 2019.
    https://markpickles.wordpress.com/2019/08/01/the-arab-israeli-conflict-
    made-simple/ (Last accessed 11 June 2024).
18 W. Lacquer, B. Rubin, *The Israel-Arab Reader: A Documentary History of
    the Middle East Conflict* (New York: Penguin Books, 2008), pp.51-55.
19 See Gilbert, *In Ishmael's House*, p.186.
20 See Julius, *Uprooted*, p.93.
21 Ibid. p.131-2.
22 D. Barnett, E. Karsh, 'Azzam's Genocidal Threat', *Middle East Forum*, 11, 4
    (Fall 2011), pp.85-88.
23 D. Schmidt, 'Aim to Oust Jews Pledged by Sheikh', *New York Times*, 2
    August 1948.
24 A Schwartz, E Wilf, *The War of Return: How Western Indulgence of the
    Palestinian Dream has Obstructed the Path to Peace* (New York: All Points
    Books, 2020), p.17.
25 Ahmad Shukeiri, https://en.wikipedia.org/wiki/Ahmad_Shukeiri (Last
    accessed 31 December 2023). (Last accessed 11 June 2024).
26 E. Webman, 'Rethinking the Role of Religion in Arab Antisemitic
    Discourses', *Religions* (2019), 10(7), 415. https://www.mdpi.com/2077-
    1444/10/7/415 (Last accessed 11 June 2024.
27 B. Morris, *1948. A History of the First Arab-Israeli War* (New Haven and
    London: Yale University Press, 2008), p.408.
28 M. Küntzel, '1967: Nasser's Antisemitic War Against Israel', *Fathom*,
    (Spring 2017). https://fathomjournal.org/1967-nassers-antisemitic-war-
    against-israel/ (Last accessed 11 June 2024).
29 David Eliezrie, 'Listen to Arafat in Arabic, not in English.' *Los Angeles
    Times*, 27 February 1996. https://www.latimes.com/archives/la-xpm-1996-
    02-27-me-40531-story.html (Last accessed 11 June 2024).

30 Y. Rosenberg, 'Mahmoud Abbas: Still a Holocaust Denier', *Tablet*, 27 April 2014.   https://www.tabletmag.com/sections/news/articles/mahmoud-abbas-still-a-holocaust-denier (Last accessed 11 June 2024).

31 MEMRI TV, Palestinian President Mahmoud Abbas: Jews 'Have No Right to Defile the Al-Aqsa Mosque with Their Filthy Feet,16 September 2015.' https://www.memri.org/tv/palestinian-president-mahmoud-abbas-jews-have-no-right-defile-al-aqsa-mosque-their-filthy-feet (Last accessed 11 June 2024).

32 R. Emmott, D. Williams, 'Abbas says some Israeli rabbis called for poisoning Palestinian water', *Reuters*, 12 October 2022. https://www.reuters.com/article/us-palestinians-israel-idUSKCN0Z91J8 (Last accessed 31 December 2023).

33 N.J. Zilberdik, 'PA Spokesman vows to continue "Pay-for-Slay" terror rewards'. Palestinian Media Watch, 7 February 2022. https://palwatch.org/page/30204 (Last accessed 11 June 2024).

34 I. Tabarovsky, 'Soviet Anti-Zionism and Contemporary Left Antisemitism', *Fathom*, May 2019.

35 D. Polisar, 'What Do Palestinians Want?' *Mosaic*, 2 November 2015. https://mosaicmagazine.com/essay/israel-zionism/2015/11/what-do-palestinians-want/ (Last accessed 11 June 2024).

36 H. Neuer, D. Rovner, 'Alternative Report of United Nations Watch to the 99th Session of the Committee on the Elimination of Racial Discrimination for its review of State of Palestine' (Geneva: United Nations Watch, 2019), p.1.

37 See Lewis, *Semites and Anti-Semites*, pp.190-1.

38 MEMRI TV, 'Sheik Yousuf Al-Qaradhawi Incites against Jews, Arab Regimes, and the U.S., and Calls on Muslims to Boycott Starbucks, Marks and Spencer', June 2009. https://www.memri.org/tv/sheik-yousuf-al-qaradhawi-incites-against-jews-arab-regimes-and-us-and-calls-muslims-boycott (Last accessed 11 June 2024).

39 J. Herf, 'Nazi Antisemitism & Islamist Hate', *Tablet*, 6 July 2022. https://www.tabletmag.com/sections/history/articles/the-nazi-roots-of-islamist-hate?utm_source=substack&utm_medium=email (Last accessed 31 December 2023).

40 Anti-Defamation League (New York), 'ADL/Global 100.' https://global100.adl.org/map (Last accessed 11 June 2024).

41 See Laqueur. *The Changing Face of Antisemitism*, p.198.

42 Benjamin Weinthal, 'Iran regime's 'Jewish Studies Center' published over 1,000 antisemitic articles', 3 June 2022, https://www.jpost.com/diaspora/antisemitism/article-708487 (Last accessed 11 June 2024).

43 See Zografos, 'Genocidal Antisemitism', p.23.

44 Jewish Virtual Library, 'Quotes from Islamic and Arab Leaders Regarding Jews and Israel', https://www.jewishvirtuallibrary.org/myths-and-facts-quotes (Last accessed 11 June 2024).

45 Twitter, Khameini.ir, 3 June 201, cited by Bari Weiss 12 December 2022. https://twitter.com/bariweiss/status/1602370518585221120/photo/1 (Last accessed 11 June 2024).

46 Centre for Combating Antisemitism, 'The Antisemitism of the Iranian Establishment – in View of the Statements Made by Iran's Vice President.' https://www.jewishvirtuallibrary.org/jsource/anti-semitism/Antisemitism%20of%20the%20Iranian%20Establishment.pdf (Last accessed 11 June 2024).

47 Anti-Defamation League (New York), 'Teaching Antisemitism and Terrorism in Hezbollah Schools,' 19 May 2020. https://www.adl.org/antisemitism-and-terrorism-in-hezbollah-schools (Last accessed 31 December 2023).

48 See Jewish Virtual Library, 'Quotes from Islamic and Arab Leaders Regarding Jews and Israel.' https://www.jewishvirtuallibrary.org/myths-and-facts-quotes (Last accessed 11 June 2024).

49 D. Aaron, *In Their Own Words* (Santa Monica, CA: RAND Corporation, 2008), p.113. https://www.rand.org/pubs/monographs/MG602.html (Last accessed 11 June 2024).

7

Global Responses: How Anti-Israelism has been Internationalised

In 2002, the final year of his first term as Malaysian prime minister, Mahathir Mohamad evoked a classic antisemitic trope: 'The Europeans killed six million Jews out of twelve million. But today the Jews rule this world by proxy. They get others to fight and die for them.'[1] This shocking remark made little impact on his popularity and in 2018 he was re-elected, making him the country's longest serving prime minister.

Mohamad's paranoia about Jews was unexceptional in the Muslim world and increasingly in non-Muslim countries. The international response to the Arab-Israeli conflict has been moulded by antisemitic ideation that is both intrinsic and extrinsic to the conflict itself. The former is presented by Arab-Muslim actors to the international community (mainly via the UN and its branches) who serve as facilitators – an uncritical Greek chorus who project an amplified version of the antisemitism to a vast global audience. Before long, such ideas are internalised by numerous partner organisations, politicians, the media, academics and the public. The result is the internationalisation of antisemitic anti-Israelism.

The New Antisemitism: a Global Phenomenon

Historian and antisemitism expert Deborah Lipstadt alludes to the overlap between traditional antisemitism and anti-Zionism in the way that extremists of both the far right and far left deploy the term 'Zio' as a synonym for 'Jew'[2] whom both agree operates within a cunning and covert network designed to extend Jewish power and replace whites or displace Palestinians. As with all forms of antisemitism, the hypothesised conspiracies are illusory, but the Internet offers a conducive culture medium for anti-Jewish and anti-Israeli fantasies, however absurd, to gain traction and, in many eyes, credibility.

In relation to Israel, many people – both in the Middle East and elsewhere but most vociferously in progressive circles in Europe and the

USA – have adopted a belief system by means of a process that Kahneman describes as type 1 or fast thinking.[3] These beliefs are comfortably superimposed on a pre-existing set of assumptions that form the architecture of a fantasised parallel reality comprising distorted perceptual models of Jews, Zionists and Israelis. These models are important to understand as they provide the foundation for the reflexive responses of individuals, groups and institutions to the conflict. According to this theoretical framework, the models are validated and extended by exposure to ideas that are widely prevalent and endlessly reiterated, with little or no challenge, within peer groups and online echo chambers. In theory, such beliefs can manifest themselves in an infinite variety of ways. In practice, they are predictable and homogeneous. All are hostile to Israel, her founding principles and, in many cases, her perceived 'Jewish' character – devious, conspiratorial, powerful and bloodthirsty.

This type of prejudiced 'fast thinking' is circular and self-reinforcing. Though largely extrinsic to the conflict itself, it is partially informed (or misinformed) by the antisemitic ideation of the Arab and Muslim participants. It frustrates rational discourse because it comprises a number of firmly held but demonstrably false assumptions that are assumed, by most of the adherents of the belief system, to be unassailably true. What is the explanation for this large-scale psychopathology?

The repetitious individual or group recital of these dogmas in public spaces appears to fulfil an emotional need in the participants.[4] In that sense, the mindset is comparable to a religious cult rather than a political ideology. But because it is expressed in quasi-political terms, both its doctrinal-devotional basis and its antisemitic nature – that may be unconscious – tend to be obscured from view. Its idealistic ethos, combined with an intellectual vagueness, may explain its widespread and growing popularity especially in younger people for whom peer approval is paramount.

The New Antisemitism's 'Articles of Faith'

Fourteen assertions or 'articles of faith' about Israel are prominent in the modern antisemitic discourse about Israel: that Zionism is an inherently racist and colonialist ideology; that Arabs cannot be antisemitic as they themselves are semites; that the 1917 Balfour Declaration betrayed the Arabs; that Balfour and the international community never intended the establishment of a Jewish state; that Arab hostility to Jews was a natural response to the migration of European Zionists to Palestine; that Israel was created by ethnically cleansing the Palestinians; that Zionism was responsible for the so-called Jewish *Nakba*; that Israel today is an apartheid state; that Israel violates international law through her occupation and settlement of Palestinian lands; that Israel uses disproportionate and murderous military force; that Israel is committing a genocide of the Palestinians comparable to the Nazi Holocaust; that Israel was created and only survives through US support; that Palestinian anger is caused by Israel's refusal to make peace on the basis of the two-state solution; that Arab threats against Jews are mere rhetoric.

Not all of these beliefs are held by all individuals who subscribe to an antisemitic worldview and not all who subscribe to them are subjectively antisemitic. But all of them are popular among those who seek to damage Israel and all are false – we shall review the evidence in Chapters 8 and 9. Yet the credo is difficult to dislodge even in the face of contrary evidence. That is because Kahnemanian *fast thinking* is based on a superficial knowledge of facts that are distorted or selected through a prism of conscious or unconscious prejudices, along with *priming*, or continuous reinforcement by the media (especially online), political rhetoric, and the expressed beliefs of others in the peer group.

However one seeks to explain or analyse these beliefs, there is no escaping the moral dimension. Those who adhere to them are convinced of their own moral rectitude and this may partially explain the growing appeal of anti-Israelism in a world in which religious faith, the traditional vehicle for the public expression of morality, is being replaced by the secular religion of human rights. Equally, those who hold a diametrically opposite view, based on knowledge and experience, have a collective moral responsibility to challenge dangerous falsehoods especially when they are wrapped in self-righteousness. This is more than a matter of political disagreement or competing narratives. Taken separately and together, these accusations are not only a travesty of the truth but an assault on the reputation of Israel and the Jewish people that amounts, in varying degrees, to demonisation, discriminatory double standards and delegitimisation – the Three Ds that Sharansky defined as the hallmarks of anti-Israeli antisemitism and that are reflected in the IHRA definition (see Chapter 2).

Framing the Conflict: Who is Fighting Whom?

As always, language is crucial to perception. Size matters. Advertisers know this: describing a foodstuff as *95 per cent fat-free* or *contains five per cent fat* describes exactly the same phenomenon but the former is more appealing to consumers than the latter. Message reframing is 'a communication technique that changes the conceptual and/or emotional setting or viewpoint in relation to how a brand is experienced by placing it in a different frame that fits the same brand equally well or better.'[5] This type of manipulation is part of the political propagandist's armoury too. Israel is less than one six hundredth the size of the MENA territory but is in full control of 60 per cent of the West Bank – so highlighting the latter figure is the more effective pro-Palestinian marketing strategy.

The framing of the conflict as purely *Israeli-Palestinian* is misleading as it represents only one of the many hostile fronts confronting Israel. From the start, the conflict has been between Israel and the Arab world plus, in more recent times, Islamist militias that look to Iran for leadership, inspiration and resources. Since that historical reality plays badly with those seeking to portray Israel as the overbearing Goliath against the puny Palestinian David, anti-Israel activists changed the narrative. Foreign commentators have blindly (or, in some cases, malignly) echoed that revisionism. But such propaganda obscures understanding and obstructs progress towards peace. It also feeds into the antisemitic trope of excessive Jewish power that echoes extreme traditional slurs of medieval European antisemitism. If Israel is the stronger party, she bears a double responsibility – for inflicting a high toll of casualties on the weaker side, and for failing to make the concessions that supposedly hold the key to ending the conflict. To put it another way: in the 'Israel-Palestine' framing, Israel stands accused of being the main obstacle to peace by deploying her superior power to inflict needless suffering on helpless Palestinians.

Both the premise and conclusion are flawed. Israel has been forced to confront the hostility of most of the Arab world (plus Iran and, to a lesser degree, Turkey) for decades. The Palestinian people are not Israel's enemies, despite their leaders having sought to forge a national identity based on bitterness and grievance towards the Jewish state. Accusing Israel of causing deaths and injuries to civilians through her capricious or deliberate exercise of superior fire-power – as though the relentless terrorist war against Israeli citizens does not exist – is effectively a blood libel. It evokes images of the 'massacre of the innocents', a biblical-era slaughter of newborn babies allegedly ordered by Judean King Herod in an attempt to kill the infant Jesus. The phrase underpins two millennia of Christian Jew-hatred and often surfaces in our own times as a rhetorical journalistic device, particularly when describing Israel's wars against the Hamas rulers of Gaza.[6]

How the World Views Modern Israel

Critics often describe Israel as nationalistic and ethnocentric, but these epithets are half-truths at best. While Zionism is a form of nationalism, it sits at the liberal end of the spectrum and has a proven track record of humanitarianism. Israel has provided a safe haven for hundreds of thousands of people, mostly but not exclusively Jews, who would otherwise have endured extreme suffering or perished. As for the charge of ethnocentricity (or even racism), 75 per cent of the population are (predominantly secular or traditional) Jewish, 20 per cent are Arab and 5 per cent other identities. Both the Jewish majority and non-Jewish minorities are heterogeneous, a far cry from the stereotypical portrayal of the country's population as binary, Jewish or Arab. All citizens have full civil and religious rights in law.

Israel is a hyper-democratic society with a multiplicity of political parties, NGOs and media platforms, all of which contribute to a cacophonous debate about the current state and future direction of the country. Since its foundation, Israel's electoral system of proportional representation has thrown up governments of the left (including at times some far left elements), of the right (including at times some far right elements) yet has generally pursued moderate policies regardless of the transient exigencies of coalition politics. Israel is the only MENA country characterised as free by Freedom House.[7]

Anti-Zionism and Anti-Israelism on the Left

In many political circles today, especially on the progressive left, Zionism has acquired ultra-negative connotations. Conspiracy theories about Israel, Zionism and Jews abound on social media. A popular canard, granted spurious legitimacy by American academics Mearsheimer and Walt, is that 'the Lobby' controls US foreign policy to favour Israel at the expense of American interests.[8] The notion of a powerful pro-Israel cabal manipulating public opinion and governments is a sophisticated recycling of Nazi and Soviet antisemitism honed for a twenty-first century audience. Pursuing the conspiratorial theme, Democratic US Congresswoman Ilhan Omar tweeted, in an echo of ancient antisemitic tropes of excessive Jewish financial power, 'It's all about the Benjamins, baby', referring to a hundred-dollar bill, reflecting her belief that US foreign policy is in thrall to a rich pro-Israel lobby.[9]

The phenomenon of modern left-wing anti-Israelism is especially puzzling given the ultra-conservative nature of Arab society and its history of collaboration with European fascism. Until the 1960s, liberal circles were generally sympathetic to Zionism and solidly pro-Israel. That changed when the Soviet Union condemned Israel for colluding with Britain and France in the Suez debacle of 1956 and angrily reacted to the humiliating defeat that Israel inflicted on the combined Arab armies in 1967. The liberal-left's *volte-face* on Israel is galling to many Jews given the historical reality that Zionism was established to fulfil the basic human rights of a people that had often been denied them for two millennia.

There can be little doubt that the Soviet anti-Zionist campaign of the 1980s influences large swathes of leftist and even liberal thinking to this day and helps explain the insistence by many of Israel's harshest modern critics that 'anti-Zionism is not antisemitism.' Tabarovsky argues that this position is untenable.

> One of the lessons that the late Soviet anti-Zionist campaign teaches is that anti-Zionism and antisemitism have historically been deeply and, possibly, inextricably intertwined. True to their ideological tenets, the Soviets never attacked the Jews in purely racist terms. Accused of antisemitism, they indignantly claimed that they were simply anti-Zionist. But wherever and whenever they employed anti-Zionism for their political purposes, antisemitism blossomed.[10]

Historian Jeffrey Herf suggests that the Soviet bloc and the PLO succeeded in convincing much leftist opinion that Arab connections to fascism never existed or were insignificant. 'Hence the PLO, having obscured the Nazi connections of its founding father, was able to reinvent itself as an icon of leftist anti-imperialism. While some Arab states have themselves moved away from the toxic mixture of Islamism, anti-Jewish hatred, and Palestinian nationalist rejectionism that al-Banna and Husseini implanted, their campaigns have had a continuing impact in Western universities.' Herf identifies a further (partial) reason for Western indulgence of Arab anti-Zionism: 'The refusal to indict Amin al-Husseini and put him on trial for the war crimes he committed through his hardcore allegiance to the Nazi state constituted an enormous missed opportunity to draw public attention to significant ideological sources of Arab rejection of the Zionist project.'[11]

International Responses to Israel

Zionism, the national liberation movement of the Jewish people, was a revolutionary movement and one which even some Jews have yet to internalise. The response of global intellectual elites of all political hues was initially favourable but has turned, in many circles, to disaffection or antagonism. One interpretation of this cooling is that while homeless, vulnerable and murdered Jews evoke sympathy, Israel's new breed of independent, assertive and empowered Jews generates resentment.[12] The most virulent reaction originated within the Arab world, itself seeking to forge a new identity through nationalism, but was by no means confined to it. After a series of wars in the latter half of the twentieth century in which Israel prevailed over far larger enemy forces, and despite her conclusion of peace treaties with some Arab states and the PLO, that hostility has continued to fester and feed into a global antagonism that has continued to acquire momentum. We saw that antagonism reach its apotheosis in the world's effective siding with Hamas in the terrorist group's violent orgy of October 2023 (see Chapter 5).

The result is that Israelis, and the majority of the world's Jews, now feel themselves under assault not only physically but on the battlefield of public opinion. The two fronts are interdependent as military power is only effective if it can be deployed. A small country reduced to pariah status and isolated politically, economically and militarily will eventually confront existential risks: its population suffering penury, its capacity for independent decision-making severely curtailed, and its future as a fully sovereign state under question.

One might expect that any small democratic country subjected to this degree of hostility would be viewed with a degree of sympathy. International attitudes to Israel today belie that expectation. Israel is the only state that is a permanent agenda item on the UN human rights council – meaning that she is ritually condemned in that forum at every meeting, regardless of what else is happening in the world. More than half the time of the UN is spent discussing (and criticising) Israel. She is the only country singled out by the global BDS (Boycott, Divestment and Sanctions) movement, and whose legitimacy is questioned on a daily basis. Most ominously, she is threatened with politicide and genocide by a powerful regional neighbour, Iran, with whom the West is anxious to do business. In a chilling echo of the early twentieth century, the global response to threats to Jewish safety from that country (and its allies) may be repeating itself in the twenty-first. When brutal dictators, fuelled by Jew-hatred, issue threats of expulsion and mass murder, the world seems all too ready to look the other way or to lecture Jews and Israelis for their alleged paranoia. This has been the pattern since 1948 and stands in sharp contrast with the empathy displayed towards Palestinians and other distressed peoples.

Mainstream Media and Anti-Israelism

Israel has long complained that she gets treated shabbily by the mainstream media. On the other hand, anti-Israel activists are convinced that the media are pro-Israel. Who is right? There is no possibility of achieving a consensus on this issue. Editors tend to adopt a defensive posture on the grounds that they receive complaints from both sides. That is a lame excuse. Though it seems counterintuitive, an editorial determination to avoid bias can, in certain circumstances, have the opposite result. Speaking at a literary festival in 2002, former *Sunday Times* editor Harold Evans launched a scathing attack on the way the media is complicit in promoting antisemitism by seeking 'balance':

> Reporting and comment in the West all too often, for the best of motives, ingenuously reinforces the antisemitic mindset. Israel is supported, in Lenin's phrase, like a rope supports a hanging man. Equal weight is given to information from corrupt police states and proven liars as to information from a vigorous self-critical democracy. The pious but fatuous posture is that this is somehow fair, as if truth existed in a moral vacuum, something to be measured by the yard like calico. Five million Jews in Israel are a vulnerable minority surrounded by 300 million Muslims who, for the most part, are governed by authoritarian regimes, quasi-police states, which in more than 50 years have never ceased trying to wipe it out by war and terrorism. They muzzle dissent and critical reporting, they run vengeful penal systems and toxic schools, they have failed in almost every measure of social and political justice, they deflect the frustrations of their streets to the scapegoat of Zionism and they breed and finance international terrorism. Yet it is Israel that is regarded with scepticism and sometimes hostility.[13]

Not all journalists seek the sweet spot of truthful objectivity. The Qatari-funded *Al Jazeera* news platform has been virulently anti-Zionist and anti-Israeli since its founding in 1996, a position that has extended into its English-language channel which started in 2006. It claims to reach more than 270 million households in over 140 countries The UK's BBC, perhaps the world's most respected media organisation, signed an information-sharing agreement with *Al Jazeera* in 2003,[14] and there has been much interchange of staff between the two organisations. That close connection should sound alarm bells in the liberal media community and beyond.

The BBC is bound by its charter to adopt an impartial position on contentious issues but has long been bombarded with complaints that it applies double standards in the Arab-Israeli conflict. The frequency and intensity of Israeli and Jewish protests led to the corporation establishing an internal inquiry into its reporting of Israel. In 2004, its findings (the Balen report) were presented to senior BBC managers but were never published.[15] Instead, the broadcaster spent at least £300,000 in fending off Freedom of Information requests during a period when it regularly complained of financial stress. Since then the complaints of anti-Israel bias have, if anything, intensified. In late 2022, the BBC finally accepted that their response to such complaints was unacceptable though they declined to acknowledge that their reporting on Israel was seriously problematic,[16] a position that may have prompted the launching of a UK parliamentary inquiry into the issue shortly thereafter. Concerns about the platform's flawed coverage of Israel's Swords of Iron campaign, launched on Hamas in reaction to the 7 October 2023 massacre, surged to even higher levels.

The Simon Wiesenthal Centre, a global Jewish human rights organisation, monitors contemporary antisemitism. In 2021, they ranked the BBC third in their annual global antisemitism top ten, highlighting the way the UK's prestigious broadcaster provides a platform to antisemitic journalists such as Tala Halawa who tweeted hateful views ('Hitler was right' and 'Zionists can't get enough of our blood') and was subsequently dismissed.[17] *Honest Reporting*, a pro-Israel watchdog group, has documented the way that the BBC violates its own charter by employing staff, particularly in its Arabic service, who routinely lambast Israel in ways that are overtly antisemitic.[18] Another pro-Israel media monitoring group CAMERA (*Committee for Accuracy in Middle East Reporting and Analysis*)[19] has prompted the BBC and others to correct inaccurate or misleading information but the frequency with which such 'errors' occur suggests that systematic bias rather than carelessness is the underlying problem.

The UK's *Jewish Chronicle* drew the attention of readers to a regular contributor across the BBC's news channels, Abdel Bari Atwan. He described the shooting of three Israelis in Tel Aviv as a 'miracle', called their murderer a 'hero' and said that those fleeing for their lives were 'like mice.' He also defended Mahmoud Abbas's refusal to apologise for the murder of Israeli athletes by Palestinian terrorists at the 1972 Munich Olympics.[20] The BBC's response to its broadcasting these views was to describe Bari Awan's appearance as 'editorially justified.' This woeful record has generated an unprecedented level of anxiety within the British Jewish community. The

Antisemitism Barometer of the *Campaign Against Antisemitism* reported that in 2020 two-thirds of British Jews considered the BBC's coverage of Jewish affairs unfavourable and that 90 per cent believed that media bias against Israel fuels persecution of Jews in Britain.[21]

Many other highly regarded media outlets such as *The Guardian, The Independent, The Financial Times, The New York Times, Channel 4* and *CNN* have adopted a similarly hypercritical perspective on Israel while treating her adversaries far more leniently. The reasons for this selectivity are obscure. Ignorance and incompetence are unlikely explanations as these organisations compete to employ the most highly rated journalists of their generation. Fear may play a role in specific locations such as the Gaza Strip where Hamas and other violent extremist groups have long been known to restrict and physically intimidate reporters.[22] What these media platforms all appear to have in common is their complicity, never admitted, in promoting a narrative that portrays Israelis as heartless aggressors and Palestinians as innocent victims while simultaneously claiming to be impartial and truthful.

Whether due to malice, ignorance or ideology, Western media have amplified anti-Israeli Palestinian propaganda. The editors of *The New York Times* must have realised the politicidal significance of promoting the 'right of return' narrative when they upscaled their coverage of the issue. Schwartz and Wilf chart the process: 'In the mid-1990s, the *New York Times* ran two or three articles a year on the right of return. In 1996, that number rose to four. In 2000, the newspaper published thirty-six articles on the right of return, a number that continued to rise after the outbreak of the Second *Intifada*.'[23]

Lewis acknowledges that biased reporting on Israel need not arise from antisemitic motives – but they often do. This is far from a new phenomenon. Citing the example of a Lebanese Phalangist massacre of Palestinian civilians in 1982, in which Israel was cleared of direct involvement but whose army commanders were judged 'indirectly responsible' by an Israeli commission of inquiry (the only one ever established), he writes:

> The universal execration of Israeli behaviour at Sabra and Shatila may represent the high moral principles of the outside world and the high standards of behaviour expected from the Israelis. But a comparison between this execration and the almost total indifference towards other massacres, including more recent ones carried out by the Shia in the same camps at Sabra and Shatila, raises disquieting questions concerning the sentiments and motives of the judges.[24]

The questionable 'motives of the judges' may dictate what is not reported as much as what is. The media disinterest in genuine balance in recent times is illustrated by the near total absence of critical reporting of the governance of the Palestinian Authority, especially regarding its incentivisation of violence whereby the families of terrorists serving prison sentences in Israel are rewarded financially in proportion to the number of Israelis murdered (the 'pay-for-slay' policy). Another striking example is coverage of the Iranian nuclear deal; when Israel's vigorous opposition is reported at all, it is characterised as a 'complaint' rather than as an expression of a legitimate fear of genocidal attack by a regime that insists, in language devoid of ambiguity, that its intention is to wipe 'the Zionist entity off the map.'

The evidence of an anti-Israel bias in the global media reporting of Israel, whether deliberate or unintended, is profuse. A kind of groupthink appears to have gripped the large contingent of journalists who report from Israel on a daily basis. Israeli journalist Matti Friedman bemoans the 'severe malfunction' of media editorial procedures and attributes it to a preconceived notion of the nature of the conflict in which Israelis are assumed to deploy excessive military force against unarmed Palestinian civilians. This is the rigid template that editors appear to demand of their reporters even if this is rarely expressed or acknowledged openly. Friedman believes that this amounts to a prejudice mediated by a process of psychological projection:

> You don't need to be a history professor, or a psychiatrist, to understand what's going on. Having rehabilitated themselves against considerable odds in a minute corner of the earth, the descendants of powerless people who were pushed out of Europe and the Islamic Middle East have become what their grandparents were — the pool into which the world spits. The Jews of Israel are the screen onto which it has become socially acceptable to project the things you hate about yourself and your own country. The tool through which this psychological projection is executed is the international press.[25]

While not all reporting of Israel is prejudicial, the contemporary media discourse on the subject is largely hostile to Israel. This tendency was most vividly illustrated in the depiction of the Hamas-initiated war of 2023-24. Whether or not the underlying motivation for this hostility is antisemitic will always depend on the circumstances of a specific report. The bottom line is this: unfair or biased reporting, whether through the promotion of a demonising narrative or the application of a double standard to the world's sole Jewish state, amounts to antisemitism regardless of the mindset of the individual journalists or editors.

Online Antisemitic Anti-Zionism and Anti-Israelism

Antisemites will exploit whatever means of communication becomes available to them. Social media offer activists an attractive mechanism for the dissemination of hatred as it tends to be easily accessible and poorly regulated. 'X', Facebook, Instagram and similar platforms have become major weapons in the hands of antisemitic individuals and groups who are quick to launch online attacks on those who dare to oppose them.[26] These messages can suddenly 'go viral' and reach enormous numbers of readers within hours. Antisemites are able to appropriate newsworthy events, such as the coronavirus pandemic and the brutal killing of a black civilian by US police, to spread calumnies about alleged Jewish or Israeli involvement. In both those cases, as in many others, sinister conspiratorial links are invented between Israel and tragedies that afflict humanity, or sections of it, whether in the Middle East or anywhere else.

Drawing a distinction between Jews and Zionists has never much appealed to antisemites, although their public rhetoric appears to do so for their own self-serving purposes. British comedian David Baddiel has highlighted the online 'trolling' (attacks) to which he has been subjected simply because he is Jewish. Some of these hate-filled comments use the term 'Zionist' though Baddiel goes to great pains to stress that he has expressed no strong views one way or the other about Israel.[27]

North America was, until recently, considered the world's safest haven for diaspora Jews. That optimism is undergoing a re-evaluation, accelerated by a Pittsburgh mass shooting in 2018 when a white supremacist who had been a radicalised online entered the Tree of Life Synagogue, opened fire and killed eleven worshippers (as well as wounding several others). In 2022, with antisemitic attacks surging across the US, the Mapping Project (supported by the anti-Israel BDS movement) set alarm bells ringing in Jewish communities by identifying the location of Jewish institutions including synagogues, youth clubs and schools in Massachusetts. Its stated purpose was to build a database of 'corporations, institutions, and other entities that are sustaining the colonisation of Palestine, US imperialism, policing, displacement, and other interlocking systems of oppression.'[28] Pro-Israel activist Jacob Baime writes: 'Make no mistake: what the Mapping Project has built is a plan for a pogrom. This is a code red — the incitement to harm and the intelligence are both being widely disseminated.'[29]

In a 2016 Australian report on burgeoning online antisemitism, Oboler describes how online bigotry can escalate to incitement to violence against Jews and Israelis and how dangerous this phenomenon has become:

> Promoting violence against Jews is the most direct form of antisemitic hate expressed online. This also applies when the violence is expressed as being against 'Israelis' or 'Zionists', as both terms are used to refer entirely or predominantly to Jews in this context of this violence. The ubiquity of such content on the Internet has played a role in the increase in violent attacks against Jews and Jewish establishments around the world, and particularly in Europe, in the last few years. Violent speech encourages violent actions, and when people read, see and hear calls for violence against Jews, it normalises the concept.[30]

Social media companies vary in their response to online incitement and are anxious to preserve the right of their subscribers to the free expression of opinions. All insist that they do not tolerate incitement to hatred or violence and that they accept their responsibility to ensure that inflammatory and racist content is removed. To date they have appeared unwilling or unable to do so unless threatened with draconian legal sanctions. More effective regulation is obviously needed to erase online antisemitism (and bigoted content generally) as the current methods have proved inadequate.

The Role of the UN in Promoting Global Anti-Israelism and Antisemitism

For decades an anti-Israel animus has permeate all branches of the UN, including the General Assembly, the Human Rights Council, UNESCO and the World Health Organization. Two standing committees – the Committee on the Exercise of the Inalienable Rights of the Palestinian People (CEIRPP), and the Division for Palestinian Rights (DPR) – were established with the ostensible purpose of supporting the Palestinians but have instead devoted their energies and resources to attacking Israel. A third – the Special Committee to Investigate Israeli Practices Affecting the Human Rights of the Palestinian People and Other Arabs of the Occupied Territories (SCIIHRP) – was formed in 1968 with an exclusive focus on alleged Israeli misdeeds: its mandate is renewed every year with barely a murmur of dissent. These propagandistic groups receive a regular funding stream of millions of dollars each year. No comparable bodies have been created for any other state.[31]

The UN's position as an impartial organisation is so self-evidently compromised in the operation of its Human Rights Council that successive Secretaries General – and several countries (including the US) – have denounced the body for its bias against the Jewish state (without taking any remedial measures apart from changing its name from the Human Rights Commission in 2006). The UNHRC's special permanent agenda item seven on Israel is the only one to critique a single country. In 2021, the Council set up an unprecedented open-ended Commission of Inquiry – with no defined time scale or budget – to probe alleged Israeli abuses of Palestinians, including within Israel itself. Its findings will undoubtedly portray Israel as a criminally repressive state as its members – including its leader, Francesca Albanese, an Italian lawyer[32] – are known to have expressed anti-Israel and, at times, antisemitic positions, making a mockery of its claim to objectivity and fairness. As the General Assembly voted for its establishment, most Western democracies abstained, in keeping with their consistent and hypocritical determination to avoid offending the initiative's Arab sponsors. (To its credit, the US voted against).

UN's Discriminatory Treatment of Refugees

The UN's discriminatory treatment of Jews and the Jewish state has continued uninterrupted since 1948. Nowhere is the double standard with which the UN treats Israel more startling than in that body's contrasting treatment of the Jewish and Palestinian refugee problems.

Ignoring the Jewish *Nakba* while devoting attention and resources to the Arab exodus demonstrates a disturbing degree of institutional bias; treating the Palestinian refugees differently *to all other refugees in the world* reveals a level of discriminatory behaviour that reduces the organisation to Swiftian parody. This discrimination operates as follows:

1. The UN has long had a refugee agency – the High Commissioner for Refugees (UNHCR) – that serves all refugees except Palestinians. The United Nations Relief and Works Agency (UNRWA) was established to serve *only* Palestinian refugees.
2. The UNHCR defines a refugee as someone who leaves out of a 'well-founded fear of being persecuted,' is outside the country of [his] nationality, and is unable or unwilling to avail himself of the protection of that country.' This accords with the 1951 Refugee

Convention By contrast, UNRWA has adopted a unique definition for a Palestinian refugee as someone 'who has lost both his home and means of livelihood as a result of the 1948 Arab-Israeli conflict' (i.e. even without a well-founded fear of persecution) and regardless of the country where he currently lives. This latter point means that *Palestinian refugees living in Palestine are still refugees*, and refugees living in Jordan (a country that absorbs them via the granting of citizenship) are still refugees.

3. The UNHCR regards a refugee as the national of his country of origin, while UNRWA defines a refugee as anyone 'whose normal place of residence was Palestine between June 1946 and May 1948' regardless of their reason for leaving.

4. The UNHCR does not extend refugee status to descendants of the original refugee, while UNRWA regards refugee status as an inherited characteristic thereby ensuring that the refugee population persists and expands in perpetuity.

5. The UNHCR is charged with the mission of finding permanent homes for refugees, while UNRWA is required only to maintain and support the refugees within refugee camps – again, if necessary, in perpetuity.

6. The UNHCR does not promote the non-existent 'right of return,' while UNRWA asserts this fictional legal right at every opportunity.

7. The support and resources provided to Palestinian refugees (disproportionately provided by the US compared to other donor countries) dwarf those devoted to other refugees such as those from Syria and Ukraine. But at least these non-Palestinian refugees received some resources, and host countries are encouraged to absorb them, provide employment and education. The UN budget for Jewish refugees is zero.

8. As a result of the skewed resource allocation, the UNHCR's staff are overstretched: 17,000 care for almost twenty million refugees in 130 countries. By contrast, UNRWA has almost double the number of employees – 30,000 staff – for a far smaller workload of around five and a half million Palestinians in Jordan, Lebanon, Syria, the Gaza Strip and the West Bank (though only about 20,000 are true refugees according to the UNHCR definition).

9. Of over 1,000 General Assembly resolutions dealing with the Arab-Israeli conflict, at least 170 refer to Palestinian refugees. The number referring to Jewish refugees is zero. When UN resolutions on the conflict (such as General Assembly resolution 194 of 1948)

have used the generic term 'refugees', Arab delegates have insisted that the prefix 'Palestinian' is implied thereby excluding Jewish refugees from its remit.

This extraordinary record is a damning indictment of the systematic bias that has pervaded the UN for decades. Quite apart from its institutional antisemitism, this scenario ensures that the Palestinian refugee problem is unlikely ever to be solved in the absence of a fundamental shift in international attitudes. The extent of this cynical political exploitation of refugees is without precedent in the annals of the international community. The media watchdog *Honest Reporting* blames UNRWA for perpetuating the crisis: 'Enabled by UNRWA, the Arab states have managed to keep Palestinians in a dismal and perpetual state of displacement, all for the sake of being used as a political cudgel to attack Israel. Rather than solve the refugee crisis, UNRWA perpetuates it, actively encouraging a so-called "right of return."'[33]

For years, UNRWA managed to conceal another dirty little secret – dozens of its staff, including teachers, have been active disseminators of antisemitism. The education curriculum has been riddled with the crudest antisemitism for many decades. A special UN expert committee in 1969 (cited by Schwartz and Wilf) discovered terms in UNRWA textbooks that denigrated Jews as 'liars', 'cheats', 'moneylenders', and 'idiots'.[34] The textbooks also made frequent use of language that issued implicit appeals to violence, such as 'the usurped homeland', 'the usurpers', and the need for the 'purification' (by removing the Jews from Palestine). Little wonder that some of the products of this racist schooling became willing recruits to terrorist organisations.

More than five decades later, and despite repeated complaints about UNRWA's institutional antisemitism, little has changed. In June 2022, *UN Watch* exposed antisemitism and incitement to terrorism propagated by ten UNRWA teachers and other employees.[35] This was in addition to more than 100 UNRWA staff previously exposed by the organisation. In a partial and inadequate acknowledgement of the report, UNRWA dismissed six teachers. This scandal, like all the others involving the agency, failed to deter international donors from pouring further resources into an organisation that has been repeatedly shown to be biased, antisemitic and a chronic barrier to peace. The revelations by the IDF in the course of the Hamas-Israel war of 2023-24 challenged the agency to account for its apparent role not only in fostering a deep-seated hatred of Jews and Israel, but also in permitting – whether by design or (less likely) inadvertently – the use of its facilities by Hamas in the preparation of attacks on Israeli civilians. Israel has even provided evidence that at least 14 UNRWA staff actively participated in the Hamas massacre of 7 October 2023.[36]

How the World Promotes Palestinian Antisemitism

UN speeches, resolutions and reports that unfairly demonise Israel are sometimes dismissed as mere hot air – unpleasant but insignificant in the wider scheme of things. That view is blinkered. The damage inflicted by that body on Israelis and Arabs reaches far beyond the back rows of the debating chambers of the General Assembly and Human Rights Council. Perhaps the most shameful distortion of the UN's founding principles is the manner in which it has systematically poisoned young minds.

In-depth empirical research has revealed that the UNRWA-sponsored antisemitic indoctrination of children – and by extension their parents – has been institutionalised since the Oslo Accords of 1993-95 through the use of official Palestinian Authority textbooks. An Israeli research and policy organisation, the Institute for Monitoring Peace and Cultural Tolerance in School Education (IMPACT-se), analyses education around the world. They have been monitoring school textbooks in UNWRA-funded schools for two decades assessing compliance with UN values such as tolerance, non-violence and peace-making. Their extensive research of PA school textbooks has consistently shown 'a systematic insertion of violence, martyrdom and jihad across all grades and subjects, with the proliferation of extreme nationalism and Islamist ideologies throughout the curriculum, including science and math textbooks; rejection of the possibility of peace with Israel; and complete omission of any historical Jewish presence in the modern-day territories of Israel and the PA.'[37] UNRWA's response to these revelations has been evasive and inadequate, as has that of its international funders, principally the US and European Union. Those two donors are effectively complicit in the UN's long record of endorsing and financing the PA's programme of antisemitic education.

Israeli journalist Ben-Dror Yemini has excoriated the European Union in particular for its negligence regarding its funding of the PA: 'It all boils down to education. And who is funding it? Mostly the European Union, and Germany, with nearly thirty million dollars in 2021. The funding was halted for a short period due to the incitement and antisemitism in Palestinian textbooks uncovered by IMPACT-se, but that did not deter the Palestinians. The Europeans ultimately capitulated and reinstated funding for antisemitic education'[38] – thereby ensuring that the poisoning of young minds continued unabated thus inflicting immeasurable further damage on future peace prospects.[39]

In 2019, *UN Watch* reported on their investigation of Palestinian and Hamas compliance with the International Convention on the Elimination of All Forms of Racial Discrimination (ICERD) to which the 'State of Palestine' purported to accede in 2014. Their findings, submitted as part of the first UN review of Palestinian adherence to the Convention, revealed widespread routine violations of many ICERD articles including extreme antisemitic incitement to violence disseminated by Palestinian officials and media and in the Palestinian education system:

> This antisemitism is rooted in the foundational documents of the PA and Hamas which classify Zionists and Jews as the enemy and call for the elimination of the State of Israel; and has made its way into Palestinian laws criminalizing the sale of land to Israeli Jews and financially rewarding terrorists for the murder of Israeli Jews. In addition, the rights of Jews to worship at religious sites in Palestinian-controlled areas are routinely violated by desecration of the sites and attacks on convoys of Jewish worshippers.[40]

Unusually, this report prompted a questioning of PA behaviour by the UN's anti-racism committee. That was, however, atypical and short-lived. Throughout the UN's history, the body that is supposed to hold member states to account for their human rights records, including on antisemitism, has pilloried Israel while turning a blind eye to much worse violations by other countries. By contrast, UN officials who deviate from the predetermined anti-Israeli line are promptly relieved of their positions.[41]

Space does not permit a cataloguing of the prejudicial behaviour of all the UN branches that have been exploited as springboards for singling out and attacking Israel, usually on entirely spurious grounds. Insiders, including several Secretaries General, are well aware of this institutional sickness yet it is ignored by mainstream media, governments and most human rights NGOs. The result is that all of these bodies continue to spread their venomous hatred – the precise opposite of their stated official remits – with impunity.

Imagine how the world would react if another small country were denounced by her neighbours as a cancerous tumour deserving nothing but public obloquy and physical extirpation, along with the massacre of most of her citizens. If Denmark, for example, were denounced in such terms over her rule of Greenland and her citizens murdered on the streets of Copenhagen by Greenland 'resistance fighters' year after year and decade after decade, there would be widespread outrage and indignation in the full glare of global media publicity. Yet Israel's experience of continuous annihilationist violence elicits little more than bored indifference. At best, diplomatic observers demand a 'balanced' approach in which all sides, including the attackers, are granted equal legitimacy. As if that failure was not serious enough, reality is often inverted to portray Israel as the author of her own misfortune. This is victim-blaming on a grand scale.

How the International Human Rights Community Promotes Blood Libels

In 2022, a brief clash between the Gaza-based faction of Palestinian Islamic Jihad and Israel caused, according to the UN, forty-eight Palestinian deaths of which twenty-two were civilians including seventeen children. Not mentioned, either by the UN or the several human rights NGOs who condemned Israel for these deaths, was the fact that twenty civilians were likely to have been killed by Palestinian rockets falling short within Gaza. The only conceivable reason for erasing this information is that the intention of these organisations was to blame Israel and exonerate the Palestinians. The Elder of Ziyon blogger writes:

> By blaming Israel exclusively for the deaths of the children, they are engaging in a blood libel, saying that Jews either purposefully target children or show a wanton disregard for their lives. In fact, every single child that was killed by Israeli airstrikes had been either a human shield or an unfortunate casualty during an attack on a legitimate military target, and there is no evidence of the slightest bit of Israeli negligence or violation of international law. Which means that these are not human rights organizations. They are anti-Israel organizations who use human rights as a weapon against the Jewish state.[42]

This is symptomatic of selective and distorted commentary on Israel whereby human rights NGOs deliberately and systematically disseminate blood libels while shielding themselves from criticism. They achieve this via what Israeli academic Gerald Steinberg of *NGO Monitor* calls their 'halo effect' whereby their avowed support for morally pristine causes – such as child welfare, social equality and conflict resolution – is taken at face value, wins reflex public and political approbation and, crucially, substantial grant funding.[43] Powerful NGOs such as *Human Rights Watch* and *Amnesty International* regularly condemn Israel for committing heinous crimes including disproportionate violence, a callous indifference to civilian casualties, war crimes, crimes against humanity, and apartheid. These serious accusations are easily refuted as they are not evidence-based yet the NGOs who make them are rarely challenged by donors.

What is unique about these 'criticisms' – apart from their mendacious nature – is their obsessive focus on Israel at the expense of demonstrably far more egregious violations elsewhere (such as China, Syria, Iran, Russia, Myanmar and Afghanistan). Through constant repetition on social media, along with a ready means of dissemination via diplomats, academics, activists, and journalists, they acquire cumulative but undeserved credibility – and wealth. These self-appointed moral guardians operate in an opaque environment in which they are subject neither to systematic peer review nor to serious financial accountability.[44] The net result is to endow these NGOs with enormous influence and a platform from which they are free to promote falsehoods that are circulated widely and acquire the status of truth. That inevitably leads to calls by activists to isolate Israel through a package of punitive measures known as BDS – Boycott, Divestment and Sanctions – a notion that gained popularity following a notorious event held in South Africa in 2001, though an antisemitic boycott had been pioneered in the Middle East first by the Grand Mufti in 1933 and then by the Arab League in 1945.[45]

The Durban Conference launches BDS

The UN-sponsored World Conference against Racism, Racial Discrimination, Xenophobia and Related Intolerance took place in September 2001 in Durban, South Africa. The choice of that city was probably deliberate as it provided what was seen as an appropriate venue for branding Israel as 'an apartheid regime' through international isolation based on the South African model. The conference comprised three parallel gatherings – an official diplomatic forum, a youth summit and a massive NGO Forum, with delegates from 1250 organisations invited by the UN Human Rights Commission.

According to *NGO Monitor*, the atmosphere and rhetoric in all three frameworks featured a high level of vitriolic antisemitism, and marked the return of the 'Zionism is racism' libel a decade after the infamous 1975 UN resolution had finally been repealed. The NGO Forum was the highest profile event of the conference. Participants included NGO superpowers such as *Amnesty International* and *Human Rights Watch* as well as several pro-Palestinian groups. Jewish and Israeli groups were informed that their presence was unwelcome. In an agreed final text, the participants signed up to a policy of complete and total isolation of Israel as an apartheid state. This was the blueprint of the strategy for the ensuing NGO-led political war against Israel using the rhetoric of human rights and international law ('lawfare'), and conducted via the UN, the media, churches, trade unions and university campuses. Around this time, British activists launched an academic boycott of Israel. The global BDS campaign had been born.

Initially, the NGO network focused on the (non-existent) 'Jenin massacre' of 2002 and the 'Apartheid Wall' (Israel's security fence built to keep out suicide bombers) but soon moved on to a campaign designed to demonise, delegitimise and isolate Israel. In the Second Lebanon War of 2006, in which Israel tried to defend herself against barrages of Hezbollah rockets from southern Lebanon, NGOs accused the IDF of indiscriminate force amounting to 'war crimes.' A similar pattern of partisan and unverified accusations emanated from the NGO network over subsequent years. This trend was reinforced by the UN Human Rights Council's flawed 'fact-finding investigation' (that former UN Human Rights Commissioner Mary Robinson declined to chair due to its unbalanced mandate) in the wake of the Israel-Hamas conflict of 2008 (*Operation Cast Lead*). The ensuing report accused both Hamas and Israel of deliberately targeting civilians. Its author, South African Judge Richard Goldstone, appeared to retract his unfounded allegation against Israel in a *Washington Post* interview a year or so later[46] but the damage had been done. The manner in which radical anti-Israel NGOs, the UN and Palestinian propagandists, following the Durban formula, cooperated in promoting this contemporary blood libel is documented in detail in a joint report by *NGO Monitor* and the *Jerusalem Center for Public Affairs*.[47]

NGO Monitor describes BDS as 'the tactics of political warfare used against Israel, based on the exploitation of human rights, double standards, comparisons to apartheid South Africa, and false accusations of war crimes. It is not an established organization or movement but is comprised of dozens of NGOs and radical activists.'[48] There is nothing in principle objectionable about calling for BDS against a country with the purpose of pressurising its government to change its policy. This was the tactic adopted with considerable success by campaigners against the South African apartheid regime, and sanctions have been applied to several other countries including Iran, Russia and North Korea for that purpose. But the BDS movement focuses exclusively on Israel and has a far more ambitious agenda than in any of these instances. It seeks to end the 'occupation and colonisation of all Arab lands' and to implement a 'right of Palestinian refugees to return to their homes and properties.' In other words, its ultimate goal is politicide – as has been openly admitted by one of its spokesmen, Omar Barghouti: 'A Jewish state in Palestine in any shape or form cannot but contravene the basic rights of the indigenous Palestinian population and perpetuate a system of racial discrimination that ought to be opposed categorically.'[49]

At a meeting marking twenty years since the Durban Conference, several speakers reflected on the shameful nature of that event – a grotesque UN-endorsed inversion of language, human rights and morality to demonise Israel and the Jewish people. Irwin Cotler, a distinguished lawyer and former Canadian Minister of Justice, who attended the conference and later served as Canada's Special Envoy on Preserving Holocaust Remembrance and Combatting Antisemitism, initially welcomed the UN's anti-racism initiative[50] until he discovered its true nature:

> What happened at Durban was truly Orwellian. That which was to be a world conference against racism, turned into a conference of racism against Israel and the Jewish people. That which was to be the first international human rights conference of the 21st century...turned into a conference which indicted Israel as the meta-human rights violator. A conference that was to commemorate the dismantling of South Africa as an apartheid state turned into a conference calling for the dismantling of Israel as an apartheid state. Durban became a festival of hate.[51]

The economic impact of the BDS movement has been minimal but that is of little concern to its proponents, their primary purpose being to inflict reputational damage on Israel that will pave the way to its demise. The term BDS is a misnomer that deliberately obfuscates its true nature – an anti-Israel grouping that seeks to destroy a sovereign state of the UN. Austria, Germany, UK, Canada and others have branded the BDS movement as antisemitic.

Antisemitic Anti-Israelism in Academia

Although there is a weak inverse correlation between the level of a society's education and its prevalence of contemporary antisemitism, universities and other scholarly institutions are far from immune from the antisemitic virus.

Following the 2001 Durban conference, an academic boycott of Israel (and only Israel) was promoted by a small circle of UK academics. After a faltering start, it slowly acquired momentum, sometimes under the radar. In campuses across Europe and North America, Israeli academics were dismissed from editorial boards or had their research papers quietly binned without proper peer review. Within a few years, Israeli and 'Zionist' speakers became 'no platformed' by student unions or subjected to abuse and disorder on such a scale that their safety could not be guaranteed. Israeli scholars were blacklisted or subjected to a loyalty test by requiring them to denounce their government's 'apartheid policies' and Zionism itself. No other countries' speakers were required to undergo this humiliating moral purity ritual as a precondition of their participation.

In Lipstadt's view, none of this discriminatory behaviour is progressive or liberal but rather the opposite: 'In America in the 1940s and 1950s, men and women who were fired or blacklisted from jobs in academia and entertainment because they had in the past been members of the Communist Party were victims of the same type of discrimination. How ironic it is that leftist BDS supporters have adopted the tactics of right-wing McCarthyites.'[52]

British antisemitism expert David Hirsh has also sounded the alarm. He has documented the unmistakeable seepage of antisemitic beliefs from fringe groups into the mainstream, driven to a great extent by a cadre of academics in the UK, Europe and the USA who are determined to demonise Israel.[53] They have met little resistance. 'Antisemitic thinking is routine in parts of the social and human sciences. Thousands of academics have signed statements affirming that Israel is uniquely apartheid, illegitimate, racist, should be boycotted and that these axioms are foundational to their scholarship and to their morality. It follows, then, that if you cannot sign up to them you are neither a scholar nor moral.'[54]

In the United States, a network of government-funded Middle Eastern Studies Centres (MESC) was established in the 1950s as part of an effort to improve American security during the Cold War. Since the 1960s, the MESC, with the help of large donations from wealthy Arab states (notably Saudi Arabia and Qatar), has been transformed into a vehicle for anti-Western and anti-Israeli activism. A report from the National Association of Scholars has described the way that academics, ideologically inspired by Edward Said's 1978 book *Orientalism*, 'have repurposed critical theory to galvanize activism on Middle East issues. For instance, they have recast the Israel–Palestine debate as a fight for "indigenous rights" against the supposed evils of colonialism.'[55] The result is that a generation of Middle

Eastern scholars have been recruited to the propagandistic libel that Israel is the racist product of European and Western colonialism.

Cary Nelson has documented extreme and irrational views about Israel among American academics (some of whom are Jewish) that appear to be predicated on a psychopathological perception of Israel. Judith Butler, a philosophy professor at the University of California, is a woman with a politicidal vision for Israel. Her ardent desire is for Jews to relinquish their hard-won state and return to a position of an 'ineradicable alterity' – pretentious language for the restoration in perpetuity of the homeless wandering Jew (a concept of medieval origin implying punishment for the alleged Jewish crime of killing Christ) or the 'rootless cosmopolitan' of Soviet propagandists' imagination. To this end, Butler urges progressives to align themselves with Islamo-fascism: 'Understanding Hamas and Hezbollah as social movements that are progressive, that are on the left, that are part of a global left, is extremely important.'[56]

Butler's preposterous opinions are moderate compared to those of Jasbir Puar, a professor of women's and gender studies at Rutgers University, New Jersey, who takes anti-Israel rhetoric to a higher level. As well as accusing Israel of 'apartheid' and 'pinkwashing' (the trumpeting of gay rights as a means of distracting attention from the state's criminality), she writes: 'Through debilitating practices of maiming and stunting, Palestinians are further literalised and lateralised as surface, as bodies without souls, as sheer biology, thus rendered nonhuman.' The IDF's efforts to minimise civilian fatalities show, she opines, that Israelis regard the Palestinians as 'not even human enough for death.'[57] Other academics have explained the rarity of rape attributed to Israel soldiers as evidence that Israelis consider Arabs inferior, and that the establishment of Israel was a crime not just against the Palestinians but against the whole of humanity.

Much of the modern academic discourse about Israel is infected with similar delusions. Conspiracy theories abound – that Zionists dictate US foreign policy, control the media, manipulate global finance, and plot to dominate first the Middle East and then the world. The IDF, it is alleged, is not a conventional army but an instrument of mass murder and terrorism; Israeli troops shoot Palestinian children for fun or for target practice, or to harvest internal organs, or because Jews are conditioned – according to award-winning British playwright Caryl Churchill[58] – to regard non-Jews as unworthy of empathy. In this foul narrative, widely internalised by swathes of the intellectual elite across the globe, Zionism is by its nature irredeemably evil, and has always sought the ethnic cleansing and ultimately genocide of the Palestinians. This is not normal criticism of the kind that is directed at other countries.

Academic researchers holding high-profile positions at prestigious universities should have nothing to do with such nonsense other than to refute it. They are regarded by the educated general public as repositories of knowledge and integrity. They are also seen as impartial purveyors of truth, or at least striving to arrive at the truth. In the case of Israel and Middle Eastern studies, this is far from the case. Why do they do this and how do they get away with it? Israeli journalist Ben-Dror Yemini provides some answers:

> The Israel depicted by these scholars bears virtually no relation to the actual Israel or its history, intentions, or influence. These scholars rely, whenever they can, on fabricated or discredited sources, on true facts taken grotesquely out of context, and on narratives that serve neither truth nor peace. They have built a web of pseudo-scholarship, a paper trail that allows each writer to cite the works of others in the circle, sharing a unified purpose that is political rather than scholarly: to discredit a country and to rally troops to that end. [59]

How do such 'scholars' internalise patent mendacity? The answer is that ideology obliterates reality – the cause is too important for them to allow themselves the luxury of being deflected by the facts. A tidal wave of antisemitic post-modernism has swept across Western academia and civil society in recent decades. This form of herd mentality asserts that history merely reflects competing narratives that are validated by subjectively defined 'lived experience' and that ideology trumps all. In the words of revisionist historian Ilan Pappé, 'Who knows what the facts are?' [60]

The World Again Ignores Genocidal Threats Against Jews

Joining the dots between the antisemitism of the past and present is rarely done. Even rarer is an acknowledgement by Western observers that antisemitism has played any part at all in the dynamics of Arab/Iranian-Israeli conflict. That failure is itself a form of antisemitism for it legitimises a poisonous world-view that belittles the impact of racism on the Jewish people. At the very least, it represents a shocking moral failure on the part of the international community and, at worst, a tacit acceptance of modern eliminationist antisemitism while virtue-signalling abhorrence of the Holocaust.

Could it be, as American-Jewish writer Dara Horn implies, that the public memorialising of dead Jews provides moral cover for endangering their living descendants?[61]. How else can we explain the sight in January 2020 of world leaders solemnly intoning *Never Again* at Jerusalem's Holocaust memorial, Yad Vashem, then immediately beating a path to embrace the Holocaust-minimiser Mahmoud Abbas who rewards terrorists financially in proportion to the number of Jews they kill? Or European powers, led by Germany, of all countries, straining every sinew to rescue the JCPOA nuclear deal with Iran's Islamo-fascist dictatorship that has not ceased for a single day to reiterate its intention to wipe Israel – 'the little Satan' – off the face of the earth?

Islamist Iran presents Israel with the greatest existential threat in her history. Even before the Trump administration's withdrawal in 2018 from the Obama-sponsored nuclear deal, Iran had unveiled its Hourglass Festival to count down the clock to the day of Israel's destruction. This obscene goal, a clear violation of the Genocide Convention (1948),[62] is barely noticed by the international community let alone confronted. On the contrary, Western democracies that never tire of reminding us of their unimpeachable Holocaust horror are not averse to rewarding Iran with a path to a nuclear bomb along with several billion dollars thrown in to emphasise their good will towards the genocidal dictatorship.

The mullahs' target is not merely 'the Zionist entity' but Jews worldwide. The well-documented call for the murder of all Jews in the founding charter of Hamas, the Iranian-backed terrorist group that has ruled Gaza by force since 2007, is hardly an isolated example.[63] Hassan Nasrallah, the leader of Hezbollah, Iran's proxy militia in Lebanon, came perilously close to offering ironic support for the Zionist ingathering of the exiles when he explained in 2002 how convenient it was that the Jews were gathering in one place where the final and decisive battle will take place.[64]

A touch of political bias here and there is barely significant but the stubborn refusal to react to the threat of a second modern genocide of a people barely recovered from the first is inexcusable. Shining a light on this murky corner of reality is the single most important thing that anyone genuinely seeking peace between Israel and her neighbours can do.

Any country facing the degree of existential danger faced by Israel would do the following: establish military deterrence through the readiness of its armed forces; ensure that hostile intentions on all fronts are continuously monitored and, if showing signs of becoming active, quickly subdued; and determine that any withdrawal from captured enemy territory does not jeopardise the security of its citizens. Despite the risks, however, Israel has always demonstrated a willingness to make major concessions for peace.

Much of the world behaves as if Israeli intransigence is responsible for the failure of peace-making and that the dark shadow of annihilationist antisemitism no longer exists. Ignorance hardly explains this perversity as the evidence is accessible to anyone with a laptop or mobile phone. More likely, it is an inconvenient truth that undermines the now near-universal narrative of permanent Israeli culpability for heart-rending Palestinian victimhood.

Notes

1   Ishaan Tharoor, 'Former Asian leader won't stop claiming Jews "rule the world"', *Washington Post*, 27 June, 2016. https://www.washingtonpost.com/news/worldviews/wp/2016/06/27/former-asian-leader-wont-stop-claiming-jews-rule-the-world/ (Last accessed 12 June 2024).

2   D. Lipstadt, *Antisemitism Here and Now* (London: Scribe Publications, 2019), p.62.

3   D. Kahneman, *Thinking, Fast and Slow* (New York: Farrar, Straus and Giroux, 2013).

4   E. Garrard, 'The Pleasures of Antisemitism', *Fathom*, Summer 2013. https://fathomjournal.org/the-pleasures-of-antisemitism/ (Last accessed 12 June 2024).

5   N. Neudecker, F-R. Esch, S. Valussi, 'Message Reframing in Advertising', *Psychology & Marketing*, 31, 11 (November 2014), pp.946-957.

6   Community Security Trust Blog, 'Robert Fisk and Immoral Equivalences', 18 December 2014. https://cst.org.uk/news/blog/2014/12/18/robert-fisk-and-immoral-equivalences (Last accessed 12 June 2024).

7   Freedom House, Global Freedom. https://freedomhouse.org/explore-the-map?type=fiw&year=2022 (Last accessed 12 June 2024).

8   J. Mearsheimer, S. Walt, *The Israel Lobby and US Foreign Policy* (New York: Farrar, Straus and Giroux, 2007).

9   Lauren Gambino, 'Ilhan Omar Apologizes after Being Accused of Using 'Antisemitic Tropes', *Guardian*, 11 February 2019. https://www.theguardian.com/us-news/2019/feb/11/ilhan-omar-antisemitic-tweets-house-democrats-apology (Last accessed 12 June 2024).

10 I. Tabarovsky, 'Soviet Anti-Zionism and Contemporary Left Antisemitism', *Fathom*, May 2019. https://fathomjournal.org/soviet-anti-zionism-and-contemporary-left-antisemitism/ (Last accessed 12 June 2024).

11 J. Herf, 'Nazi Antisemitism and Islamist Hate', *Tablet*, 6 July 2022. https://www.tabletmag.com/sections/history/articles/the-nazi-roots-of-islamist-hate?utm_source=substack&utm_medium=email (Last accessed 12 June 2024).

12 D. Horn, *People Love Dead Jews* (New York: WW Norton & C0, 2021).
13 Harold Evans, 'The Voice of Hate', *Index on Censorship*, 6 December 2002, pp10-11.   https://journals.sagepub.com/doi/pdf/10.1080/0306422020 8537129 (Last accessed 12 June 2024.
14 Ciar Byrne, 'BBC Confirms Al-Jazeera Link-up', *Guardian*, 16 January 2003.https://www.theguardian.com/media/2003/jan/16/broadcasting.bbc (Last accessed 12 June 2024).
15 Alex Green, 'Tory Peer Urges BBC to Publish Balen Report into Israeli-Palestinian Coverage', *Evening Standard*, 25 May 2021. https://www.standard.co.uk/news/uk/bbc-dyson-israeli-ofcom-hayward-b937157.html (Last accessed 12 June 2024).
16 Jonathan Sacerdoti, 'At last! BBC apologises for its "disdainful" treatment of Jewish concerns', *Jewish Chronicle*, 3 November 2022. https://www.thejc.com/news/news/at-last-bbc-apologises-for-its-'disdainful'-treatment-of-jewish-concerns-3Uo797FGdE4NfGyjMbGzqM?reloadTime=1667481903 290 (Last accessed 12 June 2024).
17 Simon Wiesenthal Center, Global Antisemitism 2021 Top Ten. https://www.wiesenthal.com/assets/pdf/global_anti-semitism_2021_top_ ten.pdf (Last accessed 12 June 2024).
18 Rachel O'Donoghue, 'Will BBC Take Action Against Journalists Who Posted Antisemitic, Anti-Israel Tweets?' *Honest Reporting*, 28 August 2022. https://honestreporting.com/will-bbc-take-action-against-journalists-who-posted-antisemitic-anti-israel-tweets/ (Last accessed 12 June 2024).
19 Committee for Accuracy in Middle East Reporting and Analysis (CAMERA). https://www.camera.org (Last accessed 12 June 2024).
20 The JC Leader, 'BBC's Defence of Atwan Makes its Hypocrisy Clear', *Jewish Chronicle* 2 September 2022. https://www.thejc.com/lets-talk/all/bbcs-defence-of-atwan-makes-its-hypocrisy-clear-7H8ogX8Xv4s9mAsZVEhxn R (Last accessed 12 June 2024).
21 Campaign Against Antisemitism, *Antisemitism Barometer* 2021. https://antisemitism.org/wp-content/uploads/2022/03/Antisemitism-Barometer-2021-2.pdf (Last accessed 12 June 2024).
22 Akiva Van Koningsveld, 'The Fix is In: How Hitler-praising Palestinians are Warping Gaza Conflict Coverage', *Honest Reporting*, 11 August 2022. https://honestreporting.com/the-fix-is-in-how-hitler-quoting-palestinians-are-warping-gaza-conflict-coverage/ (Last accessed 12 June 2024).
23 A Schwartz, E Wilf, *The War of Return: How Western Indulgence of the Palestinian Dream has Obstructed the Path to Peace* (New York: All Points Books, 2020), p. 157.
24 See Lewis, *Semites and Anti-Semites*, p.251.

25   M. Friedman, 'An Insider's Guide to the Most Important Story on Earth', *Tablet*, 26 August 2014. https://www.tabletmag.com/sections/israel-middle-east/articles/israel-insider-guide] (Last accessed 12 June 2024).

26   Lee Kern Substack, 'The Truth about Trolls', 4 September 2022, https://leekern.substack.com/p/the-truth-about-trolls?utm_medium=ios (Last accessed 12 June 2024).

27   D. Baddiel, *Jews Don't Count* (London: TLS Books, 2021), p.38.

28   Adam Horowitz, '"Our struggles are truly connected": an interview with the Mapping Project', *Mondoweiss*, 3 June 2022. https://mondoweiss.net/2022/06/our-struggles-are-truly-connected-an-interview-with-the-mapping-project/ (Last accessed 12 June 2024).

29   J. Baime, 'With Map of Jews in Boston, BDS Antisemitic Threat Now Clear and Present', *Jewish Journal*, 15 June 2022. https://jewishjournal.com/commentary/opinion/349365/with-map-of-jews-in-boston-bds-antisemitic-threat-now-clear-and-present/ (Last accessed 12 June 2024).

30   A. Oboler, *Measuring the Hate: The State of Antisemitism in Social Media* (La Trobe University: Online Hate Prevention Institute, January 2016), p.9. https://www.researchgate.net/publication/292140978_Measuring_the_Hate_The_State_of_Antisemitism_in_Social_Media (Last accessed 12 June 2024).

31   J. Muravchik, 'The UN and Israel: A History of Discrimination', *World Affairs*, November/December 2013, 176,4, pp. 35-46.

32   Luke Tress, 'UN Palestinian Rights Official's Social Media History Reveals Antisemitic Comments', *Times of Israel*, 14 December 2022. https://www.timesofisrael.com/un-palestinian-rights-officials-social-media-history-reveals-antisemitic-comments/?utm_source=Push (Last accessed 12 June 2024).

33   P. Benson, 'The UNRWA Refugee Controversy Explained', *Honest Reporting*, 17 June 2019. https://honestreporting.com/unrwa-refugees-explained/?gclid=Cj0KCQjw08aYBhDlARIsAA_gb0fn59iRxDxsfhYTYSP 4BoQTtKtVjXACJfgzAQo5hUnm_9oARdx1QLkaAuxxEALw_wcB (Last accessed 12 June 2024).

34   See Schwartz and Wilf, *The War of Return*, p.127.

35   UN Watch, 'Report: UNRWA's Teachers of Hate", 23 June2022. https://unwatch.org/exposed-un-teachers-call-to-murder-jews/ (Last accessed 12 June 2024).

36   Emanuel Fabian (and agencies), '"I captured one!"' – IDF recordings show more UNRWA staffers bragging of Oct. 7 crimes', *Times of Israel*, 4 March 2024. https://www.timesofisrael.com/i-captured-one-idf-recordings-show-more-unrwa-staffers-bragging-of-oct-7-crimes/ (Last accessed 12 June 2024).

37   I. Shalev, 'Review of UNRWA-Produced Study Materials in the Palestinian Territories', IMPACT-Se,' (Ramat Gan: January 2021). https://www.impact-se.org/wp-content/uploads/UNRWA-Produced-Study-Materials-in-the-Palestinian-Territories—Jan-2021.pdf (Last accessed 12 June 2024).

38   Ben-Dror Yemini, 'How Europe bankrolls Palestinian antisemitism', *Ynet News*, 18 August 2022. https://www.ynetnews.com/article/sjw0ndicq (Last accessed 12 June 2024).

39   UN Watch/IMPACT-Se, 'UNRWA Education: Reform or Regression?' Geneva/Ramat Gan: March 2023. https://www.impact-se.org/wp-content/uploads/UNRWA_Report_2023_IMPACT-se_And_UN-Watch.pdf (Last accessed 12 June 2024).

40   H. Neuer, D. Rovner, 'Alternative Report of United Nations Watch to the 99th Session of the Committee on the Elimination of Racial Discrimination for its review of State of Palestine' (Geneva: United Nations Watch, 2019), p.1. https://unwatch.org/wp-content/uploads/2012/01/Alternative-Report-of-United-Nations-Watch-to-the-99th-Session-of-the-Committee-on-the-Elimination-of-Racial-Discrimination-for-its-review-of-State-of-Palestine.pdf (Last accessed 12 June 2024).

41   D. Litman, 'The UN's "Independent," "Impartial," and "Objective" Inquisitors Against Israel', CAMERA, 15 August 2022. https://www.camera.org/article/the-uns-independent-impartial-and-objective-inquisitors-against-israel/ (Last accessed 12 June 2024).

42   Elder of Zyon, 'Human rights groups bending over backwards to NOT blame Islamic Jihad for killing over a dozen children', 12 August 2022. https://elderofziyon.blogspot.com/2022/08/human-rights-groups-bending-over.html (Last accessed 12 June 2024).

43   Marilyn Stern, 'Gerald Steinberg Explains How NGOs Funnel Money to Gaza Terrorists', *Middle East Forum*, 8 August 2022. https://www.meforum.org/63540/gerald-steinberg-explains-how-ngos-funnel-money (Last accessed 12 June 2024).

44   NGO Monitor, 'Watching the Watchers: The Politics and Credibility of Non-Governmental Organizations in the Arab-Israeli Conflict,' (Jerusalem: NGO Monitor, 2008). https://www.ngo-monitor.org/data/images/File/watchingthewatchers-small.pdf. (Last accessed 12 June 2024).

45   The Israeli-American Council, 'Bigotry, Discrimination, Antisemitism: *10 Things You Need to Know About BDS*.' https://www.israeliamerican.org/national-headquarters/media/bigotry-discrimination-anti-semitism (Last accessed 12 June 2024).

46   Richard Goldstone, 'Reconsidering the Goldstone Report on Israel and war crimes', *Washington Post*, 1 April 2011. http://www.washingtonpost.com/opinions/reconsidering-the-goldstone-report-on-israel- and-war-crimes/2011/04/01/AFg111JC_story.html (Last accessed 12 June 2024).

47 G. Steinberg, A. Hertzberg (eds.), *The Goldstone report "Reconsidered" – A critical analysis* (Jerusalem: NGO Monitor/Jerusalem Center for Public Affairs, 2011). https://www.ngo-monitor.org/data/images/File/The_Goldstone_Report_Reconsidered.pdf (Last accessed 12 June 2024).

48 NGO Monitor, Key Issue: BDS (Boycotts, Divestment, and Sanctions). https://www.ngo-monitor.org/key-issues/bds/about/] (Last accessed 12 June 2024).

49 David Halbfinger, Michael Wines, Steven Erlanger, 'Is BDS. Anti-Semitic? A Closer Look at the Boycott Israel Campaign', *New York Times*, 27 July 2019. https://www.nytimes.com/2019/07/27/world/middleeast/bds-israel-boycott-antisemitic.html (Last accessed 12 June 2024).

50 I. Cotler, 'The IHRA Definition: Origins, Nature and Impact', UK Lawyers For Israel Trust Webinar 24 February 2022. https://www.youtube.com/watch?v=-iRL1WFwgJA ((Last accessed 12 June 2024).

51 NGO Monitor, 'NGO Monitor Event: 20 Years of Hijacking Human Rights - The Lasting Impact of Durban', 23 June 2021. https://www.ngo-monitor.org/live/ (Last accessed 12 June 2024).

52 See Lipstadt, *Antisemitism Here and Now*, p.176.

53 D. Hirsh, *The Rebirth of Antisemitism in the 21st Century* (Abingdon: Routledge/LCSCA 2024)

54 D. Hirsh, 'Opinion: How You Can Help Oppose Antisemitism in Academia', *Jewish News*, 31 August 2022. https://www.jewishnews.co.uk/opinion-how-you-can-help-oppose-antisemitism-in-academia/ (Last accessed 12 June 2024).

55 N. Arnold, 'Hijacked: The Capture of America's Middle East Studies Centers', National Association Scholars. https://www.nas.org/reports/hijacked/full-report (Last accessed 12 June 2024).

56 C. Nelson, *Israel Denial* (Bloomington: Indiana University Press, 2019). Pp.69-116.

57 Ibid. pp.202-257.

58 Howard Jacobson, 'Let's see the 'criticism' of Israel for what it really is', *Independent*, 18 February 2009. https://www.independent.co.uk/voices/commentators/howard-jacobson/howard-jacobson-let-rsquo-s-see-the-criticism-of-israel-for-what-it-really-is-1624827.html (Last accessed 12 June 2024).

59 B-D. Yemini, *Industry of Lies*, (New York: Institute for the Global Study of Antisemitism and Policy, 2017).

60 Baudouin Loos, 'An Interview of Ilan Pappe', *Le Soir*, 29 November 1999. https://archive.ph/a9aH (Last accessed 12 June 2024).

61 See Horn, People Love Dead Jews

62 UN Office on Genocide Prevention and the Responsibility to Protect, The Genocide Convention. https://www.un.org/en/genocideprevention/genocide-convention.shtml (Last accessed 12 June 2024).

63 Yale Law School, the Avalon Project. Hamas Covenant 1988. https://avalon.law.yale.edu/20th_century/hamas.asp (Last accessed 12 June 2024)
64 Anti-Defamation League (New York), 'Teaching Antisemitism and Terrorism in Hezbollah Schools', 19 May 2020. https://www.adl.org/antisemitism-and-terrorism-in-hezbollah-schools (Last accessed 12 June 2024)

8

Counterarguments – Part 1

What Chapters 8 and 9 Are About

The central hypothesis of this book is that antisemitism is the prime cause of the Arab-Israeli conflict. Subjecting that hypothesis to evidence-based scrutiny involves a process of considering possible alternative explanations or counter-hypotheses. That requires us to explore some of the murkier waters of antisemitic argumentation.

Before proceeding, a caveat: anyone who has attempted to engage in debate with a bigot will recognise the futility of that exercise. Worse, the attempt carries a risk that addressing antisemitic falsehoods grants them undeserved legitimacy. Regrettably, some wilder accusations are aired with such frequency that they are no longer regarded as prejudiced or implausible. Research surveys reveal, for example, that a significant minority (around 40 per cent) of European adults believe that Israel is committing genocide against the Palestinians.[1] If such an extreme delusional belief has taken hold of a substantial segment of a well-educated population, it is likely that equally false notions about Israel are even more prevalent among less well-informed people, not least in the Middle East. For this reason, it is vital that falsehoods are exposed, challenged and debunked. To do otherwise would be to acquiesce in a looking-glass world in which the truth is abandoned and lies are venerated as gospel truth. In such a world, antisemitism thrives.

Hypothesis and Counter-hypothesis

The hypothesis may be tested by considering the counter-hypothesis – in scientific jargon, the null hypothesis: that antisemitism, far from being a cause of the conflict, was and is an epiphenomenon, an accompaniment or a consequence of the conflict. If that alternative explanation is valid, it will reveal antisemitism to be (at best) a red herring, or (at worst) an invented fiction (in the eyes of anti-Zionists) to distract attention from the real cause of the conflict – namely the ideologies, policies and behaviours of Zionists and Israelis. Does the null hypothesis withstand scrutiny? To answer that question, I have deconstructed the null hypothesis into two subsidiary hypotheses each of which can be tested against the evidence.

The first is that antisemitism is an unfortunate but consistent feature of the Jewish experience everywhere but has been historically, and remains today, far less prevalent in the Arab-Muslim world than in Europe; it should therefore be discounted as a critical contextual or causal factor. The second is that the upsurge in anti-Jewish hostility in the Zionist-Israeli era was an inevitable reaction to Zionist-Israeli ideologies and actions rather than to any inherent Arab-Muslim bigotry.

The thrust of the first null hypothesis is that Arab-Muslim Judeophobia prior to the Zionist era was, if it occurred at all, an insignificant backdrop to the conflagration to come and that any antisemitism associated with the conflict was a consequence of the dispute rather than an underlying causal factor. Proponents of this contention claim that Jews and Arabs lived together in relative harmony before the establishment of Israel and certainly before the arrival of Zionists in the Middle East. Is this claim true?

Testing Null Hypothesis 1: Did Jews and Arabs Live Together Harmoniously Before Israel Was Established?

Bernard Lewis, a renowned authority on Islamic history, maintains that for most of the 1400 years of the Arab-Jewish encounter the Arabs were not as antisemitic as their European Christian counterparts.[2] Islam and Judaism rarely clashed theologically as they were both monotheistic religions that shared many similarities. Both obliged their followers to adhere to divinely-ordained legal systems that regulated all aspects of daily life, including dietary laws that overlapped to some degree, and neither was ruled by a pyramidal priesthood. In the seventh century, however, the Prophet Muhammad came into violent conflict with the Jews though he emerged victorious, and that superiority is reflected in Islamic scriptures and commentaries. Judaism was considered of minor importance to Muslim theologians. For most of Islam's history, Muslims regarded Christians as the greater enemy though Jews, along with all non-Muslims, were periodically subjected to repression.

So far, so good, from the perspective of supporters of the null hypothesis. Jews undoubtedly experienced prolonged periods of acceptance and prosperity under Islamic rule, and were far more integrated into Middle Eastern societies than they had been in pre-modern Europe. Muslim leaders generally granted Jews freedom of worship and substantial autonomy in communal matters. Many productive and long-lasting Muslim-Jewish collaborations and friendships were formed. But that is far from the whole story.

Lewis is adamant that even if they were rarely persecuted Jews were never free from discrimination (with the possible exception of the 'Golden Age' of Jewish-Muslim coexistence in medieval Muslim Spain). Like Christians, Jews were second-class citizens or *dhimmis*, and though that status theoretically assured them a degree of legal protection, it was dwarfed by the disadvantages.[3] Jews often had to wear special clothing (such as a yellow badge or distinguishing headgear), were not permitted to bear arms or ride a horse or camel, had to give Muslims right of way, were obliged to pay a special poll tax (*jizya*), were not permitted to give evidence in court in their own defence, and were forbidden from having intercourse with (or marrying) Muslim women. Like Christians, they were due a degree of respect (as 'People of the Book') but the general Muslim view of the Jews was stereotypically negative: they were inferior to Muslims in every respect and should always 'know their place.' Through an illogical (and presumably unconscious) cognitive contortion, this lowly status of Jews, though not of their making, was believed by the Muslim majority to reflect an intrinsically weak and cowardly Jewish nature.

Jewish memories of their maltreatment in Arab lands remain poignantly alive through literature. The great sage Maimonides, who is often cited as enjoying harmonious relations with Muslim rulers, wrote these words to the persecuted Yemenite Jews in the twelfth century: 'You know, my brethren, that on account of our sins our God has cast us in the midst of these people, the nation of Islam, who persecute us severely and devise ways to harm us and debase us. Never did a nation molest, degrade, debase and hate us as much as they...No nation has done more harm to Israel.'[4]

Disdain for the Jew was the default position of most Muslims for many centuries. It regularly spilled over into violence: thousands were killed in pogroms in Spain (in 1066) and Morocco (in 1466), synagogues were destroyed in Yemen and Baghdad, and at times whole communities were forcibly converted. In the eighteenth and nineteenth centuries, further waves of pogroms were perpetrated in North Africa.[5] The Ottoman authorities managed to maintain a degree of order without addressing the underlying disease of antisemitism and that paved the way for a more sinister development in the MENA region.

With the advent of European colonial domination in the nineteenth and twentieth centuries, imported antisemitic tropes such as the blood libel became increasingly prevalent in Islamic lands. European antisemitic texts, including the *Protocols of the Elders of Zion* and *The Talmud Jew*, were translated into Arabic and generated a large following. Over time, the prevailing Arab-Muslim attitude to the Jewish minority slowly changed from one of contempt to fear and ultimately intense hatred. That visceral antipathy was far from universal but it was sufficiently widespread to enable the pro-Nazi Arab nationalist leader Haj Amin al-Husseini and his like-minded colleagues to follow the European playbook and whip up riots aimed at Jews ('Zionists') in Jerusalem, Hebron and elsewhere in the early twentieth century.

After the British expelled him in 1939 from Mandatory Palestine to Iraq, Husseini helped organise the Baghdad *Farhud* – sometimes called the MENA's *Kristallnacht*, a pogrom that claimed 180 Jewish lives on 1-2 June 1941. The horrors of that episode are vividly described by an eye witness, Sabih Ezra Akerib cited by Julius:

> The killing of men and children and attacks on Jewish women were rampant. Four doors down – at the home of Sabiha, my mother's good friend – a Muslim emerged carrying what appeared to be a bloodied piece of meat. We learned afterwards that Sabiha had been killed and mutilated…At the same time, Jews were scampering over the roofs, running for their lives. If not for the looting taking place below, more would have been murdered. No authorities came to help; barbarism ruled. All the anger and jealousy that had been pent up over the centuries erupted in these horrific moments. Neighbours with whom we had shared a nod, a smile – and even attended their sons' circumcisions – had metamorphosed into sub-humans intent on annihilation.[6]

Husseini's association with Hitler cannot be dismissed as a tactical move designed either to rid Palestine of the British or to shore up legitimate Arab resistance to Zionism. The Grand Mufti was a genocidal antisemite to the core and was fortunate to escape conviction as a war criminal at Nuremberg. After the British relinquishment of the Mandate and Israel's declaration of statehood in 1948, Arab antisemitism intensified, undermining the myth that the Mufti's alliance with the Nazis was a pragmatic matter of 'my enemy's enemy is my friend.' Openly anti-Jewish rhetoric by most Arab leaders has continued over the decades of conflict ever since with minimal international protest. With a few notable exceptions, antisemitic anti-Israelism – and its consequent extreme violence – shows no signs of abating in the twenty-first century.

Successive surveys have shown that the population of the MENA region, though almost empty of Jews as a result of the forced Jewish exodus, consistently harbours the most antisemitic attitudes in the world, and that the Palestinians of the West Bank and Gaza Strip occupy the top of this league table of ignominy.[7] In such circumstances, it would be odd if antisemitism played no part in influencing the policies of MENA governments, including the Palestinian Authority, towards Israel and towards internationally-brokered peace-making initiatives. As the evidence set out throughout this book has shown, endemic antisemitism provides the only plausible accounting for the continuation of the hate-fuelled Arab-Israeli conflict despite innumerable and fair-minded attempts to end it. Null hypothesis 1 is not supported by evidence.

Testing Null Hypothesis 2: Are Israelis Responsible for Arab-Muslim Hostility to Jews And Israel?

The second null hypothesis, that Zionist or Israeli ideologies and actions rather than antisemitism, explain Arab-Muslim hostility to Jews and Israel, is widely held to be true. At first sight, this appears a form of victim-blaming that echoes traditional European antisemitism – that the Jews are responsible for their own misfortune. But because the Arab-Israeli conflict is political in nature, the notion of *justifiable hatred* – sometimes euphemistically downplayed as *legitimate criticism* – has to be taken seriously. If it is ignored, critics will exploit that refusal to engage as an admission of the validity of their case.

Is hatred of an entire group ever justifiable? In extreme cases, perhaps – what decent human being could do other than hate Nazis? Israel is, in the eyes of much of the public, just such an extreme case, a monstrous entity that deserves nothing but pariah status, a group of Jews whom (*pace* Isaiah Berlin) it is 'absolutely necessary' to hate. Consigning Israel to that fate is the motivation of anti-Israel activists who deliberately label Israelis Nazis or 'Zio-Nazis' in order to elicit revulsion. How have they succeeded in making that appalling label stick? The question may be reformulated: what specific aspects of Jewish/Zionist /Israeli behaviour might have provoked in Arabs such a justifiable anti-Jewish backlash? Israel's critics are not short of suggestions.

In support of the 'justifiable hatred' argument are fourteen frequent assertions or 'articles of faith' enumerated in Chapter 7. Because these are such popular elements of the polemical armoury deployed against Israel, they demand close critical scrutiny. I have divided them somewhat arbitrarily into two groups (though there is some overlap between them). The first seven are largely related to history while the second seven are more relevant to the current situation.

Anti-Israel 'Articles of Faith' Group 1:

- that Zionism is an inherently racist and colonialist ideology;
- that Arabs cannot be antisemitic as they themselves are semites;
- that the 1917 Balfour Declaration betrayed the Arabs;
- that Balfour and the international community never intended the establishment of a Jewish state;
- that Arab hostility to Jews was a natural response to the migration of European Zionists to Palestine;
- that Israel was created by ethnically cleansing the Palestinians;
- that Zionism was responsible for the so-called Jewish *Nakba*.

Anti-Israel 'Articles of Faith' Group 2:

- that Israel today is an apartheid state;
- that Israel violates international law through her occupation and settlement of Palestinian lands;
- that Israel uses disproportionate and murderous military force;
- that Israel is committing a genocide of the Palestinians comparable to the Nazi Holocaust;
- that Israel was created and only survives through US support;
- that Palestinian anger is caused by Israel's refusal to make peace on the basis of the two-state solution;
- that Arab threats against Jews are mere rhetoric.

This charge sheet relates to the two most recent historical phases of Arab-Muslim antipathy to Jews that were set out in Chapter 6, from the advent of modern Zionism through to the current Israeli era. The accusations are used, separately and collectively, to argue that intense anti-Zionist and anti-Israeli sentiment is not only justified but is a moral imperative, and that those promoting it cannot in any sense or to any degree be considered antisemitic. It is necessary to put those oft-cited arguments to the test.

This chapter covers the seven historically-oriented assertions, the next chapter the seven that have stronger contemporary relevance.

Is Zionism an Inherently Racist and Colonialist Ideology?

The accusation that Israel is an ethno-religious state, due to the inherently racist and colonialist nature of Zionism, was once mostly confined to the Arab and Muslim world. That changed in 1975 when the UN General Assembly passed its shameful resolution equating Zionism with racism. Through the bullying of the Arab League, the resolution was reiterated annually until 1991 when it failed to pass. Ten years later, the libel was resurrected at the UN sponsored Durban anti-racism conference that turned into an anti-Israel jamboree riddled with antisemitism. The charge is now recycled as the 'apartheid' smear by several NGOs, including *Human Rights Watch* and *Amnesty International.*

The idea that Arab antisemitism was a natural reaction to Jewish anti-Arabism bred by the 'racist ideology of Zionism' – putting aside the objectionable notion that one wrong justifies another – is easily disproved. Despite their experience of discrimination at the hands of Islamic rulers, Jews always respected Arab and Muslim culture. Zionist leaders across the political spectrum emphasised this position at every opportunity since the days of the British Mandate that brought them into conflict with violent anti-Zionist militias. Ze'ev Jabotinsky, leader of the more stridently nationalistic stream of Zionism, maintained that the struggle was not between right and wrong but between two rights, and that 'the political, economic and cultural welfare of the Arabs will always remain one of the main conditions for the well-being of the Land of Israel' – hardly the sentiments of an anti-Arab racist. He told the Peel Commission in 1937 'I have the profoundest feeling for the Arab case.'[8] On the Zionist left, the approach was even more conciliatory. David Ben-Gurion, Israel's first prime minister, spelled out his philosophy in 1947 in the midst of Arab violence prompted by the UN partition resolution: 'If the Arab citizen will feel at home in our state . . . if the state will help him in a truthful and dedicated way to reach the economic, social, and cultural level of the Jewish community, then Arab distrust will accordingly subside and a bridge will be built to a Semitic, Jewish-Arab alliance.'[9]

At least two false (and mutually contradictory) premises underpin the Zionism-is-racism smear – that Jews are undeserving of any form of national self-determination as they are adherents of a religion not a nation, and that even if there is a Jewish people or nationhood, it is an inherently racist construct. Either way, they are not entitled to self-determine their identity. Note the multiple ironies here: Jews are told by others who they are and are not, and how they may or may not self-identify - in the name of 'human rights.' Consider the converse scenario: some Jews and Israelis insist that the Palestinians are not a people deserving of statehood – they are rightly granted no veto on Palestinian self-identity.

Current political realities also contradict the Zionism-is-racism charge. Though Israel defines itself as a Jewish state, around a quarter of its citizens are non-Jews (mainly Arabs) who enjoy full and equal rights, while the putative Palestinian state (essentially Area A of the Oslo Accords' arrangement) permits no Jewish residents whatsoever and has made it clear that it will never have any Jewish citizens.[10] The Palestinian Authority has declared Islam as its sole state religion while Israel has five recognised state religions to ensure pluralism and equality of worship. Regarding immigration, Israel's opponents insist on a 'right of return' for Palestinians while denouncing as racist Israel's Law of Return which is similar to the practice of many other liberal democracies that grant preferential (though non-exclusive) rights of citizenship to those with a background or heritage connecting them to the state.

This tangled knot of inconsistency, double standards and hypocrisy arises from the fundamental falsity of the original accusation. Zionism is not and never has been a form of racism. On the contrary, it is an antiracist endeavour that was born out of the direct Jewish experience of racism and one that history shows was long overdue.

The 'colonialist' charge is equally ludicrous. Ample historical, archaeological and genetic evidence supports the view that Jews ('Judeans') were the original indigenous inhabitants of today's Israel, the Palestinian Authority and part of Jordan.[11] In the second millennium BCE, the Israelites arrived in that territory where they established sovereignty (see Chapter 3) and then had to contend with a succession of occupying colonial powers until the twentieth century. Seventeen imperial powers conquered Israel throughout the Jewish exile – that is a minimum figure as the Babylonians and Arabs each invaded at least twice and Napoleon's ill-fated campaign of 1799 could also be added. Some of these regimes employed cruel tactics including deportations, enslavement and massacres. Two examples will turn the strongest stomachs: Roman Emperor Hadrian's brutal suppression of the Bar Kochba revolt in the second century is believed to have cost around 600,000 Judean lives, either through violence or starvation, while the eleventh-century Crusaders murdered tens of thousands of European Jews en route to the Holy Land where they displayed a predilection for incarcerating Jews inside their synagogues and burning them alive.

This long history of dispossession, suffering and death reached a joyful (if precarious) ending. The rebirth of a sovereign Israel in the ancestral

Jewish homeland is testament to the capacity of the oppressed to overcome the oppressor. It also exposes as false the allegation that Zionism is an imperialist, colonialist venture, a tool of the Great Powers who invaded foreign territories to enhance their hegemony and wealth. Yet many otherwise sensible and moderate commentators, such as the UK *Open Democracy* political website, jump on the ahistorical bandwagon by announcing: 'The foundations of Israel are rooted in a colonial project that has modernized its face but continues to subject Palestinians to military occupation, land dispossession and unequal rights.'[12] Though this statement is pure fiction, millions apparently believe it.

The Zionist pioneers of the nineteenth century were not emissaries of colonial powers but refugees from persecution. The Palestinians, by contrast, are relative newcomers. Though a minority were indigenous, modern Palestinians are believed to have originated from three main groups: Muslim invaders, Arab immigrants and local converts to Islam. The Muslim conquest of Byzantine Palestine in the seventh century is a textbook example of settler-colonialism. This is not just an Israeli claim: Hamas minister Fathi Ḥammad, cited by Joffe, asserted that 'half the Palestinians are Egyptians and the other half are Saudis.'[13] That history of inward migration does not invalidate the contemporary Palestinian self-definition of peoplehood, nor have most Zionist or Israeli leaders sought to deny their right to self-determination in the context of peaceful co-existence with Israel.

A key question that the anti-Zionist accusers have never answered is posed by American lawyer Alan Dershowitz: 'If the Jewish refugees who immigrated to Palestine in the last decades of the nineteenth century were the tools of European imperialism, for whom were these socialists and idealists working?'[14] The Zionist pioneers had to overcome opposition from Turkish, British and pan-Arab imperialists to achieve their goal of self-determination (or even, as many sought at that time, basic autonomy). It took the mass upheaval of the First World War to undermine and eventually overcome the hostility of the imperial powers.

For anti-Zionists, steeped in a fake history of Zionism-as-colonialism, the revelation that in 1917 Britain was only one of several countries that recognised the right of the Jews to sovereignty may come as a surprise. The geopolitical *zeitgeist* that shifted the tectonic plates of the post-war order was not colonialism but its polar opposite – self-determination for all peoples. If Israel is an illegitimate child of imperialism, then logic dictates that so must also be Syria, Lebanon, Iraq and innumerable other countries in the Middle East and elsewhere. Moreover, in the Jewish case the hard graft was performed by the Jews themselves. The Jewish national home was not a gift granted to Jews by imperialists; Zionist aims were achieved through Jewish persistence and self-sacrifice as they sought to revive the fortunes of an arid, disease-ridden and neglected terrain containing almost no natural resources. That effort was combined with a sustained global charm offensive conducted by Weizmann, Sokolow and other Zionist leaders. Their advocacy proved irresistible because it was based on truth and justice. International approval followed their labours, not the other way round.

The Balfour Declaration of 1917 and the San Remo Resolution of 1920 were unambiguous anti-imperialist statements. Both documents prioritised the rights of the indigenous inhabitants with three millennia of attachment to the territory over those of the imperial Turkish occupiers. It is tragic that the British, who had trailblazed the principle of self-determination, should have then turned their backs on this principle, reneging on their legal commitments enshrined in the Palestine Mandate. The effects of the British U-turn on the Jews of Europe, struggling to survive under the Nazi jackboot, were disastrous. The United Kingdom became the final – and perhaps most pitiless – colonial occupier of the Jewish homeland. Throwing off the suffocating straitjacket of British rule became the most urgent (and ultimately successful) battle of the long Jewish war against imperialism.

Related to the imperialist-colonialist charge is the rewriting of history to depict Israel as an expansionist land-grabber. The original Jewish national home, as embodied in international law by the San Remo Resolution and confirmed by the Treaties of Sèvres and Lausanne (that disposed of the Ottoman empire), comprised two of today's countries, Israel and Jordan. In 1922, the British created Transjordan out of 78 per cent of the Mandate (east of the Jordan river) to which mainstream Zionist leaders reluctantly agreed, renouncing further territorial claims. Mandatory Palestine was divided into a prospective Jewish state and a much larger Arab state – and the Jewish leadership accepted it. The future Jewish state had contracted to 22 per cent of the Jewish national home.

In 1937, the British Peel Commission proposed a further partition, in which the Jews would be granted a derisory 20 per cent of Western Palestine or about 5 per cent of the original Jewish national home. The Jewish leadership was unhappy with the idea but again accepted territorial compromise as a basis for negotiation if it would lead to peace. In 1947, the UN Special Commission on Palestine (UNSCOP) offered the *Yishuv* a more reasonable 55 per cent of Western Palestine. This was denounced as unfair by the Arabs on demographic grounds. But that was doubly illogical: the

Jews were a majority in the areas allocated to them (just as the Arabs were a majority in the areas of the proposed Arab state), and, based on their population in the former Ottoman Empire, the Jews should have been granted seven times that offered by UNSCOP. The *Yishuv* again accepted a plan that fell far short of their aspirations and would have deprived them of their historical heartlands of Judea and Samaria (that the occupying Jordanians would rename 'the West Bank') and of Jerusalem, their most sacred city and the focus of two millennia of yearning. True to form, the Arab leaders rejected this plan too.

In the period following the Yom Kippur War of 1973, Israel gave up vast swathes of territory (much of which was strategically important and in which she had invested substantial resources), dismantled hundreds of settlements in Sinai and Gaza and offered to remove even more in an attempt to achieve peace. In returning the whole of Sinai to Egypt, Israel (under the nationalistic Menachem Begin) relinquished close to 90 per cent of the land she had captured in 1967 – this was equivalent to almost three times Israel's pre-1967 land mass. And she did it in exchange for nothing more than a paper agreement.

In 1994, Israel withdrew from parts of the northern West Bank to clinch a peace treaty with Jordan. The Jewish state had contracted again, this time giving up historically and militarily important territory that had been part of the Jewish national home, as enshrined in international law. In 2000, prime minister Ehud Barak ordered the withdrawal of the IDF from all of South Lebanon (from where Israel had ousted the PLO in 1982), since re-occupied by Hezbollah, an Iranian proxy militia sworn to Israel's obliteration. Barak also offered to trade the Golan (that was also part of the original Mandate) for peace with Syria, and East Jerusalem (that Jordan had ethnically cleansed of Jews in 1948) for peace with the Palestinians. In 2005, prime minister Ariel Sharon – in a reversal of his hawkish political past – pulled all Israeli troops, along with all 9,000 civilian settlers, out of the Gaza Strip, instantly creating a power vacuum. It was filled by Hamas, the genocidal Iranian-backed terrorist organisation, that has been attacking Israeli civilians ever since with a panoply of lethal weapons, including rockets, tunnels, and incendiary balloons.

Such large-scale withdrawals are unprecedented in modern geopolitics. Far from being expansionist, Israel has repeatedly contracted in the interests of peace despite her small dimensions. In the words of journalist Brett Stephens: 'In proportion to its size, Israel has voluntarily relinquished more territory taken in war than any state in the world.'[15] All countries that take territory in the course of defensive wars have been permitted to retain a substantial part of it – except Israel. Even the Temple Mount – the holiest site to Jews – is not under Israeli control today, despite being located in the country's capital city, but remains under the supervision of the Jordanian-Islamic *Waqf.*

Zionism epitomises the right of all peoples to self-determination as articulated by President Woodrow Wilson over a century ago and subsequently incorporated into international law. The Arab perception of Zionism as colonialist may be sincere but is far removed from reality; Zionism is arguably the most determinedly anti-imperialist, anti-colonialist and anti-expansionist movement in history. Zionists never denied the right to self-determination of any other people but simply demanded that the same right be granted to the Jewish people in accordance with the principle of universality.

If Jewish self-determination is racist, so is the demand of the Palestinians for sovereignty – along with every other expression of self-determination in history, as manifested by the existence of the almost 200 sovereign states that today are members of the United Nations.

Can Arabs be Antisemitic as they are Semites?

The idea that Arabs, being semites, cannot be antisemitic is absurd. First, the descriptor 'semite' has no meaning when applied to ethnicities as heterogeneous as Arabs and Jews, though the group of languages (including Hebrew and Arabic) known as 'semitic' have close linguistic similarities. Second, antisemitism has never been concerned with anyone but Jews since the term was popularised by German Jew-hater Wilhelm Marr in 1879. Marr's purpose was to invent a linguistic expression that reflected his racial rather than religious hostility to Jews. Almost immediately, the word entered the lexicon of Jew-hatred though with variations. In English, hyphenated versions, *anti-semitism* or *anti-Semitism*, gained traction. The hyphenated form is favoured today by Israel's Arab adversaries who argue that 'we are also semites' as a device to accuse Israelis of antisemitism directed at Arabs.

Lipstadt explains that she rejects the hyphen because it diverts attention from its real meaning – hatred of Jews:

> It does not mean hostility toward a non-existent thing called 'Semitism.' When Marr coined the word, he was most definitely not referring to people who spoke Arabic, Aramaic, Amharic, Akkadian, or Ugaritic. That is why I find it particularly offensive when people

> who speak any of these languages claim that they cannot possibly hate Jews because the language they speak is linguistically linked to Hebrew.[16]

Lipstadt adds a further reason for rejecting the idea: it wrongly assumes that members of a group are incapable of being prejudiced against their own. Examples abound: there are racist African-Americans, sexist women, homophobic gays, antisemitic Jews, and – unbelievable as this may seem to us today – Jews who even (initially) supported Nazism and Hitler. Though disturbing, it is a well-recognised phenomenon that affects all groups subjected to protracted periods of hostility and discrimination.

When this argument is used to defend antisemitic anti-Zionism or anti-Israelism, it must be called out for what it is – an attempt to conceal hatred of Jews behind linguistic sophistry. Again, this is not just a Jewish issue: antisemitism impacts negatively on Arabs through its fanning the flames of conflict and its corrosive impact on the body politic of the MENA region. As with any form of racism, antisemitism is injurious to all who are sucked into its orbit.

Did the Balfour Declaration Betray the Arabs?

Two sets of notepaper – the 1915 correspondence of Sir Henry McMahon (the British High Commissioner in Cairo) with Sharif Hussein of Mecca (the principal Arab leader of the day) and the 1917 Balfour Declaration – committed Great Britain to support Arab and Jewish self-determination respectively. The former related to the Hejaz (roughly the western part of modern Saudi Arabia) and the latter to the Palestine district of Southern Syria. Neither statement specified the precise boundaries of these future geopolitical entities. Anti-Israel commentators have alleged that McMahon's promise included Palestine while British officials – including McMahon himself and Lord Peel who chaired the 1937 Royal Commission – repeatedly maintained that the letter had explicitly excluded 'portions of Syria lying to the west of the districts of Damascus' i.e. Palestine.[17] For its part, the Balfour Declaration stated that 'nothing shall be done which may prejudice the civil and religious rights' of Arabs in Palestine.

Regardless of the varying interpretations of those two documents, there was nothing in either that obstructed the essential realisation of both. Moreover, it is inconsistent to argue that one promise was legitimate while the other was not. Neither document (unlike the Mandate) had international legal status, and nor did the parallel, and subsequently abandoned, secret Sykes-Picot agreement of 1916 between Britain and France that attempted to delineate those countries' post-war spheres of influence.

The Zionist leadership regarded the Balfour Declaration as symbolically important in that it was the first time that a major power had acknowledged the eternal historical connection of the Jewish people to their homeland, from which they had been forcibly wrenched, and to which they were entitled to return. Though the Declaration created neither Zionism nor Israel, it endorsed the developing reality of a reconstituted Jewish homeland on the ground. Its subsequent incorporation, via the San Remo Resolution of 1920 into the League of Nations' Palestine Mandate (finalised in 1922), placed the Zionist enterprise on an internationally recognised legal footing that paved the way for the eventual (if belated) creation of the state of Israel without in any way obstructing the expression of Arab sovereignty or impinging on the rights of Palestine's Arabs.

In keeping with the Balfour Declaration, the Mandate guaranteed legal protection of the civil rights of the non-Jewish residents of Palestine. Some historians have argued that this discriminated against that group as it failed to grant the Arabs of Palestine a comparable collective right to self-determination as that offered to the Jews. The historical record points in the opposite direction. The British government's interpretation of the Mandate rapidly evolved to include national self-determination for the Arabs of Palestine as manifested by the creation in 1922 of Transjordan east of the River Jordan (in 78 per cent of the original Mandate territory) as an Arab state with no indigenous historical, national, ethnic or cultural basis and from which Jews, from the outset, were excluded – a racist policy that has been maintained to this day by the modern state of Jordan. Britain appointed Abdullah (son of Sharif Hussein of Mecca, Weizmann's fleeting peace partner in 1919) as ruler of Transjordan, and his brother Faisal as ruler of the emerging state of Iraq, in reward for the Hashemite clan's role in fomenting the Arab revolt against the Turks towards the end of the First World War. Eventually a total of twenty-two Arab states were established.

Within a few years, the British government attempted to assuage further the growing Arab hostility to Zionism by re-interpreting both the Balfour Declaration and the Mandate as implying the establishment of a Jewish national home *in* Palestine rather than in *all of* Palestine. But this had no bearing on the ultimate objective of restoring full Jewish sovereignty, albeit in the far more restricted geographical area of the Mandate in all or part of the territory west of the River Jordan. Tragically, that did not happen in time to save Europe's Jews from the Holocaust.

If anyone was betrayed in the aftermath of the Balfour Declaration, it was the Jews. A diluted version of the Mandate's vision for Jewish self-determination was revisited (alongside a proposed second Palestinian Arab state within Palestine) by both the 1937 British Peel Commission and the 1947 partition plan of the successor body to the League of Nations, the United Nations. Both proposals offered the prospect of establishing, peacefully, a Jewish state (in those parts of the territory that had a Jewish majority) alongside an Arab one – the two-state solution – many decades ago. The Zionists accepted both, with reservations, but both were violently rejected by the Arabs. That rejection (reiterated by Palestinian leaders up to the present day), rather than the Balfour Declaration and the restoration of Jewish sovereignty that flowed from it, is the essence of the Arab-Israeli conflict.

Did Balfour and the International Community Intend the Establishment of a Jewish State?

Why did both Balfour and the San Remo Resolution that created the British Mandate use the phrase 'Jewish national home' rather than 'Jewish state'? The issue was not one of style but of substance. The wording was carefully constructed to reflect the fact that full sovereignty for Jews would have to await their demographic transition from a minority to a majority and that they would be assisted in that process by the legal instruments of the Mandate.

Opponents of Zionism sometimes express a willingness to tolerate a Jewish presence in the Middle East short of full sovereignty. They seek to justify this minimalist concession – that was never a realistic option given the appalling treatment the Jews endured in Arab lands – by referring to the wording of the Balfour Declaration in which the phrase 'Jewish state' did not appear. The logic of this argument is thin to put it mildly. It was obvious to all at the time that the Jewish national home was intended to lead to full statehood once a Jewish majority had been achieved. The rapid incorporation of the Declaration into the League of Nations Mandate system, out of which several sovereign states emerged, lends support to this view. Article 22 of the Covenant of the League of Nations (1919) leaves little room for ambiguity. Class A mandates were to be applied to certain communities in parts of Ottoman Empire, including the (Syrian) district of Palestine, 'that reached a stage of development where their existence as independent nations can be provisionally recognised subject to the rendering of administrative advice and assistance by a Mandatory until such time as they are able to stand alone.'[18] It requires an excessive degree of mental gymnastics to interpret the words 'existence as independent nations' as anything other than a commitment to ultimate statehood.

The translation of the universal principle of self-determination to the scattered Jewish people was, in one aspect, *sui generis* and therefore a source of great contention and misunderstanding. Although Jews were indigenous to Palestine, the majority of Jews in the pre-Zionist era resided outside of that territory for historical reasons, including forcible expulsion from their homeland and the subsequent erection of insurmountable barriers to their return. Accordingly, they constituted a minority of the population of Palestine at the outset of the Mandate. These were extraordinary circumstances over which they had no control. In recognition of this unusual degree of disadvantage that demanded special measures to rectify, the Mandate was clear: Article 6 required Britain to 'facilitate Jewish immigration....and encourage close settlement by Jews in the land...'[19] Britain's failure to fulfil these crucial obligations was a clear breach of international law, a betrayal of the promise to the Jews enshrined in the Balfour Declaration, and the principal reason for the Jewish demographic disadvantage in the Mandatory territory occasioned by the avoidable consignment of millions of Jews to their fate at the hands of Hitler.

Whatever its motivation, the Balfour Declaration marked a key moment on the tortuous path to revived Jewish sovereignty. But it did not create Zionism, nor did it hand a foreign territory to the Jewish people; it expressed and endorsed the principle of self-determination – that the already well-established *Yishuv* embodied – and recognised the right of Jews to revive their sovereignty in their historical homeland to which they had retained a close emotional connection, as well as an almost continuous physical presence, for over two millennia.

Was Arab Antisemitism a Natural Response to the Migration of European Zionists to Palestine?

Anti-Zionists tend to regard Jewish immigrants to Palestine in the late nineteenth and early twentieth centuries as alien invaders of an Arab territory. This view is based on either an ignorance or a distortion of history.

A review of the origin of the name 'Palestine' provides important context to this question. In the second century, the Romans expelled most of the Jews from the Jewish homeland and renamed it '*Syria Palaestina*,' though the Jews continued to call it Judea or *Eretz Israel*. After the Roman Empire gave way to Byzantine then eventually Ottoman rule, the Christian

West generally used the term 'The Holy Land' while the Arabs called it southern Syria. Contrary to the claim of revisionist historians, Arab leaders at that time referred neither to a Palestinian people nor to a country called Palestine. George Antonius, author of *The Arab Awakening*, testified before the Peel Commission in 1937 in Jerusalem and argued that 'Palestine has always been an integral part of Syria and that what was common to Syria was common to Palestine.'[20] This view has been confirmed by other Arab historians. Rewriting history weakens rather than strengthens the Palestinian case.

The first time the term Palestine was widely used to denote a political entity was when the League of Nations established the British Mandate in 1920. The largest proportion of this territory was part of an Ottoman *vilayet* (administrative unit) that had been governed from the Syrian capital, Damascus, since the sixteenth century. In the early nineteenth century, the Egyptians briefly occupied the area and divided the original southern Syrian *vilayet* into two parts: the *vilayet* of Beirut in the north (that stretched down to today's Tel Aviv) and the *sanjak* (semi-autonomous district) of Jerusalem in the south (that also encompassed much of today's southern Israel).

The emergence of a distinct Palestinian Arab identity in the mid-twentieth century was primarily a response to Zionism and Israel. In 1947, despite the virtual absence of a Palestinian Arab national consciousness, the Zionist leadership voted for partition thereby recognising the existence of the case for Palestinian Arab sovereignty even as the Arab leadership withheld reciprocal recognition of Jewish rights. That Israeli position has continued ever since, with varying degrees of enthusiasm, tempered by an understandable fear of the security threat that a hostile Palestinian state might pose to Israel.

Arab anti-Zionism is often attributed, in part at least, to the rapid demographic change produced by the influx of Zionist European Jews to Palestine. There is some truth to this view but it is a partial one. The first modern-era *olim* (immigrants) to *Eretz Israel* were Yemenite Jews who arrived in numbers in the final decades of the nineteenth century, though they were soon eclipsed by Russian and eastern European Jews fleeing pogroms and destitution. Although the Balfour Declaration of 1917 boosted Jewish immigration to Palestine, it also boosted non-Jewish immigration from all corners of the Ottoman Empire: the Arab population grew from around 600,000 to 950,000 between 1920 and 1936. This occurred in response to Jewish capital investment that brought in its wake employment opportunities, improvements in agriculture and industry, better socio-economic conditions, and advanced healthcare associated with the development of the Jewish national home. Over the same period, Arab emigration declined steeply for the same reason.

Although Jewish immigration to Palestine provoked a degree of Arab enmity, that response was not inevitable. Jewish immigration was actually welcomed by Prince Faisal in his (short-lived) agreement with Chaim Weizmann in 1919, and by King Abdullah of Jordan both before and after the 1948 war until he was murdered in 1951. The Arab population (many of whom were of non-Arab origin) grew rapidly from the first day of the Mandate. The opposition to Zionism was whipped up by Arab nationalists, Haj Amin al-Husseini foremost among them, who exploited xenophobic and antisemitic tendencies in Arab society to that end.

To reiterate: when the League of Nations decided to recognise the right of the Jewish people to self-determination, and to mandate a mechanism for its fulfilment through immigration and settlement, they acknowledged the fact that Jews were a minority in their homeland. Though the proposed Jewish state fell far short of Jewish expectations by excluding Jerusalem, Judea and Samaria (the Jewish capital city and ancestral heartlands respectively), the Zionist leadership accepted the UN plan. Had the Arab leadership done the same, there would have been two states (in addition to Transjordan), no conflict and no refugees, Arab or Jewish. They rejected it, violently.

Was Israel Created by Ethnically Cleansing the Palestinians?

Pro-Palestinian activists are quick to the point the finger of blame at Israel for causing the exodus of hundreds of thousands of Arabs from the area that came under Israeli control in the course of the war of 1947-49. The Israelis vehemently deny responsibility for this human displacement. What actually happened?

Following the historic UN partition resolution of November 1947 that recognised the right of the Jews to statehood, the last thing the Jewish leadership wanted was a war and they appealed to their Arab neighbours to join them in accepting the resolution and building peaceful relations. But the default reaction – first established by Husseini in 1920 and continued ever since – kicked into play and the Arabs went to war. As always in such circumstances, many people (both Jews and Arabs, though mainly the latter) fled their homes to escape the fighting. To put it starkly, the Arab refugee problem was caused by Arab aggression against the Jews that turned into a full-scale war.

The most respected authority on the events of this period, and one widely (if selectively) quoted by authors unsympathetic to Israel, is Israeli historian Benny Morris. Originally a 'revisionist' proponent of the ethnic cleansing charge against Israel, Morris changed his mind on reviewing the evidence, including papers eventually released from British Foreign Office archives. In *1948*, his voluminous account of the War of Independence, he rejected the widely-touted allegation of a premeditated Zionist intention to expel the Arabs of Palestine. To defend Israelis from invaders, the *Haganah* (the pre-state Jewish army) had drawn up and partially implemented measures (*Tochnit Daled* or Plan D) to seize and hold Arab villages but expulsion was to be a last resort should the population offer resistance.

The flight of the vast majority of the Palestinian Arab refugees was motivated by fear – much of it generated by Arab propagandists who circulated lurid and exaggerated accounts of alleged Jewish atrocities. It was not caused by any Jewish policy or practice of ethnic cleansing but was the result of the failed 'war of extermination' promised by the Arab Higher Committee (AHC) and their supporters. Writes Morris, 'Even Christian Arabs appear to have adopted the jihadi discourse.' Matiel Mughannam, a Lebanese-born Christian who headed the AHC-affiliated Arab Women's Organisation in Palestine, told an interviewer early in the civil war: 'The UN decision has united all Arabs...[A Jewish state] has no chance to survive now that the "holy war" has been declared. All the Jews will eventually be massacred.'[21]

Morris did concede that a minority (around 50,000 or 7%) of the roughly 740,000 Palestinian Arab refugees were expelled by Israeli forces for tactical military reasons though they were expected to return when the war ended; sadly they became pawns on the political chessboard of the unresolved conflict and that outcome was never achieved. Again, this was not Israel's fault: at the war's end, Israel offered to take back 100,000 of the refugees immediately and unconditionally to kickstart peace negotiations but the idea was rejected outright by the Arab leadership who insisted that any return of the refugees was contingent on the demise of Israel. The Secretary of the Arab Higher Command, Emile Ghoury, (cited by Dershowitz), told a Beirut newspaper that 'it is inconceivable that the refugees should be sent back to their homes while they are occupied by Jews... as it would serve as a first step toward their recognition of Israel.'[22] The politicidal implication of the 'return' policy was spelled out by the Egyptian foreign minister: 'It is well known and understood that the Arabs, in demanding the return of the refugees to Palestine, mean their return as masters of their homeland, not as slaves.'[23] In any case, most Arab refugees fled to territories that today are claimed as Palestinian – namely the West Bank and Gaza – and cannot therefore be refugees from Palestine; furthermore, the large majority of those many millions registered today with the UNRWA are not the original exiles but their descendants, rendering their refugee status bogus according to the standard UN definition of a refugee (see Chapter 7). In the immediate aftermath of the war, a few Arab spokesmen acknowledged these facts. But the Arab leadership as whole were never interested in a truthful accounting of events and viewed the 'ethnic cleansing' charge – subsequently merged with the '*Nakba*' narrative – as an invaluable propaganda weapon against Israel.

What Was the 'Nakba'?

Much confusion surrounds the *Nakba* (Arabic for 'disaster' or 'catastrophe'). The widespread assumption that it refers to the tragedy of the Arab refugees from Mandatory Palestine boosts sympathy for the Palestinians but flies in the face of the evidence.

According to Israeli military analyst Raphael Bouchnik-Chen, the term was coined by Syrian Arab historian Constantin Zureiq to describe the failure of the Arab armies in 1948 to prevent the establishment of Israel; it was this event rather than the accompanying humanitarian cost of the war, that was viewed as a disaster by the Arab world at the time and ever since. Here is Zureiq's verdict from his 1948 pamphlet *Ma'na al-Nakbah* ('The Meaning of the Disaster'): 'When the battle broke out, our public diplomacy began to speak of our imaginary victories, to put the Arab public to sleep and talk of the ability to overcome and win easily until the *nakba* happened … We must admit our mistakes … and recognize the extent of our responsibility for the disaster that is our lot.'[24]

In 1988, PLO chief Yasser Arafat confirmed this interpretation by declaring the establishment of an annual *Nakba* Day to be marked every 15 May, the day Israel declared her independence. Israeli journalist Adi Schwartz has pointed out the revealing nature of this behaviour – that the Palestinians view the establishment of Israel, rather than the refugees, as the real disaster: 'The fact that the Palestinians still commemorate *Nakba* Day – and now ask the entire international community to do so as well – reflects their worldview. Those who want to understand why the peace negotiations have failed in recent decades, need only listen to the Palestinians: for them, the mourning for the establishment of Israel still continues.'[25]

Arafat, always attuned to the tastes of his international audience, went further and redefined the *Nakba* by inverting its original meaning (and historical veracity) to blame Israel rather than the Arabs for both the war of 1947-49 and its consequences. An Arab defeat was thereby refashioned into an injustice to the Palestinians.[26] The world accepted this revisionism and the *Nakba* became synonymous with the alleged Israeli mass expulsion of the Palestinian refugees. In 2022, Mahmoud Abbas Palestinians demanded that the UN recognise *Nakba* Day to coincide with Israel's independence day and a pliant General Assembly duly agreed.

While the false narrative that condemned Israel for creating the refugee problem may have been a cynical contrivance, what is not in doubt is the human suffering experienced by the fleeing Arabs. A compassionate response by the international community was unsurprising and appropriate, even if the problem had been caused by needless Arab aggression. Yet the Palestinian Arabs were not the only victims of their leaders' – and seven Arab states' - irresponsible war against the Jews. In the decades following Israel's declaration of Independence, authoritarian Arab and Islamic regimes unleashed a vicious assault on their Jewish communities. When the scale of this larger Jewish *Nakba* was revealed, the world's compassion for victims mysteriously evaporated.

Was Zionism Responsible for the Jewish Nakba?

Following Israel's rebirth in 1948, the position of Jews throughout the MENA region, where many of them had resided for more than a millennium, became untenable. Their mass exodus – the Jewish *Nakba* – had begun. Unlike the Palestinian refugees, these 900,000 Jews were not caught up in the heat of battle but were rendered homeless, stripped of their rights and possessions, and often subjected to violence as a result of a deliberate, premeditated Arab League policy of extreme anti-Zionist antisemitism. While the Arab refugee problem arose from an Arab-initiated civil and international war of aggression, the Jewish *Nakba* occurred in peaceful domestic circumstances and cannot therefore be viewed as a comparable collateral effect of the war. Furthermore, unlike the Palestinian refugees, the Jewish refugees were quickly absorbed, mainly into poverty-stricken Israel, and denied even a fraction of the financial aid that flowed to the Palestinians.

Anti-Israel propagandists claim that the establishment of Israel caused the destructive dynamic of anti-Zionism across the MENA and have offered a range of pseudo-explanations for the Jewish *Nakba* either to deny that it happened or to offer partial justifications. These include claims that the Jews left their native lands willingly as ideological Zionists, that Mossad agents acted as *agents provocateurs* to cause enmity to Jews, and that all non-Muslim minorities were equally persecuted. Julius demolishes all these assertions, none of which is supported by evidence.[27] Their purpose is a cynical one: to exonerate Arab states for their aggressively antisemitic behaviour and shift the blame onto the victims. An objective reading of history points to a different conclusion: Israel's declaration of independence sparked a pre-existing long-term animosity. As Julius writes: 'The root cause of the post-1948 exodus of around 900,000 Jews from the Middle East and North Africa was pan-Arab racism, itself influenced by Nazism. Before the first Arab-Israeli war broke out, saturation Nazi propaganda on an illiterate and gullible population had already destroyed any prospect of peaceful coexistence between Jews and Arabs.'[28]

Why have the victims of this forgotten Jewish *Nakba* received so little recognition and support? In part, it may have been due to reticence by the *Mizrachi* Jews themselves. Some regarded their self-identification as refugees as undignified and irrelevant, especially as so many had become Israelis, though not without difficulty. But another psychological factor may have been involved. Julius describes the sense of nostalgia that many of these Jews felt for their former homes in MENA countries.[29] Egyptian-born writer Bat Ye'or calls this a kind of *dhimmi* syndrome whereby unpleasant memories are suppressed: 'Reduced to an inferior existence in circumstances that engender physical and moral degradation, the *dhimmi* perceives and accepts himself as a devalued human being.'[30] That mindset is a well-recognised reaction of persecuted minorities everywhere; even Jews who suffered at the hands of the Nazis sometimes expressed a yearning to return to their former lives.

The facts are clear: 'justifiable hatred' did not cause antisemitic anti-Zionism and anti-Israelism in the Arab world. The null hypothesis is again rejected.

Notes

1 Zick A, Küpper B, Hövermann A. Intolerance, Prejudice and Discrimination. A European Report. Berlin, Friedrich-Ebert-Stiftung, 2011] https://ec.europa.eu/migrant-integration/library-document/intolerance-prejudice-and-discrimination-european-report_en. (Last accessed 12 June 2024)

2 B. Lewis, *Semites and Anti-Semites: An Inquiry into Conflict and Prejudice* (New York: WW Norton & Company, 1999), p.117.

3 W. Laqueur, *The Changing Face of Antisemitism.* (New York: Oxford University Press, 2006), p.193.

4   Cited by L. Julius. *Uprooted* (London: Vallentine Mitchell, 2018), p.35.
5   See Laqueur, *The Changing Face of Antisemitism*, p.193.
6   See Julius. *Uprooted*, p.289.
7   Anti-Defamation League (New York), 'ADL/Global 100', https://global100.adl.org/map (Last accessed 12 June 2024)
8   O. Kessler, 'Mandate 100: 'A Clean Cut' for Palestine: The Peel Commission Re-examined', *Fathom* (March 202). https://fathomjournal.org/mandate100-a-clean-cut-for-palestine-the-peel-commission-reexamined/ (Last accessed 12 June 2024)
9   E. Karsh, 'Israel's Arabs v. Israel', BESA Center Perspectives Paper No. 2,029, May 14, 2020. https://besacenter.org/wp-content/uploads/2021/05/2029-Israeli-Arabs-v.-Israel-Karsh.pdf (Last accessed 12 June 2024)
10 Noah Browning, 'Abbas Wants "not a single Israeli" in Future Palestinian State', *Reuters World News*, 30 July 2013. https://www.reuters.com/article/us-palestinians-israel-abbas-idUSBRE96T00920130730 (Last accessed 12 June 2024)
11 R. Bellerose, 'Are Jews Indigenous to the Land of Israel?' *Tablet*, 9 February 2017. https://www.tabletmag.com/sections/israel-middle-east/articles/bellerose-aboriginal-people (Last accessed 12 June 2024)
12 D. Avelar, B. Ferrari, 'Israel and Palestine: a story of modern colonialism', Open Democracy, 29 May 2018. https://www.opendemocracy.net/en/north-africa-west-asia/israel-and-palestine-story-of-modern-colonialism/ (Last accessed 12 June 2024)
13 A. Joffe, 'Palestinian Settler Colonialism', (Ramat Gan: BESA Centre, 2017). https://besacenter.org/wp-content/uploads/2017/08/577-Palestinian-Settler-Colonialism-Joffee-final.pdf (Last accessed 12 June 2024)
14 A. Dershowitz, *The Case for Israel* (Hoboken: John Wiley & Sons, 2003), p.14.
15 Bret Stephens, The Progressive Assault on Israel', *New York Times*, 8 February 2019.
16 D. Lipstadt, *Antisemitism Here and Now* (London: Scribe Publications, 2019), p.23-24.
17 A. Shapira, *Israel: A History* (London: Weidenfeld & Nicolson, 2015), p.71.
18 Yale Law School, The Avalon Project, The Covenant of the League of Nations. https://avalon.law.yale.edu/20th_century/leagcov.asp (Last accessed 12 June 2024)
19 Laqueur W, Rubin B (eds), *The Israel-Arab Reader* (London: Penguin Books, 2008). P.31.
20 Steven Zipperstein, 'Back when Palestinians insisted there's no such place as Palestine', *Times of Israel*, 4 September 2022. https://blogs.timesofisrael.com/back-when-palestinians-insisted-theres-no-such-place-as-palestine/ (Last accessed 12 June 2024)

21 B. Morris, *1948, A History of the First Arab-Israeli War* (New Haven Yale University Press 2008), p.395.
22 See Dershowitz, *The Case for Israel,* p.85.
23 Ibid.
24 Rafael Bouchnik-Chen, 'The False Nakba Narrative,' *Jewish News Syndicate,* 5 December 2022. https://www.jns.org/opinion/the-false-nakba-narrative/ (Last accessed 12 June 2024)
25 Adi Schwartz, 'Palestinians help Israel when they focus on "Nakba Day",' *Israel Hayom,* 5 December 2022. https://www.israelhayom.com/opinions/palestinians-help-israel-when-they-focus-on-nakba-day/ (Last accessed 12 June 2024)
26 Shany Mor, 'The UN is distorting the meaning of the Nakba,' *Unherd,* 15 May 2023. https://unherd.com/thepost/the-un-is-distorting-the-meaning-of-the-nakba/ (Last accessed 12 June 2024)
27 See Julius. *Uprooted*, pp.119-128.
28 See Julius. *Uprooted*, p. 104
29 See Julius. *Uprooted*, p.25.
30 B. Ye'or, *The Dhimmi: Jews and Christians Under Islam* (London: Associated University Press, 1985), p.143.

9

Counterarguments Part 2

Chapter 8 addressed seven historically-referenced – and demonstrably false – beliefs about Zionism and Israel that are used justify the adoption of hostile attitudes to both. A further seven currently popular assertions, taken individually or collectively, can inflict serious reputational damage on Zionism and Israel unless vigorously rebutted. They are:

- that Israel today is an apartheid state;
- that Israel violates international law through her occupation and settlement of Palestinian lands;
- that Israel uses disproportionate and murderous military force;
- that Israel is committing a genocide of the Palestinians comparable to the Nazi Holocaust;
- that Israel was created and only survives through US support;
- that Palestinian anger is caused by Israel's refusal to make peace on the basis of the two-state solution;
- that Arab threats against Jews are mere rhetoric.

We can test the validity of these statements by scrutinising the evidence.

Is Israel an Apartheid State?

The 'apartheid' charge did not originate with Israel's occupation of the West Bank following the Six Day War in 1967. Both the Arab League and the PLO used the term in the early 1960s, based on Israel's self-definition as the Jewish state, long before the first settlement was constructed. The 'apartheid' smear, then as now, was detached from reality and was simply a device to delegitimise Israel. 'Apartheid' is the Afrikaans term for the systematic, legally enforced racial segregation and discrimination that was violently imposed on the black population by white minority governments in South Africa from 1948 to 1994. The UN defines apartheid as 'policies and practices of racial segregation and discrimination as practised in southern Africa...for the purpose of establishing and maintaining domination by one racial group of persons over any other racial group of persons and systematically oppressing them.'[1] Its application to Israel, a multi-ethnic liberal democracy that guarantees equal rights to all its citizens, is wholly inappropriate. Over three-quarters of the 20 per cent of Israelis who are Arabs say that they prefer living in Israel to any other country.[2]

The apartheid charge against Israel has a unique attraction for Israel-haters because opposition to racism commands near-universal support.[3] It is the modern liberal shorthand for the epitome of evil, an offence against the most basic political morality, and has been declared a crime against humanity by the UN. The success attributed to the Anti-Apartheid Movement (formed in the UK in 1960) in bringing down South Africa's apartheid system offers an inspirational model for achieving the same result with Israel. Activists base the apartheid charge on two key circumstances: Israel's presence (including her defensive measures) on the West Bank, and her status as a Jewish state. Neither reflects a policy of Israeli apartheid.

As a consequence of the Oslo Accords that Israel signed with the PLO in 1993-95 and signed off by the international community, an unusual and complex transitional politico-legal scenario was implemented. The West Bank was divided into three areas: A, under the exclusive authority of the newly created Palestinian Authority and where the majority of Palestinians live; C, under the exclusive authority of the Israeli government and where the majority of West Bank Jewish residents ('settlers') live; and B, a mixed demographic area under joint control. Area C contains both Jews and Arabs who have different rights and responsibilities to each other: Jews are subject to Israeli civil law from the other side of the Green Line (the 1949 armistice boundary) and vote in Israeli elections while Arabs live under Israeli military law and vote in PA elections. The reason for this anomalous system is simple: Area C contains both Jews and Arabs, posing security challenges for the Israeli administration, while in Area A there are no Jews, nor are any permitted by Palestinian law to reside there. In addition, in the wake of the terrorist campaign known as the Second *Intifada* that started in 2000, Israel built a security barrier to stop the entry of Palestinian suicide bombers into Israel proper. This was a highly successful defensive measure that anti-Israel activists call the 'Apartheid Wall' despite the fact that over 95 per cent of it is a fence. None of these circumstances amounts to apartheid and none of the signatories to the Oslo Accords regarded them as such.

The Oslo arrangements were arrived at by mutual Israeli-Palestinian agreement and endorsed by the international community. They were intended to be temporary pending final status negotiations that the Palestinian leadership has repeatedly declined to enter (or has briefly entered before exiting) while simultaneously violating the Accords on a daily basis. These have included unilaterally changing the political status of the West Bank and Gaza (to the 'State of Palestine'), refusing to amend the Palestinian national covenant that brands Israel as illegitimate, and – most seriously – inciting the murder of Israelis via religious sermons, the media and financial inducements ('pay-for-slay' policy). In these circumstances, Israelis are wary of entering into further agreements (even if they were on offer) with such a capricious 'peace partner.'[4]

As indicated in the previous chapter, Israel's Jewish status is frequently misrepresented. There is a widespread perception that Israel is or aspires to be an exclusively Jewish state. A cursory glance at the demographic nature of her citizenry reveals this to be nonsense: a quarter of the country's citizenry is non-Jewish and growing at the same rate as the Jewish population. Contrary to popular belief (even among some Jews), Judaism is not the official religion of Israel but it is one of several (including Islam and Christianity) that are recognised by the state – in contrast to most MENA countries in which Islam is the sole state religion. Israeli religious plurality contrasts favourably with many Western countries including the United Kingdom, where Anglicanism is the sole state religion, and the USA, a nominally secular state where public reference to religious faith is so ubiquitous that it has become an unspoken requirement for aspiring candidates for high office.

In pre-1967 Israel (i.e. within the Green Line agreed at the Rhodes Armistice conference in 1949), most of the laws relating to religion are rooted in the historical *Status Quo* regarding religious communities. These regulations date back to the Ottoman Empire and were sustained during the British Mandate and by successive Israeli governments. For Israeli minority faith groups, the *Status Quo* is valued as a constitutional protection for their modes of worship and their communities – a state of affairs unknown in most Arab states.

As in most countries, elements within Israeli society sometimes express prejudiced views and these can lead to tension between Jews and Arabs. Given the history of antagonism (including civil war) between the two groups over many decades, it would be surprising if a degree of mutual antipathy between them was absent. But Israeli law does not discriminate in any way against her non-Jewish citizens. On the contrary, Jews are the one group that face officially sanctioned discrimination. There are numerous examples.

Only Orthodox strands of Judaism are recognised by the Chief Rabbinate thus creating difficulties for non-Orthodox Israeli Jews in the realms of citizenship, marriage and burial. Israel (unlike the PA) strives to grant access to the holy places of all faiths, particularly following her entry in 1967 into the areas historically known as Judea and Samaria (renamed 'The West Bank' by Jordan in 1950 and containing today's Area A of the PA). While Christians and Muslims are guaranteed the right to worship at their holiest sites by Israeli law, Jews are not. On religious festivals, Christians flock to the Churches of the Holy Sepulchre and Nativity, and Muslims pray at the *Haram al-Sharif* (the Islamic name for the Temple Mount); by contrast, Jews can hold prayer services only at the foot of the Western Wall – a structure that lies close to but not within the Temple Mount precinct itself, the most sacred spot in Judaism. Jews are also banned from visiting most of Hebron, the second holiest city of their faith, and one that was for centuries home to a substantial Jewish community until the Jewish inhabitants were massacred or expelled by Muslim extremists in 1929.

As for residency, only Jews face restriction: the Israeli Supreme Court has ruled that Jews are not permitted to exclude non-Jews from any of their communities while Arabs may exclude Jews from theirs. In the West Bank, under the Oslo Accords Jews are not permitted under any circumstances to live in large swathes (40 per cent) of Judea, the historical Jewish homeland that is largely located in areas A and B. West Bank and Gaza Arabs, on the other hand, may (and do) live throughout all of these areas except in the 1 per cent of those territories (located mostly adjacent to the Green Line in Area C) where Israeli settlements have been established and are vulnerable to terrorism.

Regarding military service, the burden of defending the country falls almost exclusively on Jewish shoulders. Conscription is compulsory for all Jewish Israelis except *Charedi* (ultra-Orthodox) Jews – and efforts to remove that exemption are ongoing. In addition to the obvious physical dangers to which soldiers are exposed, the disruption to family life, education, career advancement and economic well-being that is caused by both regular and reserve army service is considerable. Non-Jews (other than Druze and Circassian men) are not required to serve though they can (and many do) volunteer.

That is the reality of the so-called 'apartheid state': only Jews are prevented, by a raft of domestic and international legal instruments, from pursuing the kind of lifestyle that most people regards as a fundamental human right. That extraordinary state of affairs begs a question: why have draconian restrictions on Jewish rights been imposed over many decades by successive governments of the Jewish state? The answer is commendable though rarely acknowledged: to avoid infringing Arab-Muslim sensibilities. This is a unique policy: where else in the world has a government voluntarily renounced the rights of the majority of its citizens to live in their historical homeland or to pray at or visit their holiest sites, solely in the interests of achieving peaceful relations with their neighbours?

Apartheid is alive and well in the Middle East; it is inflicted by Arab states on Palestinians who have been systematically deprived, by law, of fundamental civil rights in Jordan, Lebanon, Syria, the Gulf and elsewhere in the MENA region. The 'apartheid' charge against Israel is pure projection. It is also built on fabrications rather than evidence.[5,6] But the truth does not interest the accusers. Alan Johnson is unequivocal that 'whatever the good intentions of some supporters of the Apartheid Smear, in the minds of its hard-core promoters there is a darker purpose: the demonisation of Israel as a pariah state in order to prepare the ground for its eventual destruction.'[7]

Does Israel Violate International Law Through her Occupation and Settlement of Palestinian Lands?

Opposition to Israeli occupation and settlements – even if based on misinformation – is not, of course, in itself antisemitic, but there are two circumstances in which it might be: deliberately distorting or inventing legal principles in order to demonise Israel; and applying a double standard by singling out Israel in a discriminatory fashion while ignoring or downplaying all other instances, including far more egregious ones. Both of these are in play in the 'illegal occupation and settlements' charge.

'Illegal Occupation'?

Why is the endlessly recurring charge of 'illegal occupation' so significant? Arab states did not merely unleash their military might against Israel on the day of her birth in May 1948; in parallel, they initiated a propaganda war that continues to this day. Few, beyond the direct participants, are aware of its existence. Instead, large sections of public opinion have swallowed the malign accusation of illegality hurled at Israel as though it were gospel truth. The starting point is the UN's depiction of the West Bank, Eastern Jerusalem and the Gaza Strip as 'Occupied Palestinian Territories' (OPT) since 1967. This is a politicised phrase as these territories – more accurately described as disputed – were never part of a state of Palestine (though some of them might have been had the Arabs accepted, like the Jews, the UN partition resolution of 1947). Nor was such a designation applied by anyone in the nineteen years (1948-67) of the occupation of these territories by Jordan and Egypt, though Israel, even behind the pre-1967 Green Line, was subjected to the accusation of 'occupation' by the Arab League that regarded every part of Israel since 1948 to be illegally occupied and settled by Jews. In any event, Israel withdrew entirely from Gaza in 2005 thereby unequivocally ending her belligerent occupation there according to the Hague Conventions of 1907, though the UN (and thus most of the rest of the world) insists on maintaining the fiction that both the West Bank and Gaza remain part of the OPT.

The post-1967 purpose of the term 'occupation' is to disadvantage Israel diplomatically by nullifying any Israeli claim to even a centimetre of the disputed territories thus pre-empting the negotiations that the UN itself (through Security Council Resolutions 242 and 338) insists must take place. The OPT descriptor effectively endorses the Palestinian rejection of territorial compromise or peace negotiations. If unchallenged, the current impasse will become permanent.

The 'illegal occupation' charge is also unfounded. Robbie Sabel, an international law professor at the Hebrew University in Jerusalem, writes: 'The West Bank has not been incorporated into Israel, and therefore those areas of the West Bank not part of the Palestinian Authority are administered by Israel in accordance with the international rules on administering occupied territory. This is a crucial point: though the term has negative connotations, occupation is legal in times of armed conflict.'[8] (Notwithstanding her objection to the term 'occupation,' Israel has always accepted *de facto* responsibilities as an occupier under international humanitarian law). The International Court of Justice, in its advisory opinion (not a judgement) in 2004 on the Legal Consequences of 'The Wall,' refrained from characterising the Israeli occupation as illegal. And former ICJ President, Rosalyn Higgins, has stated that 'there is nothing in either the [UN] Charter or general international law which leads one to suppose that military occupation pending a peace treaty is illegal.'[9] The 'illegal occupation' charge is not only false but is damaging to diplomacy by branding Israel a criminal state – and no civilised person negotiates with criminals.

The United Nations is frequently cited as the final arbiter of international law and the repository of all moral authority in international affairs. This view is based on a misunderstanding of the nature of the organisation (as opposed to its Charter). The UN General Assembly is a political tool of its constituent members. It has been implacably hostile to Israel for decades and is in thrall to the wishes of the Arab League that bullies and cajoles member states with economic and political threats and inducements. It has often issued hate-filled, irrational statements (such as annual the 'Zionism is a form of racism' resolution from 1975 to 1991). But pronouncements of the UN General Assembly neither constitute international law nor acquire the force of international law by repetition. As for the Security Council, only Chapter VII resolutions are legally binding – and the Council has never passed one in relation to Israel. With rare exceptions, it has relied on one key resolution since 1967 to try to end the conflict, namely the aforementioned Resolution 242 Israel accepted that resolution while the Arab world rejected it.

Israel's entry into those territories during the Six Day War of 1967 was an act of self-defence under Article 51 of the UN Charter and was therefore legal pending the signing of peace treaties between the warring parties. Resolution 242 implicitly recognised the legality of the occupation as it did not require Israel's withdrawal from all the territories but 'from territories' to 'secure and recognised boundaries free from threats or acts of force' because at that time the Security Council acknowledged that the 1949 ceasefire lines – that resulted in Israel having a narrow waist nine miles wide – were indefensible. This is a crucial point because Resolution 242 has been the starting point for all attempts to negotiate peace agreements between Israel and her neighbours since 1967. While those efforts bore some fruit with Egypt and Jordan, they have floundered in relation to the Palestinians due to the intransigence of successive Palestinian leaders.

What is the legal status of these disputed territories? International law is primarily determined by mutually agreed undertakings incorporated into multinational treaties and conventions. Two groups of twentieth century treaties are especially relevant to the territories. First, the 1919 Paris peace conference and subsequent summits established, in a series of declarations, the right of Jews to revive their national home under the terms of the Palestine Mandate. The Mandate comprised (even in its truncated form after the creation of Transjordan) all of the territory west of the Jordan River, including what is today designated the West Bank and East Jerusalem. Second, the 1993-95 Oslo Accords (that are linked in principle to Resolution 242) have the status of an international treaty that is legally binding on all participants.

The Oslo Declaration of Principles set out the Israeli-Palestinian consensus, backed by the international community, on the nature of the new arrangements. These included the establishment of the Palestinian

Authority in Area A (parts of the West Bank and all of Gaza), bringing 98 per cent of the Palestinian population under PA control, and Area C where about 80 per cent of the Israeli residents of the West Bank lived. The term 'occupation' is nowhere to be found in those agreements. The Oslo Accords thus created a post-occupation reality that was accepted by the parties as a transitional stage towards a final status agreement that would end the conflict. Following Oslo, the state of belligerent occupancy – such as it was – came to an end. This was affirmed in 2013 in a case brought by the PLO against a company connected to the light railway in Jerusalem; the French Court of Appeal in Versailles ruled that the alleged occupation was not illegal.[10]

'Illegal Settlements'?

Following Israel's entry to the West Bank, Gaza and East Jerusalem in the Six Day War, Israel's Labour-dominated government established a network of strategically located army installations and Jewish communities in these territories. Their purpose was threefold: to bolster the state's security in the face of the ongoing refusal of her enemies to abandon violence and negotiate peace; to restore Jewish access to historically and religiously significant sites (such as the Jewish Quarter of Jerusalem) from which Jews had been unlawfully ejected by Arab forces in the War of Independence of 1947-49; and to hold as bargaining chips in the event of future peace negotiations.

Following the election of the Likud in 1977, Israel approved the construction of additional settlements even if they served a minimal security need. This encouraged militant Greater Israel groups who attempted to 'create facts' by initiating unofficial settlements across the newly acquired territories. The Israeli government and Supreme Court responded by specifying strict conditions for a settlement to be formally recognised. First, its establishment had to be based on a government decision. Second, it could be built only on state-owned land or on land legally acquired by an Israeli citizen. Third, it had to accord with planning laws supervised by a municipal authority. If any of these conditions were not met, a settlement was deemed illegal and had to be removed, and thousands of such settlements have been evacuated and demolished over the years. Unauthorised settlements are clearly different from those that have been officially sanctioned by the state. For political reasons, the UN (most blatantly in Security Council Resolution 2334 of 2016) and the wider international community have chosen to blur this distinction. Three main arguments are offered to justify the blanket designation of *all* Israeli settlements as illegal: that the occupation is illegal and therefore so are the settlements; that settlements violate the Geneva Convention; and that the Rome Statute (that established the International Criminal Court) outlaws settlements. The previous section offers a firm rebuttal of the first; Israel's response to the other two has been equally robust and evidence-based.

The 1949 Fourth Geneva Convention, formulated in response both to Nazi atrocities directed primarily against Jews and to the post-war displacement of millions of Europeans, outlawed the forcible transfer of civilians across the international borders of sovereign states ('High Contracting Parties'). These conditions are not met by the settlements as a) all Israeli settlers relocated themselves voluntarily, b) no settlers have crossed internationally recognised borders, c) no Palestinians have been displaced to make way for settlements, and d) prior to 1967, no states held legal sovereignty over the so-called OPTs – to which the Jordanians renounced all claims, excluding the Islamic holy sites, in 1988.

The legal status of the settlements was transformed in 1993 when Israel signed the Oslo Accords with the Palestinian Authority, thereby ending her 'belligerent occupancy' and thus the (theoretical) applicability of the Fourth Geneva Convention. The terms of these accords, formally endorsed by the international community, relegated a resolution of the settlement problem to final status negotiations, all attempts at which have floundered on the rock of Palestinian rejectionism. Moreover, the right of Jews and Arabs to live peaceably and lawfully anywhere is enshrined in international treaties such as the International Covenant on Civil and Political Rights (1966), and the discriminatory denial of either Jewish or Arab rights violates the UN Charter.[11] The Rome Statute of 1998 (that established the International Criminal Court) declared that 'indirect transfer' of civilians was a war crime – a novel notion that had no precedent in international relations. The clause, inserted by the Arab states to attack Israel (given their disappointment at the unsuitability of the Geneva Convention for this purpose), was the reason for Israel's refusal to sign the Statute.

Respected Canadian international lawyer Jacques Gauthier explains that historical events established today's Jewish legal rights in the reconstituted Jewish homeland. The key decisions were taken by the Principal Allied Powers at San Remo in April 1920, endorsed at the Treaty of Sevres in August of that year and then accorded full legal force by the League of Nations Palestine Mandate of 2022.[12] All point to Israel's overriding legal rights to the territories she has held since 1967. The legal Jewish title to Western Palestine (i.e. from the River Jordan to the

Mediterranean Sea), including the right of 'close settlement' (Mandate Article 6), is extant under the UN Charter (Article 80), and is not nullified, as alleged, by military conquest. Declarations by the UN and others that the settlements are illegal reflect political opinions that are not evidence-based.

Three further arguments are relevant here. First, all of the states, with one exception, that emerged from the Mandate system adopted borders derived from the territorial frontiers of the Mandates based on the doctrine of *uti possidetis juris*; that one exception was Israel. Since the UN Charter requires that all states and conflicts be treated equally, Israel has a legitimate claim to sovereignty based on the territorial frontiers of the Palestine Mandate as of May 1948 when she became an independent state. Second, many settlements are located in areas (including Greater Jerusalem) that had not been allocated to the putative Arab state in the 1947 UN partition resolution that was accepted by the Zionist leadership and rejected by their Arab counterparts. Consequently, these areas cannot be retrospectively defined, in legal terms, as 'Palestinian territory'. Third, many settlements are located in places from which Jews were forcibly expelled in 1948 despite having lived there for centuries and to which they held legal title (e.g. Gush Etzion and Jerusalem's Jewish Quarter). None of this information features in pronouncements of the UN and other bodies that declare Israel's settlement policy to be illegal. Meanwhile, clear legal violations of the Oslo Accords by the PA are not just ignored but actually supported by the EU that subsidises illegal settlements in Area C (that is under full Israeli control) to the tune of hundreds of millions of euros.[13]

This unfair treatment of Israel is part of a long-term pattern of discrimination. Such selectivity is a violation of the principle of equality before the law as enshrined in Article 2(1) of the UN Charter and declared by the International Court of Justice to be a fundamental pillar of international law. But for the sake of argument, let us assume that the accusations of illegality hurled against Israel are true. Several governments and international bodies (including the EU) have issued guidance discouraging trade involving Israel's settlements. Yet such no such guidance has been issued in relation to Northern Cyprus, Western Sahara, Tibet and other occupied territories on which settlements have been built.[14] According to both the IHRA definition of antisemitism and the UN charter, criticising Israel for illegal (or other forms of reprehensible policy) behaviour is legitimate and is not antisemitic – provided she is treated in the same way as any other country. There can be no doubt that she is not.

Israel's settlement policies are nevertheless controversial both within Israel and internationally. Putting aside the biblically-inspired rhetoric of religious fundamentalists, there is a legitimate debate to be had about the political wisdom of continuing to encourage Israelis, for military, economic or ideological reasons, to set up home beyond the Green Line (the ceasefire boundaries of 1949). While permitting Jews the right to live peacefully in any part of the world may appear a reasonable manifestation of universal human rights, the consequent irritant effect of such settlement in the context of a volatile and often violent dispute between Israel and her neighbours should not be ignored. But differing political perspectives should be recognised and discussed for what they are. Those who conduct 'lawfare' against Israel deliberately conflate the legal and political arguments surrounding the disputed territories, the settlements and other issues. Statements of law are different from statements of policy or morality.[15] A cruel irony lies at the heart of this matter: if the false legal assertions were put aside, politics might stand a chance. The majority of Israeli settlers live in the large settlement blocs of the West Bank, such as Ma'ale Adumim and Ariel, located close to the 1949 ceasefire lines. This means that almost all of the West Bank could be relinquished to the Palestinians as part of a future peace agreement, while the settlement blocs could be integrated into Israel in a land swap.

Does Israel Use Disproportionate Force Against Palestinians?

The accusation that Israel employs 'disproportionate force' is so widespread that it has acquired sacrosanct status in many quarters including the mainstream media. Again, we see a familiar pattern of inverted, projected emotion at work, for it is Israel's enemies who threaten – and regularly deploy – indiscriminate force against her population. Successive Israeli governments have declared their willingness to eschew the use of force entirely should peace with her neighbours be achieved. Equally, all have insisted on their obligation to protect their people against military attack, terrorism and other existential assaults.

Just War Theory posits that there are circumstances in which war is acceptable and even necessary. From St Augustine in the fourth century to the UN Charter in the twentieth, theologians, philosophers and diplomats have sought to define the conditions under which war is justifiable. First and foremost of these is the principle of defending one's country against an aggressor. Despite its long record of antipathy towards Israel, the UN itself offers legitimacy for Israel's military record. Article 51 of its Charter states: 'Nothing in the present Charter shall impair the inherent right of collective or individual self-defence if an armed attack occurs against a member of the United Nations.'[16]

In all the major conflicts between Israel and Hamas since 2008, Israel has been accused of inflicting avoidable civilian casualties. The laws of war comprise three key principles: distinction, proportionality and caution. The first principle outlaws the targeting of civilian objects such as homes, schools and hospitals but a civilian object may become a legitimate military target if it is used to launch attacks or store weapons. Proportionality requires the use of minimum lethal force to counteract the threat; it does not mean that casualties should be numerically equal on both sides. Finally, caution is necessary to reduce the risk to civilians in or near a military target. The IDF strives to fulfil all three principles: it avoids attacking civilians and ensures that its commanders and troops are aware of that policy; in selecting military targets, it carefully assesses the risks to civilians versus the military advantage, unless returning life-threatening fire, which is legal; and it acts with caution by giving warning to civilians of an impending attack and by aborting missions when a high risk to civilians is discovered. At least until the most recent Hamas-Israel war following the 7 October massacre, the civilian-to-combatant fatality ratio was generally one-to-one or less – considerably better than the average (at least three-to-one) of Western armies involved in asymmetric urban warfare in modern times.

The IDF's strong commitment to ethical standards and adherence to international humanitarian law has been confirmed by external military experts from NATO and other democratic countries.[17] By contrast, Hamas and other terrorist groups are legally responsible for the civilian casualties on both sides by initiating conflict and by breaching all three principles – through targeting civilian objects, seeking to maximise harm to civilians, and recklessly placing its own population, as well as Israel's, at risk by using civilians as cover.

Regarding both the decision to go to war and the protection of civilians in the course of combat, Israelis have always set the bar for war high for themselves while their critics, true to their discriminatory tradition, set it – for Israel alone – virtually beyond reach. Why does the world tolerate this double standard? An even more important question is too rarely asked: what motivates and sustains the enduring belligerence of Israel's enemies? The answer is depressingly straightforward: the violent rejection of the Jewish right to self-determination behind any borders, an unyielding weapon forged on the anvil of antisemitism.

The result is terrorism and asymmetric warfare between the IDF and Palestinian militias (usually Hamas, Hezbollah or Islamic Jihad). These erupt periodically with extreme violence directed at both Israeli soldiers and civilians, particularly the latter as they offer softer targets (as we saw in October 2023). Palestinians invariably justify these incidents as 'resistance operations.' Israel often responds vigorously though she takes meticulous care – probably unmatched in modern warfare – to minimise non-combatant Palestinian casualties even when this places her own personnel at heightened risk. In the full knowledge of that ethical context, foreign governments, for reasons best known to themselves, lecture Israel on her obligation to respond 'proportionately', citing casualty figures of a higher death toll on the Arab and Palestinian sides than on Israel's. 'The numbers speak for themselves' is a favoured mantra, particularly in relation to the conflicts between the IDF and Hamas in the Gaza Strip.

This is illogical, as revealed by expert analyses of Hamas tactics.[18] Firstly, militia fighters are often instructed to dispense with uniforms, in part as a ruse to inflate the apparent number of civilian casualties on their side. Secondly, terrorist militias operating from within Gaza deliberately expose their population to increased risk of injury by placing rocket launchers in densely populated areas, building little or no defensive infrastructure, and denying their residents the opportunity to shelter in the numerous underground tunnels that are the exclusive preserve of the ruling elite and its forces. Israel, by contrast, seeks to protect civilians on both sides, and has invested heavily in a nationwide network of bomb shelters, early warning systems and anti-missile technologies such as the Iron Dome. In Shepherd's words: 'One side treats its people as expendable. The other side treats its people as the top priority for protection. Under such circumstances, equal levels of military action would inevitably lead to greater casualties on the side of Israel's opponents.'[19] Despite that risk, the IDF's careful of analyses of enemy casualties repeatedly show an epidemiological pattern that accords with combatant rather than civilian demographics.[20] A final point demolishes the 'scorecard' argument: the higher fatality rates of the Germans compared to the Allies during the Second World War might lead one to conclude that the fascist Third Reich held a higher moral ground than the democracies that opposed it.

Some critics have moved beyond the debate about proportionality to accuse Israel of premeditated mass murder and a cavalier attitude to Palestinian health and welfare. In a letter to *The Lancet*, a prestigious UK medical journal, a group of doctors denounced Israel's 2014 *Operation Protective Edge*, that was launched against Hamas in response to barrages of rockets fired indiscriminately at her civilians, in terms that amounted to a modern blood libel: 'We challenge the perversity of a propaganda that justifies the creation of an emergency to masquerade a massacre, a so-called "defensive aggression." In reality it is a ruthless assault of unlimited duration, extent, and intensity.'[21] They also alleged the use of 'weaponry known to cause long-term damages on health' and hinted at the 'use of gas.' None of these statements was evidence-based yet that troubled neither the journal nor the more than 20,000 readers who rapidly expressed their support, via an online button, for the letter. The editor, Richard Horton, eventually offered a partial apology but the diatribe was never retracted. This is unsurprising as *The Lancet* has a long track record of demonising Israel, including giving a platform to activists who accuse the country of deliberately neglecting Palestinian healthcare; an in-depth analysis of public health indicators in the West Bank and Gaza post-1967 revealed that the opposite was the case.[22] The field of health, where one might expect to find minimal standards of professional integrity, is just one example of the way an extreme and false narrative about Israel has entered the mainstream.

Is Israel Committing a Genocide of the Palestinians?

At an event marking the fiftieth anniversary of the massacre of eleven Israeli athletes at the Munich Olympic games in 1972, Palestinian President Abbas held a joint press conference in Berlin with German Chancellor Scholz. Abbas not only refused to condemn that atrocity but accused Israel of perpetrating 'fifty holocausts of Palestinians.'[23] That sparked Israeli outrage (though the international response was muted) and he later partially withdrew the remark.

Abbas was following a script first written by his predecessors, the founding fathers of the PLO shortly after it was created in 1964. One booklet lambasted the 'Zionist colonial state for its chosen pattern of racial exclusiveness,' while another compared what it called the Zionist 'chosen race' with the Nazi 'Aryan race.'[24] This theme was taken up by Soviet propagandists in the 1970s. Having adopted the 'Zionism is racism' slogan, it was but a short step for PLO spokesmen to accuse Israelis, without a shred of evidence, of seeking to exterminate the Palestinians. The baseless and obscene idea that Israel is committing genocide is deployed not only by Palestinian leaders and terrorist groups such as Hamas and Hezbollah but by propagandists, intellectuals, religious figures and academics throughout Palestinian society and the wider Arab world.

The genocide libel has spread to the West (and long predated the 2023-24 Hamas-initiated war that re-energised the charge). A 2008 poll of a representative sample non-immigrant European adults (1,000 in each country) found that an average of 40 percent of respondents in participating countries (France, Germany, Great Britain, Hungary, Italy, the Netherlands, Poland and Portugal) affirmed the view that 'the Israeli state is conducting a war of extermination against the Palestinians.' In Poland 63 percent of respondents shared that opinion.[25] Anti-Israel demonstrations in European capitals as well as in the Middle East frequently depict Israeli leaders as Hitler and the Israeli flag merged with a swastika. The deliberate comparison of Israeli defensive actions against Palestinian violence with the mass murder of six million Jews and the sadistic maltreatment of all Europe's Jews, some of whom survived and are alive today in Israel, is *Holocaust inversion*. This casting of 'the victims as perpetrators' is one of the most pervasive examples of contemporary antisemitism in which both reality and morality are inverted.[26]

Projection is again at work: Israel's enemies – including Iran and the proxies that country funds to the tune of at least a billion dollars per year – are explicitly genocidal in their intentions and behaviour. That pattern can be traced back to the Grand Mufti's attacks on unarmed civilians in the 1920s, his alliance with Hitler, and the genocidal threats of successive Arab and Palestinian leaders. And throughout the decades of Israel's existence, the Israeli Arab population has increased tenfold, as has the Arab population of the West Bank and Gaza. What kind of 'genocide' could possibly account for these figures?

Dershowitz writes that one side has attempted genocide during the Arab-Palestinian-Israeli conflict.

> The self-proclaimed Arab War of Extermination in 1948, the targeting of Israeli cities by Arab armies during the 1948, 1967 and 1973 wars, and the continuous terror attacks that have killed thousands of Israeli, Jewish, and other civilians can be characterised as attempted genocide. Israel's efforts to protect its citizens from these mass murders by attacking Arab military targets can only be labelled genocide by a bigot willing to engage in Orwellian turnspeak against a people that was truly victimised by the worst form of genocide.[27]

Shepherd suggests that the allegation of Israeli genocide against the Palestinians is so grotesque and divorced from reality that its purpose is purely to heap scorn, contempt and hatred upon Israel, the most potent symbol of modern Jewry.[28] The radical left are particularly fond of the Nazi smear as it is emblematic of the ultimate 'fascist' evil. When *The Observer* published a poem[29] comparing the Israeli army to the SS, and a distinguished Nobel laureate for literature compared the suffering Israel inflicts on Palestinians to the Nazi persecution of Jews,[30] all red lines had been crossed. The seepage of this type of demonising discourse into the mainstream media would have been inconceivable in the immediate aftermath of the Second World War but it is now such a regular occurrence that it would be a mistake to underestimate its impact on public opinion.

Was Israel's Creation – and Survival – Due to the Support of USA?

On 9 June 1967, In the midst of the Six Day War, Egyptian President Nasser broadcast these words to his people:

> In the morning of last Monday, 5 June, the enemy struck. If we say now it was a stronger blow than we had expected, we must say at the same time and with complete certainty that it was bigger than the potential at his disposal. It became very clear from the first moment that there were other powers behind the enemy.[31]

Nasser was referring to the UK and, especially, the USA. In the jargon of his political backers in Moscow, who had exploited dysfunctional authoritarian regimes throughout the Middle East for their own geostrategic purposes, the Arab defeat was a result of the intervention of the 'imperialists' in the early hours of the war. That scenario was, of course, fictional. It had been invented to save the faces of both the Soviet and Arab leadership. The Soviet Union viewed Israel as a US outpost, a colonial creation of the capitalist West, and one that had severely embarrassed their Arab allies to whom they had supplied state-of-the-art weaponry for many years. Israel's victory in 1967 compromised the reputation of the USSR itself and so any alibi, however implausible, was useful.

Nasser's speech was revealing in another way: it exposed the contempt with which the Egyptian leader, schooled in all matters Jewish by the antisemitic Muslim Brotherhood, viewed Israelis. That contempt had deep roots. For most Arabs, it was axiomatic that Jews – an inferior *dhimmi* minority throughout the Muslim world for centuries – were cowards incapable of winning a war without the help of a powerful ally. To this day, the 'Arab street' believes two specific fabrications: that America, forced into action by the Jewish lobby, won the Six Day War for Israel and that, as a result of American hesitancy, Egypt and Syria won the 1973 (Yom Kippur) War for the Arabs.

In the twenty-first century, the idea of Israel and the US scheming in lockstep to dominate the Middle East is a core belief of the progressive left that seeks to apply the intersectionality principle to Zionism, imperialism, slavery and other forms of oppression. On this issue, ideologists of the far left and far right converge (the Horseshoe Effect), are cheered on from the side-lines by Islamists, and are of one mind – that Jews control the US government through the dark arts of an all-powerful pro-Israel lobby. In their racist paranoia, they are buttressed by a coterie of Western academics such as Mearsheimer and Walt who invoke the classic antisemitic trope of a Zionist conspiracy manipulating American foreign policy to serve Israel's interests.[32]

The US is a strong ally of Israel but the bond between the two countries is far from the unshakeable constant that is widely assumed. As so often, the historical evidence points to the need for a more nuanced view. Although the US supported both the Balfour Declaration of 1917 and the subsequent League of Nations Mandate that instructed Britain to re-establish a Jewish national home in Palestine, it declined, at the Evian conference of 1938, to offer the trapped Jews of Europe sanctuary from Hitler. As for Jewish efforts to reverse the British betrayal of the Mandate and establish a safe haven for the remnants of their people after the Holocaust, the US was unenthusiastic about the UN partition plan of 1947 and offered no assistance whatsoever to Israel during her War of Independence. As historian George Simpson explains:

> Washington's actual support for the Zionists was ambiguous, halting, and limited. Its support for partition followed that of Moscow and was virtually confined to the White House, which acted against the staunch opposition of the Department of State and the Pentagon. Indeed, not only did the State Department collaborate with the British to exclude the Negev from the territory of the prospective state of Israel (only to be foiled by Truman), but in late 1947, State [Dept] orchestrated a regional arms embargo that left the Palestine Jews highly disadvantaged.[33]

After that unpropitious start, the American posture towards Israel lurched back and forth in the succeeding decades. Yet the much-touted economic, military and diplomatic US-Israel alliance is often regarded as the ultimate secret weapon in Israel's armoury. Middle East analyst Sean Durns disagrees:

> It is a common, albeit false, assumption that the United States and Israel closely cooperated since the Jewish state's recreation in 1948. The State Department and the Pentagon had argued that US support for Israel would be a strategic liability. America, in turn, often kept Israel at arm's length, both forcing the Jewish state to give up territory won in the 1956 Suez War against Nasser and prohibiting weapon sales until 1962.[34]

The US remained pointedly cool to Israel – to the point of maintaining an arms embargo on the country – throughout the 1950s, when first Czechoslovakia and then France provided crucial military support at a period of greatest danger to the renascent Jewish state. In a stunning revelation by Irish diplomat Conor Cruise O'Brien, the US abandoned Israel at least three times in the face of veiled threats by the Soviet Union to annihilate the tiny country – in 1956, 1970 and 1973 – by declining to offer Israel protection under its nuclear umbrella.[35] This alarming fickleness on the part of her closest ally must have been a major factor in Israel's (presumed) decision to develop an independent nuclear deterrent. In the 1980s, the pro-Israel President Reagan publicly criticised Israel's actions in Lebanon and annexation of the Golan Heights. He punished Israel by holding up arms deliveries and suspending strategic cooperation. Reagan also clashed with prime minister Menachem Begin over the sale of AWACS (an airborne early warning system) to the Saudis. As for formal alliances, Israel's claim on US support in times of crisis is weaker than that of Montenegro or Albania – both NATO members, unlike Israel. If Turkey, an increasingly Islamist and anti-Western NATO country, is threatened with attack, the US is obliged to help. Israel has no such protection.

US diplomatic support for Israel in the UN is often characterised as obstructive to progress towards a fair settlement between Israel and the Palestinians. This is untrue. When President Barack Obama, one of the most pro-Palestinian US leaders, refused to veto the harshly anti-Israel UN Security Council resolution 2334 in 2016, it was followed by no discernible progress towards peace – if anything, Palestinian positions hardened. Obama may have been influenced by the growing culture of anti-Zionism in his academic circles. In this respect he resembled his predecessor, Jimmy Carter, whose expressed policy of creating 'daylight' between the US and Israel led to his rejection by a majority of Jewish voters, whom Carter then falsely blamed for his 1980 re-election defeat. According to former Israeli ambassador to the US Michael Oren, Obama (like Carter) saw Israel as persecutor rather than victim.[36] And (also like Carter), he blamed US peace-making failures on Israel – despite the previously hawkish Begin's agreement in 1978 to withdraw from all of the strategically and economically important Sinai peninsula to secure a peace treaty with Egypt.

What about financial support for Israel's armed forces? Does not the US Treasury virtually underwrite Israel's purchases of advanced weaponry to maintain her qualitative military edge? That is another half-truth, at best. The US only provided substantial financial support to Israel after 1978 – and then it was conditional on recycling most aid back to the US. Currently 75 per cent of US military aid to Israel must be spent in the US – a figure that will rise higher in a few years – and thus supports the American rather than the Israeli economy. Much of the rest is spent in joint projects (such as the Iron Dome missile defence system) that benefits US as well as Israeli security.

Few commentators seem aware that US military support to the Arab and Muslim world dwarfs (by a factor of around six) that given to Israel. Even Donald Trump, said to have been the most pro-Israel president in US history, insisted on selling a massive package of F-35 fighter jets and MQ-9 unmanned systems to the United Arab Emirates as part of the 2020 Abraham Accords – with more lucrative arms sales to Arab states in the pipeline – riding roughshod over the Israeli defence establishment's explicit opposition. In summary, while many US presidents have publicly expressed sympathy for Israel, US foreign and defence policy is generally moulded by the State and Defence departments that have been consistently cool and at times openly hostile to Israel's predicament.

Shepherd contends that a combination of anti-capitalism, anti-Americanism, antisemitism and anti-Israelism form a tangled cluster of New Left ideologies that draw on the Cold War polarisation in which Israel, having started out as a *cause celebre* of the liberal left, was relocated to the other side of the political spectrum.[37] Progressives now enthusiastically peddle the counterfactual Soviet-era myth of an Israel created by a capitalist-Jewish-American alliance. For their tribe, this sinister collusion 'explains' what they see as an all-powerful and unbreakable US-Israel axis, forged by the hidden tentacles of a global Zionist conspiracy and sustained by an irresistible American pro-Israel lobby. They should be called out for what they are: purveyors of an antisemitically motivated falsehood.

Is Palestinian Anger Caused by Israel's Rejection of the Two-state Solution?

Calling for a Palestinian state is not antisemitic but demanding the destruction of Israel is, and blaming Israel exclusively on its absence – in the face of easily accessible, extensive contrary evidence – is a form of demonising antisemitism. Anyone who has witnessed a pro-Palestine demonstration will have heard this slogan being chanted: 'From the river to the sea, Palestine will be free!' Those words assert that all of Israel plus the West Bank are Palestinian and that Israel is an illegitimate entity. They also imply that the Palestinian nation is being held captive by Israel that occupies their land. In other words, the absence of freedom from which the Palestinians suffer is attributable to the existence of Israel. The corollary is that Israel must disappear to enable the Palestinians to acquire freedom.

Sympathetic as many Israelis are towards the Palestinians' aspirations to freedom, they are understandably reluctant to commit suicide to pave the way for the fulfilment of this goal. If the demonstrators' vision is accepted, it consigns Israelis and Palestinians to endless conflict, or at least until one side prevails over the other – the classic zero-sum-game. Fortunately for Israelis and Palestinians, there is an exit strategy. All that is required is for each side to acknowledge the right of the other to self-determination – the famous two-state solution or, more accurately, the 'two states for two peoples' solution. What is more, one side – Israel (and the pre-state Zionist movement) has done exactly that for close to a century – while the other has not.

Two years after the Balfour declaration of 1917, the Zionist leader, Chaim Weizmann, reached an amicable agreement with Faisal, son of Emir Hussein of Mecca and the undisputed leader of the Arab world, whereby the right of self-determination of both Jews and Arabs was recognised. (Faisal later tore up that accord). When Great Britain was granted the Palestine Mandate by the League of Nations in 1920, the territory allocated to the embryonic Jewish national home spanned both sides of the Jordan. In their desire to defuse Arab hostility to the Mandate, the British decided to enforce a discretionary clause in the Mandate to create a large Arab state, Transjordan, that had no prior historical, political or cultural identity, in 78 per cent of Palestine. That decision (to which the Americans are believed to have given a discreet green light) was taken without consultation with the Zionist leadership who were, understandably, displeased – particularly as this new country, carved out of the prospective Jewish homeland, was barred to Jews. But in the interests of peace, Chaim

Weizmann adopted a policy of territorial compromise that would characterise all key future Jewish decision-making in the region, and reluctantly agreed to what was, in effect, the first partition plan. Unfortunately, the Arab leadership was far less inclined to adopt a similar strategy and conflict became inevitable.

Although a Palestinian Arab state had existed since 1922, the pre-Israel Zionist leadership twice more accepted proposals for a second Palestinian state – first in 1937 (the Peel Commission) and again in 1947 (the UN partition plan). In both cases, the Arab leadership rejected the 'two-state solution.' Despite their reservations, the Zionists accepted proposals (on more than one occasion) for a Palestinian state alongside Israel decades earlier than anyone else in the Middle East.

A long litany of missed opportunities for peace and mutual coexistence followed.[38] A few examples: the Rhodes Armistice Conference of 1949 that was supposed to lead to peace treaties but was frustrated by Arab intransigence; UN Security Council resolutions 242 (1967) and 338 (1973) that were met by the Three Nos of the Arab League; the 1978 Camp David accords (between Sadat, Begin and Carter) where an empty chair for Arafat symbolised his abrogation of responsibility for the future of his people; the 1993-5 Oslo accords that Arafat appeared to embrace – following his 'recognition' of Israel in 1988 that was contradicted by his simultaneous demand for the 'right of return' – but refused to follow through with a negotiated peace; the 2000 Camp David summit where Israeli PM Ehud Barak offered Arafat at least 92 per cent of the West Bank and shared sovereignty of Jerusalem; the 2001 Taba event where Bill Clinton set out his Parameters for Peace and was snubbed by Arafat who was too busy whipping up the deadly Second 'Intifada'; the 2003 initiative of US President George W Bush who set out a Roadmap for Peace; the 2008 conference at Annapolis when Israeli PM Olmert offered Abbas even more than Barak had offered Arafat – 94 per cent of the West Bank plus 6 per cent in land swaps; the recurrent efforts throughout 2014-16 during the Obama administration when the Kerry-Allen and Biden plans were tabled and dismissed by Abbas; the 2020 Trump administration's Deal of the Century, rejected in advance by Abbas, that provided for a Palestinian state in most of the West Bank plus ultimately Gaza.

Every attempt to grant the Palestinians their freedom was ground to dust by the Palestinian leadership's irresponsible posture of hostility to the idea of a Jewish state behind any borders. Israel unilaterally withdrew from all of the Gaza Strip in 2005 in an attempt to test the waters of Palestinian self-rule that might have led to Palestinian statehood. None of these opportunities created by Israel has ever been reciprocated. On the contrary, they have been met by increased aggression and terrorism.

Recognition of rights has to be mutual or it is meaningless. Arab and Palestinian leaders have remained steadfastly opposed to the existence of Jewish sovereignty anywhere in the Middle East for over a hundred years despite some latterly professing approval not of the 'two states for two peoples' solution but of the 'two-state solution,' a hollow phrase that would, if implemented, result in two Arab states at the expense of Israel.

Far from opposing Palestinian freedom, Israelis have consistently accepted the right of the Palestinian Arabs to achieve their national goals, while the Palestinians and most Arab leaders (plus some Muslim countries led by Islamist Iran) have repeatedly refused to accord reciprocal rights to Israelis. This double standard is indefensible and discriminatory. It also acts as an obstacle to peace though it is rarely recognised as such by an international community whose vision is clouded by its obsessive focus on Israel as the sole party that is held perennially responsible for the deadlock.

Are Arab Threats Against Jews Mere Rhetoric?

Some commentators regard spine-chilling antisemitic threats from Middle Eastern leaders as colourful Arab rhetoric that need not and should not be understood literally. History permits us to judge the folly of that complacency; mass murder, wherever it occurs, is often preceded by verbal incitement. That had been the experience of Europe's Jews and Israel was intent on avoiding a repeat performance a few years later. The world as a whole remained coldly indifferent to the new state's plight as a chorus of Arab threats of impending slaughter were heard in all their nightmarish clarity only by its intended targets. Israel's protests were ignored even by her hypocritical fair-weather 'friends.'

The relative rarity of Arab massacres of Jews in the 1947-49 war has been cited as evidence that Arab rhetoric is all hot air. Leading Israeli revisionist historian Benny Morris suggests that this reflects the course of the war: 'Arab rhetoric may have been more blood curdling and inciteful to atrocity than Jewish public rhetoric – but the war itself afforded the Arabs infinitely fewer opportunities to massacre their foes.'[39]

Regarding ethnic cleansing, Morris has this to say:

> Both national movements entered the mid-1940s with an expulsionist element in their ideological baggage. Among the Zionists, it was a minor and secondary element, occasionally

entertained and enunciated by key leaders, including Ben-Gurion and Chaim Weizmann. But it had not been part of the original Zionist ideology and was usually trotted out in response to expulsionist or terroristic violence by the Arabs....Nonetheless, transfer or expulsion was never adopted by the Zionist movement or its main political groupings as official policy at any stage of the movement's evolution – not even in the 1948 war.[40]

The victorious Jewish forces had ample opportunity to conduct massacres or mass expulsions of Arabs from the territories over which they gained control; they chose not to do so. By contrast, when an opportunity presented itself to Arab forces, Jews were ethnically cleansed from Jerusalem and Judea and Samaria (the West Bank) by Jordanian troops in 1948 and by most MENA states between 1950 and 1972, and massacred without hesitation (in, for example, Hebron in 1929, and at Gush Etzion and Mount Scopus in 1948) when circumstances permitted.

Threats of mass murder or genocide should never be dismissed lightly. In case of scepticism, the Hamas murderers of 7 October 2023 proved more than willing to banish any remaining doubts as to their intentions.

Counterarguments: Summary of the Evidence

Where does this review of the evidence pertaining to these allegations lead? Any fair-minded observer would dismiss the charges out of hand, for they are not only unsupported by evidence but in many cases the inverse of the truth. Establishing their falsity is a necessary undertaking in itself but a second, related insight is equally valuable: disseminating falsehoods about Israel on such a scale can have only one purpose – the demonisation of Zionism and Israel to the point where any sympathy demonstrated for either is denounced as complicity with a criminal, racist and homicidal state.

The evidence is unequivocal, offering no support for the null hypotheses. All fourteen of the Israel-related 'articles of faith' reviewed in this and the previous chapter are false.

Notes

1   United Nations, International Convention on the Suppression and Punishment of the Crime of Apartheid, G.A. resolution 3068, 1974. https://www.un.org/en/genocideprevention/documents/atrocity-crimes/

Doc.10_International%20Convention%20on%20the%20Suppression%20a
nd%20Punishment%20of%20the%20Crime%20of%20Apartheid.pdf
(Last accessed 12 June 2024)

2 Weiss Reuven, 'Poll: 77 per cent of Arabs say they won't replace Israel', *Ynet News*, 23 June 2008. http://www.ynetnews.com/articles/0,7340,l-3559045,00.html (Last accessed 12 June 2024)

3 D. Rich, *The Left's Jewish Problem* (London: Biteback Publishing, 2018), p. 34.

4 Elder of Ziyon blog, 'A Short List of Palestinian Violations of Agreements Signed with Israel', 12 September 2022. https://elderofziyon.blogspot.com/2022/09/a-short-list-of-palestinian-violations.html (Last accessed 12 June 2024)

5 S. Aizenberg, *Amnesty International's Cruel Assault on Israel: Systematic Lies, Errors, Omissions and Double Standards in Amnesty's Apartheid Report* (Jerusalem: NGO Monitor, April 2022). https://www.ngo-monitor.org/reports/amnesty-internationals-cruel-assault-on-israel/ (Last accessed 12 June 2024)

6 S. Aizenberg, *A Threshold Crossed: Documenting HRW'S "Apartheid" Fabrications* (Jerusalem: NGO Monitor, November 2022). https://www.ngo-monitor.org/reports/threshold-crossed-hrw-apartheid/ (Last accessed 12 June 2024)

7 A. Johnson, *The Apartheid Smear* (London: BICOM, 2014), p.5.

8 R. Sabel, 'International Legal Issues of the Arab-Israeli Conflict: An Israeli Lawyer's Position', *Journal of East Asia and International Law* 2010, 3,2. p.415.

9 R. Higgins, 'The Place of International Law in the Settlement of Disputes by the Security Council', *American Journal of International Law* 1970, 64, pp.1-15.

10 J-P. Grumberg, 'Israel is the legal occupant of the West Bank, says the Court of Appeal of Versailles', Dreuz, 13 January 2017. https://www.dreuz.info/2017/01/israel-is-the-legal-occupant-of-the-west-bank-says-the-court-of-appeal-of-versailles-france-124054.html (Last accessed 12 June 2024)

11 United Nations Charter (Full Text), Preamble, Article 2(1). Geneva, United Nations, 1945. https://www.un.org/en/about-us/un-charter/full-text (Last accessed 12 June 2024)

12 H. Sela, 'Dr Jacques Gauthier – The Jewish Claim to Jerusalem: The Case Under International Law', CAMERA 23 November 2013. https://camera-uk.org/2013/11/23/dr-jacques-gauthier-the-jewish-claim-to-jerusalem-the-case-under-international-law/ (Last accessed 12 June 2024)

13 A. Koningsveld, 'How European Union Funding of West Bank Activities Breaches International Law and Undermines Peace', *Honest Reporting*, 31

March 2022. https://honestreporting.com/honestreporting-exclusive-how-european-union-funding-of-west-bank-activities-breaches-intl-law-under mines-peace/ (Last accessed 12 June 2024).

14 E. Kontorovich, 'Unsettled: a global study of settlements in occupied territories', *Journal of Legal Analysis*, Winter 2017, pp.285-350. https://doi.org/10.1093/jla/lax004 (Last accessed 12 June 2024).

15 M. Blois, A. Tucker, *Israel on Trial: How International Law is Being Misused to Delegitimize the State of Israel* (The Netherlands: thinc.,2018), p.352.

16 United Nations Charter (Full Text), Chapter VII, Article 51. Geneva, United Nations, 1945. https://www.un.org/en/about-us/un-charter/full-text (Last accessed 12 June 2024).

17 High Level Military Group, 'Israel's Security Challenges Today: An Assessment', HLMG April 2019, p28-29. http://www.high-level-military-group.org/pdf/hlmg-israels-security-challenges-today.pdf (Last accessed 12 June 2024).

18 Y. Cohen, J. White, 'Hamas in Combat: The Military Performance of the Palestinian Islamic Resistance Movement', Washington Institute for Near East Policy, Policy Focus 97, October 2009. https://www.washingtoninstitute.org/media/3416 (Last accessed 12 June 2024).

19 R. Shepherd, *A State Beyond the Pale.* (London: Orion Books, 2009), p.139-140.

20 Haviv Rettig Gur, Adiv Sterman, 'IDF indiscriminately killing in Gaza? Data says no', *Times of Israel*, 8 August 2014. https://www.timesofisrael.com/idf-indiscriminately-killing-in-gaza-data-says-no/ (Last accessed 12 June 2024).

21 P. Manduca, I. Chalmers, D. Summerfield et al, 'An open letter for the people in Gaza', *Lancet*, 23 July 2014 http://www.thelancet.com/journals/lancet/article/PIIS0140-6736(14)61044-8/fulltext (Last accessed 12 June 2024).

22 D. Stone, 'Has Israel damaged Palestinian health? An evidence-based analysis of the nature and impact of Israeli public health policies practices in the West Bank and Gaza', *Fathom*, Autumn 2014. https://fathomjournal.org/has-israel-damaged-palestinian-health/ (Last accessed 12 June 2024).

23 Philip Oltermann, 'Uproar after Mahmoud Abbas in Berlin accuses Israel of 50 Holocausts', *Guardian*, 17 August 2022. https://www.theguardian.com/world/2022/aug/17/uproar-after-mahmoud-abbas-in-berlin-accuses-israel-of-50-holocausts (Last accessed 12 June 2024).

24 See Rich, *The Left's Jewish Problem*, p. 19-20.

25 A. Zick, B. Küpper, A. Hövermann, *Intolerance, Prejudice and Discrimination. A European Report* (Berlin: Friedrich-Ebert-Stiftung, 2011), pp.57-58. https://library.fes.de/pdf-files/do/07908-20110311.pdf (Last accessed 12 June 2024).

26 L. Klaff, 'Holocaust Inversion and Contemporary Antisemitism', *Fathom*, Winter 2014. https://fathomjournal.org/holocaust-inversion-and-contemporary-antisemitism/ (Last accessed 12 June 2024).

27 A. Dershowitz, *The Case for Israel* (Hoboken: John Wiley & Sons, 2003), p.152-3.

28 See Shepherd, *A State Beyond The Pale*, p.116.

29 Tom Paulin, 'Killed in Crossfire', *Observer*, 18 February 2001. https://www.theguardian.com/books/2001/feb/18/poetry.features1 (Last accessed 12 June 2024).

30 See Shepherd, *A State Beyond The Pale*, pp. 60-61.

31 W. Laqueur, B. Rubin B (eds), *The Israel-Arab Reader* (London: Penguin Books, 2008), p.104.

32 J. Mearsheimer, S. Walt, *The Israel Lobby and US Foreign Policy* (New York: Farrar, Straus and Giroux,2007).

33 G. Simpson, 'Revisiting the US role in three Middle East crises', *Middle East Quarterly*, Summer, 2018.

34 S. Durns, 'Black September remembered: how the PLO forged the modern Middle East', *The National Interest*, 21 August 2020.

35 C.C. O'Brien, *The Siege* (London, Paladin Books, 1988).

36 M. Oren, *Ally* (New York: Random House, 2015).

37 See Shepherd, *A State Beyond The Pale*, p.53.

38 D. Ross, *The Missing Peace: The Inside Story of the Fight for Middle East Peace* (New York: Farrar, Straus and Giroux, 2005).

39 See B. Morris, *1948*, p.405.

40 Ibid. p.407.

10

Time to Confront the Elephant – and End the Conflict

Ending the Arab-Israeli conflict is self-evidently a major challenge. No effective prescription – the much-touted 'two-state solution' included – is readily available or it would have been dispensed long ago. Nevertheless, the evidence outlined in this book suggests that there is unrealised potential in taking the following two interlinked steps: reviewing the evidence to enhance understanding of the root causes of the conflict rather than its myriad manifestations, and using these insights to take remedial action. Academia has a special responsibility for the first; all of us have a role in the second.

Antisemitic Anti-Israelism Drives the Conflict

Post-1945, the expression of Jew-hatred, while no longer acceptable in polite society, had to find an outlet; it may have mutated not just into anti-Zionism but into quasi-psychotic beliefs about the Jewish state. A psychosis is a mental disturbance characterised by a cognitive and emotional loss of contact with reality. This is an apt descriptor of the delusional suite of malevolent accusations launched against Israel on a daily basis; some of these have been discussed in detail in previous chapters.

The evidence is compelling that a hatred of Jews, conscious or otherwise, lies at the root of the vilification of Israel. Antisemitism is a mass psychosocial disorder that has never disappeared but continuously evolves. It expresses itself in various ways depending on the circumstances. A peculiar set of circumstances arose in the MENA region in the twentieth century that generated a new and dangerous version of antisemitism.

Goldhagen's hypothesis concerning German antisemitism may be reformulated with respect to the overlapping hostility to Israel of both Western intellectual elites and Arab-Muslims. A number of *culturally shared cognitive models of Jews* may have evolved over centuries in both the Christian West and the Islamic MENA region. The models may differ in their nature and chronology but they appear to share common features: both viewed Jews as contemptible, alien and dangerous, and both provided a substrate for toxic mutations that created conducive conditions for genocide in the twentieth and twenty-first centuries. In the MENA region, a specific antisemitic mutation – forged by an ideological fusion of Islamism and Nazism – continues to promote an uncompromising version of anti-Zionism and anti-Israelism, both of which have attracted numerous admirers (including, disturbingly, a minority of Jews) in every corner of the globe.

Two examples illustrate the phenomenon. The late Portuguese Nobel Laureate José Saramago updated the old blood libel via a form of Holocaust inversion: 'What is happening in Palestine is a crime we can put on the same plane as what happened at Auschwitz,'[1] a view enthusiastically echoed by Israeli writer Yitzchak Laor: 'Gas chambers are not the only way to destroy a nation, it is enough to develop high rates of infant mortality.'[2]

To describe such fulminations as irrational would be an under-statement. Yet these and similarly bizarre opinions are regarded as normal in the MENA region and those who share them have found welcoming platforms throughout the world to disseminate their crackpot theories. Many of these so-called experts, who cavalierly ignore evidence to promote their fictional narrative of a brutal and illegitimate Israel, include university professors who receive lavish praise from peers and have become global celebrities. This dislocation from reality appears – to those looking in from the outside – a form of mass insanity; reverse the roles and imagine how it looks to those on the inside looking out, and it all makes sense. That is the nature of delusional thinking. For those experiencing it, the fantasies are real and those who challenge them are mistaken, or part of a conspiracy to suppress the truth.

An alternative explanation is that the proponents of grotesque fabri-cations about Israel are cynical liars, peddling falsehoods for propagandistic or political reasons. Both interpretations may be simultaneously true but in either case the end result is the demonisation of Israel that attracts a large and unsavoury following of antisemites who are all too willing to join the fray. Social media, as Israeli writer Shoshanna Keats Jaskoll has observed, have added a new dimension to the disease: 'What we see online is a mass of misinformation…. The result is that masses of people around the world think that Israel feeds on the blood of Palestinian babies just as the Nazis – and Christians before them – believed that we fed on the blood of their babies.'[3]

Human rights organisations such as *Human Rights Watch*, *Amnesty International* and *Oxfam*, never slow to criticise Israel, turned venomous in 2001 after the NGO Durban 'antiracism' conference, effectively an anti-Israel hate-fest that incubated the BDS (Boycott, Divestment and Sanctions) movement. Many BDS supporters proclaim their devotion to universal human rights yet appear unmoved by BDS spokesman Omar Barghouti's call to 'euthanise' Israel.[4] Demanding the destruction of a state and condemning most of its inhabitants to homelessness or worse should be ethically unacceptable to all.

The outcome of such discourse is the normalisation of hateful views about Jews and Israel. Ben-Dror Yemini puts the matter starkly: 'When these statements are circulated in an atmosphere that is antagonistic to Israel, created as a result of similar lies made by other lecturers and journalists, the lies become truth.'[5] Wider public opinion, shaped by ill-informed or malicious journalistic filtering of extreme ideas into the mass media, inevitably follows suit. That is as dangerous to Jews as previous incarnations of classic antisemitism. The extensive dissemination of a warped view of Israel drags moderate opinion towards extremism that increasingly appears acceptable. What should have been dismissed as an unimportant lunatic fringe has been warmly embraced by NGOs, the media, politicians, academia, churches and trade unions. These are all strong influencers of public opinion. In 2003, at the height of Arafat's terrorist campaign against Israelis, a European survey found that 60 per cent of respondents regarded Israel as the greatest threat to world peace.[6] In 2005, Clare Short, a UK cabinet minister, asserted that 'the oppression of the Palestinian people is the major cause of bitter division and violence in the world.'[7] There we have it – the classic Nazi trope of the Jewish threat to all of humanity has morphed into the scapegoating of Israel as the root of all evil.

Another damaging effect of this delusional mindset is a dysfunctional international political response to the conflict. The UN and its agencies have been recruited as combatants in the continuation of the Arab war against Israel of 1948. An organisation that was created in the wake of the horrors of the Holocaust and is ostensibly committed to peace, equality and human rights for all, condemns the Jewish state more than any other country.[8] The UN Human Rights Council, for example, appoint individuals well-known for their extreme anti-Israelism as special advisors; they then exploit their position to demonise Israel. The same behaviour occurs in other branches of the UN such as UNESCO (that erases the Jewish historical connection to Judaism's holiest sites), the Economic and Social Council (that accuses Israel of being the world's foremost violator of women's rights), and the World Health Assembly (that claims Israel denies Palestinians healthcare).

Most producers and consumers of news or commentary about the Arab-Israeli conflict have no awareness that antisemitic ideation about Israel even exists. They therefore cannot be expected to understand its origin – the destructive cultural cognitive model of Jews that pollutes the intellectual environment of the MENA region and much of the rest of the world. This all but guarantees that the boundary between fact and fiction in all matters relating to the conflict remains semi-permeable. Until that ignorance is banished, a false narrative will cripple all diplomatic initiatives and effective peace-making will prove impossible.

Academia: a Hostile Environment for Jews

Universities are breeding grounds for the future intellectual and political leaders of our planet and so play a critical role in determining the fate of all of us. They are also repositories of knowledge and laboratories of research designed to assist our understanding of the world around us. But academia today is a hostile environment for the evidence-based exchange of ideas about Jews, Zionism, Israel and the dynamics of the Arab-Israeli conflict. Reasoned debate is no longer tolerated. Many Jews feel alienated and rejected on the grounds that they are maliciously labelled 'Zionists' and even no-platformed. The university campus, the one place that an honest and nuanced examination of evidence should be encouraged, has become a cesspit of prejudice and intolerance.

Higher education has been hijacked by a 'progressive' ideology that proclaims itself to be antiracist but is in effect hostile to Jews and their aspirations to freedom and security. What is to be done? American academic Cary Nelson calls for a robust response to attempts to silence pro-Israeli voices:

> The standard for appropriate academic conduct has long been that the speakers invited by a bona fide campus academic group deserve to give a public lecture uninterrupted. People can protest quietly by holding signs during a lecture or standing to signal their disapproval. I believe a brief noisy demonstration before a lecture begins, perhaps a minute in length, is also acceptable, but that repeatedly interrupting a lecture or trying to apply a heckler's veto and preventing a lecture from taking place should be a punishable offence.[9]

Hirsh, a UK scholar of antisemitism, offers a suggestion: 'The task is nothing less than to change the intellectual weather and to turn around some powerful and enduring intellectual tendencies that have been building for decades; that threaten Jews, and that weaken the democratic state.'[10] How can the intellectual weather be changed? Hirsh is circumspect about this. It is a task that will take years of sustained effort in the face of apathy, scepticism and hostility. Building a critical mass of academics who are committed to meeting the challenge will be necessary. That includes promoting major research initiatives such as the opening in 2022 of the London Centre for the Study of Contemporary Antisemitism[11] and granting it the academic status and financial support it deserves.

Towards Resolving the Conflict

Identifying the cause of a problem is only half-way to solving it. Even if the evidence that a culturally determined antisemitism is the key driver of the hostility to Israel is credible, how should it be confronted and, ideally, removed from the equation? There is no panacea but a strategic approach is necessary. The so-called two-state solution is often cited as the key. This concept, as it is usually understood, requires critical scrutiny, as does the related (but not always synonymous) 'two states for two peoples.'

Two States for Two Peoples – or Two Arab States?

The Arab-Israeli conflict is usually defined as a territorial one between two peoples struggling to establish sovereignty over the same small geographical space. All attempts to mediate over the past eight decades have proposed an obvious answer: share it. This should not be a zero-sum game. Even if we set aside the British division of the original Palestine Mandate (roughly the area comprising today's Israel and Jordan) into two embryonic sovereign territories for Jews and Arabs in 1922, the two-state solution could have been brought into existence between the river Jordan and the Mediterranean Sea decades ago. Why did it not happen? The answer is that one side accepted the idea while the other rejected it, as described in previous chapters. Though the Arab position was hypocritical, it was consistent – no Jewish state within any borders would ever be acceptable because Jews were not entitled to one. That rejectionism is only compatible with the two-state solution if both states are Arab.

Rejecting Jewish sovereignty – a modern political incarnation of antisemitism – is the reason the 'two states' formula has failed to date as a solution even to the narrowly-focused Israeli-Palestinian element of the conflict. It could still work its magic – on one condition. As soon as the

Palestinians and their international backers abandon antisemitism and accept a Jewish sovereign presence as of right, the 'two states for two peoples' solution might finally deliver peace. That condition has not yet been met.

Beyond Oslo

To rewind to the 1990s: the Oslo Accords offered a transient chink of light amidst a gloomy landscape. Mutual recognition beckoned, briefly and tantalisingly, across the diplomatic horizon but remains an unfulfilled aspiration. The arrangements that the Accords produced were designed to be temporary pending the conclusion of negotiations on the final status issues – borders, security, settlements, refugees, Jerusalem and an end to the conflict.

Repeated attempts to resolve these issues have failed for various reasons, the most important of which has been the Palestinian insistence on a non-existent 'right of return' of the Palestinian refugees from the 1947-49 war. This unrealistic aspiration – that of all the world's refugee problems is exclusive to the Palestinians – has been wilfully and cruelly reinforced by UNRWA, the special UN agency established to deal with this issue, and by the international donors (led by the US) who fund it. The antisemitic rejectionism embodied into the institutional culture of UNRWA is now arguably the single most intractable impediment to peace.[12] That is exactly its purpose. What was created as a temporary humanitarian agency is now the standard-bearer of antisemitism, the underlying cause and continuing driver of the conflict. The 'right of return' is the backstop, the last line of defence against what remains an unthinkable scenario for most Arabs – a legally binding, mutually agreed Jewish sovereign state living peacefully with its neighbours in the Middle East.

It is not credible for Palestinian leaders to protest that they support two states while simultaneously demanding the 'return' to Israel of over five million Palestinian descendants of the original refugees. If Israel were to accept such a condition, she would be committing demographic suicide as a Jewish state – Israel's internationally endorsed *raison d'être*.[13] Israeli leaders have never been opposed in principle to Palestinian sovereignty. While it is true that several Israeli governments and leaders have expressed opposition to the establishment of a hostile Palestinian state on their doorstep, five of the last seven Israeli prime ministers have publicly expressed support for 'two states for two peoples.' We await the first Palestinian leader to do the same.

In 2020, an apparent breakthrough in Israeli-Arab relations occurred with the signing of the US-mediated Abraham Accords between Israel and two Gulf states (United Arab Emirates and Bahrain) plus Morocco and (somewhat precariously) Sudan. Other similar agreements may follow. While undoubtedly welcome, the long-term implications of this partial Israeli-Arab reconciliation for the future of the Israeli-Palestinian dimension of the conflict remain unclear. These treaties fail to address the heart of the problem – not the lack of a Palestinian state, as so often claimed, but the persistent collective Arab (and Iranian) inability to set aside their antisemitic prejudices and affirm the Jewish right to sovereignty in a portion of the historical Land of Israel once and for all. That failure has been compounded by a second one – the international community's indulgence of antisemitic rejectionism. Both will have to be addressed to enable a genuine peace process to proceed successfully.

A Conflict Too Complex?

It is often said the Arab-Israeli conflict is one of unmanageable complexity for which all sides bear responsibility. That is, at best, a misreading of history. The consequences of Arab rejectionism are legion and mistakes have indeed been made by all sides. Provocative announcements at sensitive moments of Israeli settlement building in the West Bank have had a corrosive influence on peace prospects by gifting opportunities to the Palestinians to retreat further from negotiations as well as reinforcing a perception of Israeli bad faith. But Israel's settlement policy is and always was a distraction, a pretext for the Palestinians to cry foul. The conflict raged for half a century before the first settler took up residence and continued long after settlements were dismantled in all of Sinai and Gaza and in parts of the West Bank. Repeated settlement freezes have never unlocked the diplomatic logjam.

The historical record outlined in this book shows that the original sin was not Israel's. Nor does the oft-repeated 'cycle of violence' mantra stand scrutiny as it promotes a false narrative of equally shared blame. Arab politicians – so-called moderates included – are culpable for the initiation and continuation of the conflict through their persistent refusal to accept the legitimacy of Jewish sovereignty anywhere within the territory of former Mandatory Palestine. That intransigence has long fanned the flames of violence, and is responsible for all that flowed from it over the past century.

If today's Arab (and Iranian) leaders change that posture, the conflict will cease and its consequences will be manageable.

The denial of the Jewish right to self-determination is always antisemitic. An important question is this: apart from Israel and her supporters, who has called out that denial of Jewish rights and exposed it for the discriminatory attitude that it is? The answer is – almost no-one. This collective silence is extraordinary, a unique form of mass self-censorship by the global community. This perennial enemy of peace is scarcely mentioned in commentary around the subject; it is the bigotry that hardly anyone sees, the hatred that dare not speak its name. That is not just a Jewish view but one that is endorsed by the many governments and other bodies, Jewish and non-Jewish, that have adopted the IHRA definition of antisemitism.

Antisemitism is the elephant in the Middle Eastern room. If, as seems likely, it cannot be removed from this latest scene of its crimes, it will have to be tamed. But first its destructive presence must be acknowledged.

Ending the Conflict

What are the essential ingredients of peace? There is no mystery here – mutual recognition by Arabs and Jews of the right of both peoples to self-determination. Why has that recognition failed to materialise? Because Arab leaders – especially Palestinians – have stubbornly declined, in principle and in practice, to accept the right of Jews to self-determination behind any borders in their homeland. All peace-making efforts, from the Faisal-Weizmann Agreement in 1919 to the numerous failed negotiations in the early twenty-first century, have crashed into that single seemingly immoveable barrier. The only way to achieve peace is first, to recognise that barrier's existence, and second, to take concrete steps to dismantle it through concerted international pressure, if necessary via a Chapter VII (mandatory) Security Council resolution. Arab leaders – starting with the President of the Palestinian Authority – must meet the relatively modest demand to fulfil their obligations under the UN Charter.

Because antisemitic anti-Zionism and anti-Israelism arise from a destructive culturally-shared cognitive disorder, the long-term goal must be to cure the disorder. Meanwhile Israelis and Arabs continue to suffer. In the short-term, other measures designed to mitigate that suffering should be applied, starting with the Palestinians.

UN Watch has offered the UN a series of practical recommendations[14] as to how this process might begin within the PA:

- ending all practices of racial segregation and apartheid, including by removing racist laws that criminalise the sale of property to Israeli Jews;
- terminating all legal proceedings and discrimination against Palestinians suspected of involvement in land sales to Israeli Jews;
- ending the practice of financial rewards to terrorists for killing or attempting to kill Israeli Jews;
- ending all antisemitic and terrorist incitement by government officials by enacting and enforcing appropriate legislation;
- eliminating all antisemitic and terrorist incitement from the media and the education system by criminalizing such incitement and punishing perpetrators;
- reforming the educational curriculum;
- providing appropriate training to educational and media personnel;
- respecting the rights to freedom of thought, conscience and religion for Jews, Christians and Samaritans by ensuring protection for places of worship and worshipers, criminalising intimidation, harassment, and violence against members of these faiths, and holding perpetrators to account;
- criminalising violence against all persons on grounds of race, colour, descent, or national or ethnic origin, and holding perpetrators to account.

The effectiveness of these measures will be contingent on the PA meeting a further wholly reasonable and modest demand: to accept the historical connection of the Jews to the land of Israel, and the rights of Jews to self-determination in the state of Israel. In this way, the Palestinian leadership will have demonstrated that they have abandoned their antisemitic perception of Jews and Israelis.

None of these recommendations is likely to be implemented in the absence of concerted and sustained international pressure on the Palestinians to abandon their antisemitic ideology as part of a realistic strategy, that must include the reform or dismantling of UNRWA and the detoxification of Palestinian society of its antisemitic culture, to resolve the conflict. Maintaining the fiction that Israel is exclusively or largely responsible for the failure of the so-called two-state solution – which Palestinian leaders have repeatedly rejected (with little or no domestic, Arab or global criticism) – does nothing to promote peace. If the principle of equality in the upholding of universal human rights means anything,

Israelis and Arabs have a right to demand truth, moral clarity and fairness from each other and from the international community.

That means granting credit and apportioning blame in accordance with facts not fantasies. It also means ridding Palestinian and wider Arab society of its ingrained and violent antisemitism. Then we can move on to real peace making.

Notes

1   José Saramago, 'The militant magician', *Guardian*, 28 December 2002. https://www.theguardian.com/books/2002/dec/28/featuresreviews.guardia nreview11 (Last accessed 13 June 2024).
2   Y. Laor, 'After Jenin', *London Review of Books*, May 2002. https://www.lrb. co.uk/the-paper/v24/n09/yitzhak-laor/after-jenin (Last accessed 13 June 2024).
3   Shoshanna Keats Jaskoll, 'The Whack-A-Mole model of Israel advocacy', *Jewish Chronicle*, 3 December 2020.   https://www.thejc.com/lets-talk/all/the-whack-a-mole-model-of-israel-advocacy-1.509344   (Last accessed 13 June 2024).
4   C. Nelson, *Israel Denial* (Bloomington: Indiana University Press, 2019). p.19.
5   B-D. Yemini, *Industry of Lies: Media, Academia, and the Israeli-Arab Conflict* (New York: Institute for the Global Study of Antisemitism and Policy, 2017).
6   Chris McGreal, 'EU Poll Sees Israel as Peace Threat', *Guardian*, 3 November 2003. https://www.theguardian.com/world/2003/nov/03/eu.israel (Last accessed 13 June 2024).
7   The Skies Are Weeping, 1 November 2005. https://weepingskies.blogspot. com/search?q=clare+short (Last accessed 13 June 2024).
8   Ariel Kahana, 'UN passes 14 anti-Israel resolutions in 2021, only 4 against all other countries', *Israel Hayom*, 20 December 2021. https://www. israelhayom.com/2021/12/20/un-passes-14-anti-israel-resolutions-in-2021-only-4-against-all-other-countries/ (Last accessed 13 June 2024).
9   See Nelson, *Israel Denial*,' p.28.
10   David Hirsh, 'How you can help oppose antisemitism in academia', *Jewish News*, 31 August 2022. https://www.jewishnews.co.uk/opinion-how-you-can-help-oppose-antisemitism-in-academia/ (Last accessed 13 June 2024).
11   London Centre for the Study of Contemporary Antisemitism. https://londonantisemitism.com/about/ (Last accessed 13 June 2024).

12 A Schwartz, E Wilf, *The War of Return: How Western Indulgence of the Palestinian Dream has Obstructed the Path to Peace* (New York: All Points Books, 2020).

13 Yale Law School, The Avalon Project, United Nations General Assembly Resolution 181, November 29, 1947. https://avalon.law.yale.edu/20th_century/res181.asp (Last accessed 13 June 2024).

14 H. Neuer, D. Rovner, Alternative Report of United Nations Watch to the 99th Session of the Committee on the Elimination of Racial Discrimination for its review of State of Palestine (Geneva: United Nations Watch, 2019), p.1. https://unwatch.org/wp-content/uploads/2012/01/Alternative-Report-of-United-Nations-Watch-to-the-99th-Session-of-the-Committee-on-the-Elimination-of-Racial-Discrimination-for-its-review-of-State-of-Palestine.pdf (Last accessed 13 June 2024).

11

The Global Moral Imperative – What We All Need to Do

Working to end the Arab-Israeli conflict is one of the great moral imperatives of our day. The prize is to save lives, reduce misery and offer a renewed sense of hope to the millions of people affected. The restoration of moral clarity is a necessary precondition for resolving the conflict. That idea should not be controversial, nor should its purpose – to acknowledge and neutralise the antisemitic dynamic that sustains the violence. Yet the world may prove unwilling or unable to rise to the challenge. An alternative approach is to develop a strategy that focuses on the values that all democracies are duty bound, through international declarations and treaties, to uphold. Both point in the same direction – the need to adopt a robust global posture that favours truth and nurtures peaceful co-existence.

By any civilised standards, a democracy fighting for survival in the midst of tyranny deserves support. But the world's treatment of Israel has been and remains perverse. The 'Jew among the nations' is subjected to collective abuse that is comparable to that meted out to individual Jews or Jewish communities in previous eras. The nineteenth century slogan 'the Jew is our misfortune' translates today into 'the Jewish state is our misfortune.' Both reflect a prevalent *cognitive disturbance* in which all the perceived evils of the world are projected onto Jews, individually or collectively. This is an antisemitic belief that should be called out for the repulsive creed that it is. Until that happens, the prospects for resolving the conflict between Israel and her adversaries will remain elusive.

Antisemitism Threatens Us All

A key point about antisemitism is that it is toxic to all of humanity. To paraphrase Martin Niemöller, a Nazi-era German Protestant cleric (who was no phylosemite): 'What starts with Jews never ends with Jews.' By extension, what starts with the Jewish state will not end with the Jewish state. Hatred is contagious and can quickly engulf others as the Iranian example illustrates; Israelis and Jews are not the only victim of the mullahs' violent intolerance as Salman Rushdie[1] and the 2022 Iranian street protesters can attest.

The pernicious impact of antisemitic ideation on the Arab and Muslim world itself should not be underestimated. When the international community holds Israel to a discriminatory higher standard than any other country, Israel's enemies also suffer the consequences: the avoidable misery caused by endless conflict, the cynical exploitation of a foreign foe (the satanic 'Zionist entity') to deflect attention from corrupt and authoritarian domestic governments, and the perpetuation of dysfunctional international relations. Antisemitic anti-Israelism is doubly racist – towards both Israeli Jews and their Arab (and Muslim) neighbours – for it deprives the latter of human agency. This is patronising and disrespectful, and contributes nothing to conflict resolution.

Countering Contemporary Antisemitic Anti-Zionism and Anti-Israelism: A Strategic Approach

Strategy theory was originally invented by military thinkers as an *aide-memoire* for gaining the upper hand on the battlefield. It has been adapted to meet the needs of all human enterprises that involve the realisation of a clearly identified aim. The initial steps of strategy building are the most difficult: to define an overarching goal or *vision* of the ultimate destination, followed by a breakdown of that goal into manageable *objectives*. Once those have been agreed, the operational details for implementation and evaluation can be elaborated. The starting point should include the articulation of the vision along with the specific objectives designed to reach that goal.

A strategy to counter antisemitism in the Arab-Israeli conflict might include:

The Vision: A world liberated from the tyranny of antisemitic anti-Zionism and anti-Israelism.

The Objectives:

1. Investigate the origins and nature of antisemitic anti-Zionism and anti-Israelism.
2. Increase awareness of antisemitism in the conflict by using the IHRA definition as a tool for education, monitoring and accountability.

3. Expose the wider threat posed by antisemitic anti-Zionism and anti-Israelism.
4. Support Israel's existential struggle through Jewish and non-Jewish initiatives.
5. Alter the perception (or culturally shared cognitive model) of Jews and Israelis in the MENA region and worldwide.

Objective 1. Investigate the Origins and Nature of Antisemitic Anti-Zionism and Anti-Israelism

To counter the threat posed by antisemitic anti-Zionism, diagnosing the nature and ramifications of the phenomenon is a first step towards mounting countermeasures. Sceptics may argue that, while scholarly research into the subject is important, antisemitism matters little to the future course of the conflict itself, given that Israel has to date succeeded in staving off the threat of destruction and continues to maintain a qualitative military superiority over her enemies. While it may be tempting to belittle the hatred as nothing more than background noise, a careful appraisal of its nature suggests otherwise.

Antisemitism is not just a psychic disorder but a determinant of behaviour. That behaviour poses an existential threat to the Jewish state and to the Jewish people, who have learned from experience that antisemites, if empowered, are capable of acting out their fantasies of genocide should the opportunity arise. When Iranian leaders publicly and repeatedly declare their intention to 'wipe Israel off the map' within a few decades, it would be dangerous to ignore them.

Antisemitic ideation finds expression beyond the MENA region in various ways. The BDS movement, for example, may not pose an obvious existential or even economic danger to Israel but its intermediate aim is delegitimisation as a prelude to politicide, the destruction of the Jewish state. Even if only partially successful, it will sour every aspect of the world's relationship to Israel with a consequent negative impact on trade, tourism, culture, research, international relations and defence. Not least, it will corrode Israeli and Jewish self-respect and damage Israeli-diaspora relations at a time when the nurturing of a strong national identity is vital to the healthy development of a young democracy.

Antisemitism has ancient roots but major contemporary relevance. It impedes the objective appraisal of historical events, the holding of murderers to account, and the effectiveness of peace-making. As Yasser Arafat demonstrated following the Oslo Accords in 1993-95, Arab leaders will not hesitate to tear up signed agreements if the alternative is to abandon their ingrained antisemitism that they regard as a useful political weapon. All of these phenomena demand close attention, rigorous analysis and thoughtful debate. To date, this has not happened.

Henri Stellman, a political scientist based in London, discovered something remarkable: academic research into anti-Zionism, and its relationship to traditional antisemitism, is unaccountably neglected by scholars.[2] The evidence for Stellman's central thesis – that anti-Zionism and antisemitism are closely interlinked to the point of being indistinguishable – is substantial. This is an observation with major implications for the intellectual discourse around the Arab-Israeli conflict and how to resolve it, yet it is rarely discussed or even acknowledged. That lacuna of awareness, for which academics and Holocaust educators must accept a degree of culpability, enables many antisemites to disguise their hatred of Jews, unchallenged, behind the mask of political ideology.

Objective 2. Increase Awareness of Antisemitism in the Conflict Via the IHRA Definition

The weight of evidence in support of this book's central thesis – that antisemitism is the underlying cause of the Arab-Israeli conflict – is formidable. The evidence also strongly supports the corollary: that persistent antisemitism has been the major obstacle to successful peace-making over the past century or more. The evidence for both could aptly be described as undeniable. Yet denied it is, including by some Jews and Israelis. Julius writes: 'Too many people are in denial about Arab and Muslim antisemitism and bigotry, the engine of ethnic cleansing [of Jews] within the region. The story is not just a niche *Sephardi* or *Mizrachi* one – it is more relevant than ever to an understanding of the Arab/Islamist struggle against Israel and the non-Muslim Other.'[3]

The denialism may be inadvertent, perhaps in part due to ignorance. One example is the ritual declamation by Western politicians of the post-Holocaust mantra *Never Again* while simultaneously – and apparently oblivious to the irony – propping up an openly antisemitic Palestinian Authority (and the even more extreme Hamas movement indirectly) through diplomatic and financial support. A second is the international community's failure to treat the Jewish refugees from Arab and Muslim lands on a par with the Palestinians by creating a well-funded agency (UNRWA) only for the latter. This collective moral blind spot is both deeply hurtful for Jews and damaging to peace prospects. When President Obama addressed an Arab audience in Cairo in 2009, he called for a resetting of American-Muslim relations based on shared principles of justice and progress. André Aciman, a Jew who had left Egypt in 1964, wrote in a letter to the *New York Times* that the President 'didn't say a word about any of the 800,000 or so Jews born in the Middle East who fled the Arab and Muslim world or who were summarily expelled for being Jewish in the twentieth century.'[4]

How should this international failure of awareness, whether wilful or inadvertent, be overcome? There are no easy answers. An obvious barrier is the reluctance of Israel's opponents to admit to being influenced by antisemitic ideation. And because antisemitism is inherently irrational, the presentation of evidence, however irrefutable, will fail to persuade the antisemite. Moreover, antisemitism may be unconscious or rationalised. That places an additional burden of responsibility on anti-racists to call out Jew-hatred wherever it arises, including in the MENA region, but they may be hesitant to do so in the Arab-Israeli context due to the superficially 'political' nature of the prejudice. What this boils down to is an epistemological conundrum – how can we know what is antisemitic and what is not? Efforts to answer that question have long been bedevilled by disagreements over the precise definition of antisemitism, particularly in relation to anti-Zionism and anti-Israelism.

Those arguments may now be redundant following the publication of the non-legally binding IHRA definition (see Chapter 2). This ground-breaking document cannot solve the antisemitism problem, but it offers a practical tool, derived from the principle of universal human rights, for monitoring, research and education. Unsurprisingly, anti-Zionists and others have objected to the definition that, they claim, silences free speech (including criticism of Israel), privileges Jews over other minorities, is too vague, and is unnecessary. These complaints have been addressed in detail and thoroughly rebutted in a compendium of essays published by the online British journal *Fathom*.[5]

Organisations and governments that endorse the definition should be praised for taking that first step but should be encouraged to go further. A senior official should be designated to lead the institutional strategy for action on antisemitism, and the definition should be clearly visible on their websites (and include all the cited examples). They should also commit to incorporating the definition into their staff training programmes and complaints and disciplinary processes, and conduct periodic reviews of its effectiveness in all of these domains.

Objective 3. Expose the Wider Threat Posed by Antisemitic Anti-Zionism and Anti-Israelism

Why should the century-long dispute between Jews and Arabs concern anyone other than the protagonists? There are many reasons but two deserve special attention. One is regional, the other global.

First, Israelis are not the only people in the Middle East facing threats from political and religious extremists. Kurds and Yazidis are two groups that occasionally figure in headlines but there are many others – from LGBTQIA+ people and women in Iran and Gaza to Palestinians in Syria, Lebanon and Jordan. One in particular is a relatively large yet curiously neglected religious minority with which Western nations claim to have a strong cultural affinity. At the beginning of the twentieth century, Christians constituted 20 per cent of the Middle East population dropping to approximately 4 per cent in 2015. The twelve million Christians living today in the Middle East are predicted to decline further and are on course to disappear entirely from the region. In part, this is due to their relatively low birth rate compared to Muslims, but there is another cause – persecution. In Iraq, Syria, Libya, Egypt, the Palestinian Authority, Gaza and elsewhere, Christians live in fear and are often subjected to discrimination, harassment, expulsion, and mass murder.[6]

Most of the world has barely noticed that, in contrast to the rest of the region, Israel's Christian community is safe and flourishing. Since 1948, the Christian population of Israel, comprising around two per cent of the total, has increased more than fourfold from 34,000 in 1948 to 160,000 today. Israel is the only Middle Eastern country where the Christian population has grown in the last half-century. Christianity is one of the five official religions of the state. Israeli Christians perform as well as or better than Israeli Muslims and Jews in the education system. This did not happen by chance. Few of Israel's critics seem aware of the inclusive nature of her constitution that is based explicitly on democratic egalitarianism; this translates into the legal protection of minorities that is overseen and enforced by an independent and vigilant judiciary. Such an arrangement is unique in the MENA region, yet it is Israel that finds herself repeatedly and unfairly condemned for abusing minorities in the UN Human Rights Council and elsewhere.

The second reason that the world should pay attention to the Arab-Israeli conflict is enlightened self-interest. Israel is, and has always been, on the front-line in a global confrontation between the forces of moderation and extremism. Even Middle East specialists, with a few exceptions, fail to identify the common antisemitic thread running between the Iranian

Revolutionary Guards, Palestinian terrorists, Al Qaeda, ISIS and other jihadist militants. While these disparate groups regularly fall out with each other in their quest for hegemony, all glorify death, martyrdom and cruelty in pursuit of their grotesque interpretation of Islam, and all view themselves as waging a Manichean struggle against the Infidel, the Other – epitomised by the Jew. The incontinent fury of these radicals transcends the Shia-Sunni divide and has little to do with Western or Israeli foreign policy though they are adept at exploiting real grievances for their own ends. Islamists despise the West and seek to replace all democracies, violently if necessary, with a global caliphate. Hamas, Hezbollah and Islamic Jihad (along with other violent Palestinian organisations that shelter under the 'moderate' banner of the Palestinian Authority) loathe and attack Israel for her Western values and her original sin of existing. Since the days of Yasser Arafat, Palestinians of all political hues have made no secret of the fact that the two-state solution is, at best, an interim measure, a stepping stone towards the total liberation of 'Palestine from the river to the sea,'[7] a euphemism for the end of Israel. Western governments, especially in Europe, have failed to acknowledge let alone respond to this reality.

Antisemitism poses a moral and civilisational challenge to the entire world. If it is ignored it will proliferate, and if it undoubtedly proliferates it will undermine the foundations of democracy, human rights and peaceful co-existence everywhere. All who believe in universal human rights, including democracy and the right to self-determination, must be concerned about the future of the nation state of the Jewish people, and all have a role to play in her struggle. Israel remains capable of defending herself physically but deserves international support in countering the threat to her legitimacy. Just as hatred of Jews never ends with Jews, hatred of Israel will not end with Israel. As Lord Jonathan Sacks said: 'Those who can't see the obvious good in Israel harm themselves, not just Israel.'[8]

American philosopher Sam Harris believes that the cause of Israel is not a narrow, tribal, Jewish one; it has a resonance for all human beings. He is in no doubt that supporting Israel is a moral imperative – it is simply the right thing to do: 'The truth is that there is an obvious, undeniable, and hugely consequential moral difference between Israel and her enemies. The Israelis are surrounded by people who have explicitly genocidal intentions towards them...So, it seems to me, that you have to side with Israel here.'[9]

His French colleague, Bernard-Henri Lévy agrees:

> It is so tiresome to have to defend Israel. So distressing to have to present the same evidence over and over. Not that Israel is

irreproachable, of course. Not that it is forbidden, as the frauds endlessly assert, to 'criticise' Israel. But in the face of so much bad faith, in the face of a systematic campaign of delegitimisation that has no parallel on the world political scene, in the face of the role that this demonisation of the Jewish state plays in the construction of the new antisemitic machine, how can one not respond by proclaiming the virtues of Israel?[10]

Those who would destroy Israel would destroy us all. The roots of the jihadist massacres in France, Tunisia, Nigeria, India and elsewhere are traceable to the poisonous legacy of the Muslim Brotherhood that has inspired anti-Western, anti-democratic, antisemitic and anti-Israeli radicals since the 1920s. Today's Hamas and Hezbollah fighters, along with their brothers-in-arms in Iran, are the heirs to the fanatical Haj Amin al-Husseini, the Grand Mufti of Jerusalem from 1921 to 1948, who spent much of the Second World War as a guest of the Third Reich. These dangerous terrorist groups promote a cult of murder and martyrdom that must be confronted rather than appeased.

The emergence of the current hateful anti-Israel narrative has implications for all countries and all societies. Its apotheosis – a genocidal military assault on Israel of the kind promised by a nuclear-armed Iran – is almost unimaginable but far from implausible. The shock waves would reverberate well beyond the Middle East. Shepherd rightly views Israel's plight as a civilisational challenge.[11] Israel is the world's canary in the mine[12] and she is calling on all of us to take urgent action.

Objective 4: Support Israel's Existential Struggle through Jewish and Non-Jewish Initiatives
a) Joint Diaspora-Israeli Action

When Israel was born in 1948, her priority was for people, money and arms. The Jewish communities of the world rose to the challenge and forged a partnership with the new state that delivered those desperately needed means of survival. Later, charitable projects were (and to a large extent remain) the focus of world Jewry's assistance – for example, supporting universities, building schools and hospitals, aiding immigrant absorption – all of which were necessary to stabilise the fragile new state. As international criticism of Israel has morphed into antisemitic anti-Israelism, many Jews have demonstrated solidarity with the homeland through street demonstrations, political lobbying and advocacy. Israel, for her part, has taken great strides in improving her diplomatic corps, in training spokespeople for government and the IDF, and in nurturing constructive relations with the world's media.

But Israel faces a problem in this regard. The propaganda war is being lost, and not just within the liberal commentariat. Surveys of public opinion around the world have found that Israel is more unpopular than ever before in her history. International fora such as the UN, already intrinsically biased, have become unassailable bastions of antisemitic anti-Israelism, as have many Muslim organisations and otherwise respected humanitarian NGOs such as *Oxfam, Christian Aid, Amnesty International* and *Human Rights Watch*. Trade unions, academia, professional organisations, political parties and churches are rapidly following suit. The media reflect and reinforce this phenomenon in their unsympathetic or biased reporting of the country.

These trends pose a danger to Israel. Global public opinion was a key factor in the dismantling of apartheid South Africa, an event that most fair-minded people welcomed. That country's increasing isolation, brought about through a prototype BDS movement, was a major contributor to its downfall. Many anti-Israel activists perceive Israel to be the new 'apartheid state' and are undeterred by the counterfactual nature of the label. They are determined to ensure that Israel meets the same fate as the old South Africa within their lifetimes. To this end, they deploy three key methods in accordance with their Durban strategy launched at the NGO Forum in 2001: demonising Israel's nature, policies and behaviour, attempting to inflict economic and political damage on Israel, and pursuing 'lawfare' (the use of legalistic rhetoric and international legal procedures) to condemn and delegitimise the Jewish state. All three rely heavily on nurturing, via the mass media, a hostile climate of public opinion towards the country, her history and her people.

It is unclear if Israel's political class recognises the extent to which this deepening antipathy to their country threatens her welfare and security. In the past, Israel's priority was to survive rather than to court international approval. Today, her unpopularity may threaten that survival. Having a strong army is no guarantee of security if it cannot be deployed. Should global public opinion turn further against Israel following the war with Hamas in 2023-24, she could become a pariah state with all that that implies: a deteriorating economy, declining tourism, a growing scarcity of military supplies, an erosion of the IDF's qualitative edge and – most dangerously – collapsing domestic morale. Increasing public antipathy to Israel might further endanger Jews everywhere, with antisemitic incidents soaring with each future crisis, as well as widening internal divisions within and between diaspora and Israeli Jewish communities.

What is the answer? Conventional counter-propaganda (*'hasbara'*) is no longer sufficient. Merely reacting to unfounded criticism will rarely win back lost friends as the rebuttal never has the same impact as the accusation. A consensus may be emerging, both among Israel's supporters and within Israel, that a more effective plan of action is needed. The war of ideas must be fought pro-actively as well as reactively to achieve a step-change upwards. This will require focus, resources and organisation. Israel has many brilliant minds, but public relations is not a national forte. Just as in the early days of the state, Israel cannot solve all her problems alone. The scale of the challenge demands the launching of a joint diaspora-Israeli enterprise, staffed by committed practitioners with the knowledge, skills and motivation to prosecute it with vigour and effectiveness.[13]

b) Global Action

The status quo is unacceptable. The world's liberal democracies, if they have any awareness of history, a genuine adherence to civilised values, and a sense of responsibility to future generations, have a moral imperative to remove the major obstacles to peace between Israel and her enemies: the promotion of a false narrative, the relentless UN condemnations, the double standard towards refugees, the weaponisation of UNRWA to indoctrinate children to believe in the non-existent 'right of return' and to encourage its achievement through violence, the singling out of Israel for BDS, the ignoring of daily anti-Israeli terrorism – including its incitement and incentivisation by the Palestinian Authority – and the appeasement of a nuclear-threshold Iran. The question is how?

Education (in the broadest sense) may hold the key. Although the evidence presented in this book is easily accessible, few educationalists are familiar with it and this ignorance is antithetical to peace. Educational curricula must abandon 'woke' political dogmas and encourage evidence-based analytic approaches to Jewish, Arab and Islamic history. A specific focus on the manner in which Islamism and Nazism coalesced around antisemitic anti-Zionism from the 1920s is essential as these toxic ideologies continue to cast their shadows into the twenty-first century. The political discourse around Israel in schools, colleges and universities is increasingly unhealthy. Post-modern gobbledegook such as 'competing narratives,' and 'intersectionality' requires relentless challenge in schools, colleges and universities. A related task is to reclaim the research agenda that has been hijacked by ideologically motivated academics who promote an antisemitic ethos on campuses and the wider intellectual sphere.

A second-tier educational approach involves the utilisation of teachable moments by responding, within the limits of practicability, to instances of harsh criticism of Israel or Jews that are either clearly antisemitic (according to the IHRA definition) or demonstrably false, since the dissemination of such falsehoods feeds antisemitic ideation. Opinion formers who promote, directly or indirectly, a rejectionist antisemitic anti-Israelism, are enemies of peace who can no longer be permitted free rein. Responsible figures within the international community, including the UN, must be challenged when they promote libels rooted in antisemitic beliefs. That will require a process of continuous monitoring and responding to demonising statements, policies and behaviours of NGOs, churches, academics, trade unionists, politicians, diplomats and journalists. This is already underway though the work of watchdog groups such as CAMERA, *Honest Reporting*, *UN Watch* and *NGO Monitor*, and Jewish communal efforts at self-protection[14]; their efforts deserve support and upscaling.

A priority for attention is the chronic running sore of the *Mizrachi* Jews who were dispossessed *en masse* during an antisemitic convulsion across the MENA region following Israel's establishment. This forgotten Jewish *Nakba* will be a permanent stain on the world's conscience until their plight is recognised. The Israeli Knesset passed a law in 2010 requiring all Israeli governments to include compensation for the victims in any peace agreement with the Palestinians. As Julius emphasises, this is a matter of basic fairness:

> The 50.2 per cent of Israel's Jews who descend from refugees forced out by Arab and Muslim persecution have a right to expect that a peace deal will be signed that does not ignore their painful history. They cannot reasonably be asked to approve a peace plan that only provides rights and redress for Palestinian refugees, without providing rights of remembrance, truth, justice and redress for Jews displaced from Arab countries, as mandated under international law.[15]

While the Jewish *Nakba* – a direct result of antisemitic anti-Israelism – has been virtually forgotten, the Palestinian refugee problem – also a by-product of antisemitic anti-Israelism – has been canonised through UNRWA, a lavishly-funded, corrupt and hate-generating engine of endless conflict predicated on a legally non-existent 'right of return' of refugees and their descendants to Israel. The strikingly different and discriminatory manner in which the international community has reacted to those two refugee populations is emblematic of the antisemitism that that lies at the heart of the Arab-Israeli conflict. The deliberate erasure of the Jewish *Nakba* is a human rights scandal of the first order, as is the cynical prolongation of the Arab one. If there is one message that is capable of winning hearts and minds across an otherwise indifferent world, it must surely be this one.

In terms of more broadly focused practical action, one approach would be to establish a pro-Israel global NGO network as a kind of mirror-image of the anti-Israel Durban initiative. By working together rather than separately, pro-Israel groups may succeed in achieving the necessary critical mass to generate upward momentum in their effectiveness. The purpose of the network would be to coordinate efforts to roll back the tide of antisemitic anti-Israelism. The Appendix lists some of the organisations that might form the core of a World Coalition for Israel (WCI) modelled on the Boycott, Divestments and Sanctions (BDS) network – but with diametrically opposite aims.

Objective 5: Alter the Culturally Shared Cognitive Model of Jews and Israelis

Whether or not the details of Goldhagen's analysis of German antisemitism are directly transferable to the MENA region, it seems clear that the main driver of the Arab-Israeli conflict is a pathological and culturally shared cognitive model of Jews and Israelis. How may this model be altered? Two possible approaches may be 'borrowed' from preventive medicine and the rehabilitation of post-war Germany.

Public health professionals working in the field of injury prevention (including intentional and unintentional violence reduction) have advocated Three Es – education, enforcement of legislation (and statutory regulations), and environmental modification.[16] This template may be adapted for the present purposes.

The key educational challenge will be to erase or modify antisemitic stereotypes of Jews and Israelis. That will be a major multidisciplinary undertaking that will demand the harnessing of the expertise of social psychologists as well as teachers, sociologists, historians and political scientists. It should encompass all communities, all nationalities, all faiths (and none), and all age groups. The priority target group must be young people as from their ranks will emerge future opinion formers and political leaders.

Enforcement of existing legislation relevant to antisemitism is inadequate. In most countries, efforts to curb hate speech, Holocaust denial and discrimination need ramping up to provide more effective protection of Jews and Israelis. That enforcement should be equitable and fearless. When the UN, for example, is in clear breach of its own Charter, its officials should be held accountable. The regulatory framework for both mainstream and social media may require tightening with regards to antisemitic anti-Zionism and anti-Israelism as well as more traditional expressions of antisemitism.

Environmental measures designed to reduce the exposure of the population (especially children and young people) to antisemitic anti-Zionism and anti-Israelism will be necessary to ensure that demonising cognitive models are modified. The sources of this ideation include educational and religious institutions, community agencies, voluntary organisations, the arts, sport, and the media. This will be a complicated but manageable task. The global experience of altering public attitudes to public health hazards has demonstrated what can be achieved over relatively short timescales: smoking cessation programmes, drink-driving campaigns, and measures to enhance child safety[17] have all proved successful in changing public knowledge, attitudes and behaviour.

Penetrating the all-important sphere of intra-familial dynamics presents a more daunting challenge. The intergenerational transmission of negative stereotypes from parents to children is a subtle, covert and often decisive process that is liable to prove resistant to external intervention. The development of innovative approaches to breaching this barrier this will require creativity and research.

Following the surrender of the Axis powers at the end of World War Two, the allied embarked on a programme of denazification of the German populace.[18] This was a momentous task that was widely criticised at the time for its apparent leniency, yet there is little doubt that German society was transformed within a few years to the point that the expression of Nazi ideology, including antisemitism, became taboo.

The countering of prejudice is a long-term project that will require patience, persistence, a clear vision of the ultimate goal, and the allocation of sufficient resources. We know that such an exercise in psychosocial engineering is feasible as there are many precedents in the fields of public health and social psychology. There is no reason why such lessons cannot be applied to unhealthy and dangerous attitudes and behaviours towards Jews, Israelis and the Jewish state.

Notes

1   Reuters, 'Iran's Hardline Newspapers Praise Salman Rushdie's Attacker', 13 August 2022. https://www.reuters.com/world/irans-hardline-newspapers-praise-salman-rushdies-attacker-2022-08-13/ (Last accessed 13 June 2024).

2   H. Stellman, *What Is Anti-Zionism? (and is it Antisemitic?)*, A Short Handbook for Activists and Analysts (Soesterberg: Aspekt Publishers, 2019), p.11.

3   L. Julius, *Uprooted* (London: Vallentine Mitchell, 2018), p.xxv.

4   André Aciman A, 'The Exodus Obama forgot to mention', *New York Times*, 8 June 2009. https://www.nytimes.com/2009/06/09/opinion/09aciman.html (Last accessed 13 June 2024).

5   A. Johnson (ed.), *In Defence of the IHRA Working Definition of Antisemitism* (London: Fathom, 2021). https://fathomjournal.org/wp-content/uploads/2021/02/Fathom-eBook-In-Defence-of-the-IHRA-Working-Definition-of-Antisemitism.pdf (Last accessed 13 June 2024).

6   Patrick Wintour, 'Persecution of Christians "coming close to genocide" in Middle East – report', *Guardian*, 2 May 2019. https://www.theguardian.com/world/2019/may/02/persecution-driving-christians-out-of-middle-east-report (Last accessed 13 June 2024).

7   E. Karsh, 'Arafat's Grand Strategy', *Middle East Quarterly*, Spring 2004. https://www.meforum.org/605/arafats-grand-strategy#_ftn7   (Last accessed 13 June 2024).

8   Richard Ferrer, 'The 100-year war? Lord Sacks on defeating Islamic State and its evil ilk', *Jewish News*, 29 June 2015. https://www.jewishnews.co.uk/the-100-year-war-lord-sacks-on-the-rise-of-islamic-state-and-its-evil-ilk/ (Last accessed 13 June 2024).

9   S. Harris, 'Why Don't I criticize Israel?' 27 July 2014. https://www.samharris.org/podcasts/making-sense-episodes/why-dont-i-criticize-israel (Last accessed 13 June 2024).

10   B. Henri-Levy, 'Anti-Semitism's New Guise, Israel's Exceptional Future', *Tablet*, February 2017. http://www.thetower.org/article/anti-semitism-new-guise-israel-exceptional-future-bernard-henri-levy-the-genius-of-judaism/ (Last accessed 13 June 2024).

11   R. Shepherd, *A State Beyond the Pale.* (London: Orion Books, 2009), p.166.

12   David Stone, 'Israel – the canary in the mine the world ignores at its peril', *Times of Israel*, 1 July 2015. https://blogs.timesofisrael.com/israel-the-canary-in-the-mine-the-world-ignores-at-its-peril/ (Last accessed 31 December 2023).

13   David Stone, 'Countering anti-Israelism– needed: a joint Israel-Diaspora strategy', *Times of Israel*, 6 April 2015. https://blogs.timesofisrael.com/

countering-anti-israelism-needed-a-joint-israel-diaspora-strategy/ (Last accessed 13 June 2024).

14 Ben Bloch, 'CST issues security warning for Jewish schools after Miller's rant on Iranian TV channel', *Jewish Chronicle*, 1 September 2022. https://www.thejc.com/news/news/cst-issues-security-warning-for-jewish-schools-after-millers-rant-on-iranian-tv-channel-GSP2XKPzdNM cOaKxXBgS6 (Last accessed 13 June 2024).

15 See Julius, *Uprooted*, p.244.

16 Children's Safety Network, 'Evidence-based and Evidence-informed Strategies for Child and Adolescent Injury Prevention', U.S. Department of Health and Human Services (HHS), May 2019. https://www.childrenssafetynetwork.org/sites/default/files/Evidence-Based%20Strategies%20FINAL.pdf (Last accessed 13 June 2024).

17 D. Stone, *Injury Prevention in Children* (Edinburgh: Dunedin Academic Press 2011), pp.44

18 Denazification, Jewish Virtual Library. https://www.jewishvirtuallibrary.org/denazification-2 (Last accessed 13 June 2024).

12

Conclusions

This book has presented a body of historical and contemporary evidence highlighting the role that antisemitism – latent or active, conscious or unconscious – has played throughout the course of the Arab-Israeli conflict. The evidence is persuasive that hatred of Jews and Israel caused the conflict rather than the reverse. That evidence also supports the hypothesis that antisemitism remains the central driving force of the hundred-year war launched by the Arab and Muslim world against the Jews. The alternative or null hypothesis – that antisemitism is an epiphenomenon of the conflict – is unsupported by the evidence.

Toxic Culturally Shared Cognitive Models of Jews, Zionists and Israelis

Antisemitic ideation has been present in the MENA region for more than a millennium. It evolved over centuries from a perception of Jews as weak and cowardly to the modern genocidal Islamist (and Iranian) ambition to 'wipe Israel off the map.' The scene was set in the pre-Zionist era by the prolonged second-class or *dhimmi* status of Jews (as well as Christians) in the Arab and Muslim world. In the early twentieth century, nationalistic antagonism to Zionism was cranked up by the injection of a hybrid Islamist-Nazi ideology, all of which influences left an antisemitic legacy that remains potent today and infects the mainstream discourse about Israel in the Middle East and around the world.

Antisemitism is not the sole explanation for the Arab-Israeli conflict but it seems likely that it was always its most crucial ingredient. Drawing on scholarly research undertaken in the fields of Holocaust and Middle Eastern studies, the evidence suggests that today's virulent Arab-Muslim antisemitism is the outcome of a long-term historical process whereby anti-Jewish hostility finds expression in a variety of ways depending on specific circumstances or triggers. This conceptualisation posits that antisemitism in the MENA region evolved from religious Judeophobia in the medieval period to political and nationalistic anti-Zionism in the late nineteenth and early twentieth centuries, and finally to modern anti-Israelism that exhibits some features of classic European versions of anti-Jewish stereotyping. These variants of Jew-hatred have their specific characteristics but all share common features that act synergistically, a phenomenon that helps account for their potency.

Just as historian Daniel Goldhagen identified a generalised German cognitive disturbance that produced Nazi antisemitism, the evidence suggests a similar dynamic at work in Arab-Muslim society. If Goldhagen's theoretical framework is applied to the MENA region, the salience of Arab-Muslim antisemitism is explicable in terms of a sequential series of underpinning *culturally shared cognitive models* of Jews, Zionists and Israelis. In recent decades, following the emptying of most of the Jews from the MENA region (apart, of course, from Israel), a new antisemitic cognitive model has emerged that focuses its anti-Jewish hostility, with laser-like precision, on the Jewish state – or rather the perceived demonic nature of Israel that the model dictates. Goldhagen's work prompts another insight: the Arab-Muslim cognitive model of Jews appears disturbingly similar to that shared by most Germans in the period prior to the Nazi persecution, a commonality that is rarely countenanced let alone explored by Holocaust educators and researchers.

Although the early Muslim cognitive model of Jews placed a stronger emphasis on religion than on ethnicity, it evolved over time in response to the importation of European racist tropes first by European colonialism and then by Nazism. These external influences extended and darkened the perception of Jews from a contemptible *dhimmitude* to that of an alien intrusion into the purity of the Arab-Muslim people (the *ummat al-Islām* or *ummah*). Jews were increasingly regarded as an existential threat to the *ummah*, and – as in the German case – a consensus emerged that the only way to 'solve' the Jewish problem was to eliminate its polluting presence. That eliminationist message is communicated daily to the MENA public today in speeches, sermons, educational curricula and the media. That Hamas-ruled Gaza's children were subjected to such poison over many years will surprise few; by contrast, the role of the internationally supported 'moderate' Palestinian Authority in implanting equally extreme notions in young Palestinian minds has generally passed almost unnoticed.[1] The watchdog organisation *Palestinian Media Watch* has had some success in explaining to foreign governments four specific themes, none of which is related to the occupation, settlements, the two-state solution or any Israeli government policy, promoted by the PA: that Jews are sub-human or 'humanoids'; that Jews pose an existential danger to Palestinian lives; that

Jews are intent on destroying the Muslim holy places, notably the *Al Aksa* Mosque; and that Jews have no historical connection to Israel. These messages are deployed to justify the quest for martyrdom (*shahada*) by all Muslims who murder Israelis and are linked to explicit incitement to achieve the ultimate extermination of all Jews everywhere.[2]

The concept of a culturally shared cognitive model does not imply that every last member of a society is ruled by it; on the contrary, as with all cultural norms there are dissident minorities. The reality is that those who hold counter-cultural opinions will face greater barriers to the free expression of their views in authoritarian and socially conservative societies than in democracies. Because Israel is the only country in the MENA region that is a democracy in the Western sense, few dissenters in the region, outside of Israel, are likely to feel secure enough to question prevailing antisemitic norms their societies.

Antisemitic Cognitive Models and Mass Psychosis

Widely shared contemporary cognitive models of Jews and Israelis in the MENA region facilitate the acceptance of projected beliefs about Israel and Jews that are verifiably untrue or grotesque distortions of the truth. They include Holocaust denial or minimisation, the view of Zionism as an imperialist, colonialist and racist ideology intent on controlling the Middle East, and the depiction of Israel as an 'apartheid state' that ethnically cleanses and murders Palestinians in pursuit of Nazi-like genocidal goals. These beliefs are so divorced from reality that they could be described, despite having been incorporated into the collective understanding of the societies that harbour them, as quasi-psychotic in nature. Hirsh and Miller write: 'Contrary to appearances, antisemitism is never really about Jews, and anti-Zionism is not really about Israel. Both are ways of projecting all that is bad in the whole world onto an "other."'[3]

Having been imported in part from Nazi-dominated Europe, this relatively novel version of antisemitism has been refined and recycled back to Europe from where it has been spread to North America and elsewhere, often shorn of its overtly Islamist component. When it takes root in receptive soil, the new antisemitic model is so fervently embraced that it amounts to a secularised religious credo comprising a set of beliefs about Israel and Jews that are elevated to unchallengeable 'articles of faith' – including fabrications about Zionism and its alleged global influence, the origins of the Palestinian refugee problem, the Israeli army's ethical standards, Israeli government policy, and the nature of Israeli society generally. In some Western circles (notably the media, human rights NGOs, 'progressive' politics, and academia), this credo has been enthusiastically adopted, wholly or in part, for ideological, political or financial reasons.

Antisemitic anti-Israelism has entered global civil society in the twenty-first century to the point where it has been normalised to a disturbing degree. A delusional antisemitic discourse about Israel is facilitated and legitimised, even if the facilitators (and their institutions) are not themselves inherently or consciously antisemitic. Important sectors of the news media promote false narratives about Israel, or subscribe to a performative version of journalistic 'balance' that disseminates libels and distortions as though they were legitimate political perspectives. The result is a steady abandonment of rationality, a retreat from historical veracity, and, at times, a detachment from reality – all characteristic features of a mass psychotic disturbance that results in delusional beliefs passing unrecognised and even gaining credence.

How Antisemitism is Normalised

When a plausible but flawed cognitive model becomes the norm – 'common sense' to which a majority subscribes – it appears capable of engulfing almost everyone in a tsunami of falsehoods in a manner that transcends political and demographic categories – left and right, secular and religious, white and black, straight and gay, young and old, Jewish and Arab, Israeli and Palestinian. It may become internalised by otherwise well-meaning people who would be horrified to discover that they had, unwittingly or otherwise, adopted a prejudiced belief. We know from history that such a cultural Trojan horse can infiltrate the collective psyche of the most sophisticated countries; less educated, conservative societies are even more vulnerable.

The new antisemitism, obsessively focused on Israel, is now a global scourge that afflicts advanced and developing countries alike. Worse, the default prejudicial view of the Jewish state has become socially and politically normalised. We must come to terms with the troubling fact that it is no longer possible to separate the population into two mutually exclusive categories, the tolerant majority and the prejudiced minority; in epidemiological terms, we are dealing with a continuously distributed rather than a bimodal population variable. In the early twenty-first century, a bigoted discourse about Jews and Zionism has infected the conscious-ness of entire societies around the globe. As we know from twentieth century European history, it is but a short step from that societal defect to governmental behaviour through a process, in Shepherd's phrase, of 'agenda slippage'[4] into policy making at national and international levels.

When a pernicious stereotype achieves a critical mass, it grants legitimacy to ideas that were previously confined to the extremist fringe. The most unhinged conspiracy theories become 'reasonable' as they are viewed through the distorting prism of prejudice. These are then disseminated, embellished further and recycled. This process is amplified through mainstream and (especially) social media. When negative stereotypical perceptions of Jews and Israelis become the norm, they are easily incorporated into policy-framing (mainly at international level) and policy-making (mainly at national level) with devastating consequences: the denial of the legitimacy of Jewish self-determination in the historical Jewish homeland, the uncritical acceptance of misinformation as gospel truth, the incitement of violence ('resistance') towards Israelis and Jews, and a compulsion to shore up corrupt, totalitarian and violent Arab or Islamist regimes via diplomatic, economic, intellectual and moral support.

Eliminationist Antisemitism is the Driving Force of the Arab-Israeli Conflict

Unlike the vast majority of other conflicts over territory around the world, Israel's enemies and their (active or passive) supporters have expressed their declared aim to obliterate the country that is the object of their disapproval. They regard Israel as an illegitimate stain on the map that poses a threat to their region, their religion, and the world as a whole, often comparing the 'Zionist entity' to a malignant, metastasising cancer. They do this in the name of anti-Zionism, the denial of the right to sovereignty of the Jewish people, either explicitly (by working towards Israel's destruction) or implicitly (through the endless reiteration of the non-existent 'right of return' of the Palestinian refugees) or both. All of these openly expressed positions meet the IHRA criteria of antisemitism but denying a people the right to self-determination also violates the UN charter, as does threatening or using violence against a member state of the UN. That, however, is the thin end of the antisemitic wedge; in addition to politicide, genocide has long been firmly on the agenda.

Shortly before Israel declared her independence, Azzam Pasha, the Arab League's secretary-general promised a 'war of extermination and momentous massacre.' He was frustrated in that ambition but there is abundant evidence of the seriousness of his vow: during the first Arab-Israeli war of 1947-49, the attacking Arab militias and armies deliberately targeted civilian settlements wherever they could. This was a pattern of officially-sanctioned Arab anti-Jewish violence that had ancient historical precedents and is one that has continued to the present day. Both Julius[5] and Gilbert[6] document anti-Jewish pogroms perpetrated by frenzied Muslim mobs dating from the seventh century until modern times in Algeria, Egypt, Libya, Morocco, Tunisia, Persia, Turkey and Iraq.

Modern extremist groups such as Hamas, Hezbollah and Islamic Jihad, aided and abetted by Iran, sustain that homicidal tradition through regular terrorist attacks against Israelis and Jews. In October 2023, Hamas reiterated their aim to destroy Israel and massacre her Jewish citizens who comprise 75 per cent (chillingly around six million in 2022) of the country's population. This barbarous ambition has been fuelled by UNRWA's educational system, generously funded by the international community, that indoctrinates children from an early age to despise Jews whom they are taught to view as a scheming and less than human satanic enemy. As these brainwashed children enter adolescence, their propensity to jihadist violence is nurtured and sustained by a broad societal culture of resentment, anger and martyrdom in which antisemitic anti-Israelism is ubiquitous. Unsurprisingly, this guarantees a steady stream of willing recruits to terrorist groups operating in Gaza, the West Bank, southern Lebanon, Syria, Egypt and, at times, within Israel's borders. Israeli governments, of all political hues, have no choice but to defend their citizens from these threats. The result is that the war against the Jews launched by Haj Amin al-Husseini in 1920, and prosecuted with equally ferocious antisemitic fervour today by his Islamo-fascist successors under the leadership of Iran, continues unabated over a hundred years later.

The Deadly Cocktail of Islamist, Nazi and Soviet Antisemitism

The contemporary manifestation of antisemitic anti-Israelism has three overlapping elements all of which are rooted in history. First, the traditional bigotry towards Jews in the Arab and Muslim world, that arose around the birth of Islam in the seventh century, was revitalised by the Muslim Brotherhood in the 1920s initially in Egypt, and then disseminated as violent jihadism throughout the Middle East. Second, a toxic brand of Nazi-inspired racial hatred was imported from Europe, also in the 1920s, to turbocharge nationalist or 'political' anti-Zionism. Third, Soviet-origin far-left conspiracy theories were injected into the conflict following Stalin's lurch into antisemitism just before his death in the early 1950s.[7]

These three strands of Jew-hatred were permitted to thrive and became mutually reinforcing. The centuries-old *dhimmi* status of minorities in Muslim lands obliged Jews to wear distinctive clothing, a means of social control that inspired the Nazis to introduce the yellow Jewish star. The Muslim Brotherhood (that would become the largest political organisation in Egypt in the 1940s) and National Socialism amplified each other's conspiracy theories about Jewish plans for world domination and forged an alliance that, among other troublesome consequences, propelled Hitler's *Mein Kampf* and the antisemitic Russian forgery *The Protocols of the Elders of Zion* into Arab bestseller lists where they have remained ever since. Both Marxist-affiliated Arab nationalists and ultra-reactionary jihadist terrorists are prone to chant anti-Jewish homicidal slogans when denouncing Zionism and Israel.

All of these elements continue to make their presence felt today. This is rendered possible because antisemitism, in the form of a still evolving visceral hatred of Jews, Zionists and Israelis, has become a cultural norm in the MENA region and beyond. This perception of Jews has become so tightly woven into the fabric of the Arab and Muslim world that it presents a danger no less profound than its counterpart in Christian Europe in the early twentieth century.

The Grand Mufti's Dream of a MENA Final Solution

Specifically Palestinian Arab antisemitic violence may be traced back to the sinister figure of Haj Amin al-Husseini who was appointed Grand Mufti of Jerusalem by the British Mandatory administration in 1921. This self-proclaimed populist leader of the Arabs of Palestine was not merely a Nazi sympathiser; he forged an agreement with Hitler to extend the Final Solution to the Middle East and eradicate every Jew – not just those in Palestine but all the Jews of the MENA region. When Hitler committed suicide in his Berlin bunker in 1945, the Mufti was undeterred in his pursuit of a posthumous victory for his beloved *Führer* – the obliteration of the old-new archenemy, the Jews.

Husseini's antisemitism was extreme but hardly unique in the Arab world. In 1920, renowned pan-Arabist Awni Abdel Hadi ruled out any Jewish presence in Palestine, promising that 'we will not rest until Palestine is either placed under a free Arab government or becomes a graveyard for all Jews in the country. We will finish them off one by one: if not in a month, then in a year, if not in a year – then in ten years.'[8] Karsh reminds us of the call by the newspaper *Karmil* for 'an Arab Hitler,' as well as of Jamal

Husseini, leader of the Arab Palestinian Party, invoking one of Hitler's famous refrains: 'When we began our activity we were six, then we became 6,000 and then sixty million.'[9] These sentiments persist today across the MENA region, most obviously in Iran and its client terrorist proxies that operate on Israel's borders, and in the Palestinian Authority whose leaders – despite their avowed commitment at Oslo to engage in exclusively peaceful relations with Israel – continue to revere their antisemitic forebear, the Grand Mufti, and all he stood for.

Arab-Muslim Plans for Today's MENA Jews: the Elephant in the Room

Even in the two Arab countries that entered formal peace agreements with Israel several decades ago, anti-Jewish rants remain as popular as ever in Arab media. Here's an op-ed by Jordanian journalist Bassam Al Yassin in 2022:

> The Jew is the epitome of evil and deceit, a professor of greed and deceit, a genius who plots against creation, a superman who spies wherever he is. The Jew is selfish, self-centred, and believes that God created no one but Him, and that the goyim – other peoples – were created to serve Him. That is why the Jew lives behind a false mask of oppression and the Holocaust.[10]

What should be done about 'the epitome of evil and deceit?' Yassin does not spell this out – he has no need. Hamas have informed us in word and deed.

Hirsh, in responding to critics of the IHRA definition of antisemitism, emphasises the often-overlooked continuities of the various historical strands of Middle Eastern antisemitism, notably both from both Nazi Germany and the Soviet Union, and the way in which they have blended with Arab nationalism and Islamism in the twenty-first century:

> In its modern form it was specifically shaped by Soviet apparatchiks as a weapon against 'rootless cosmopolitans', bourgeois Zionist nationalists' and against 'imperialism'; meaning anyone who opposed the USSR. And anti-Zionism's specific history in the Middle East is significant, with an input from Berlin during the war via the Mufti of Jerusalem, with an input from Moscow via Ba'athism and Arab nationalism, and with an input from Tehran via Hamas and Hezbollah.[11]

Wistrich, writing in the early years of the twenty-first century, summarised the threat posed by antisemitic anti-Zionism globally:

> Anti-Zionism has become the most dangerous and effective form of antisemitism in our time, through its systematic delegitimization, defamation, and demonisation of Israel. Although not a priori antisemitic, the calls to dismantle the Jewish state, whether they come from Muslims, the Left, or the radical Right, increasingly rely on an antisemitic stereotypisation of classic themes, such as the manipulative "Jewish lobby," the Jewish/Zionist "world conspiracy," and Jewish/Israeli "warmongers." One major driving force of this anti-Zionism/antiSemitism is the transformation of the Palestinian cause into a "holy war"; another source is anti-Americanism linked with fundamentalist Islamism. In the current context, classic conspiracy theories, such as the Protocols of the Elders of Zion, are enjoying a spectacular revival. The common denominator of the new anti-Zionism has been the systematic effort to criminalise Israeli and Jewish behaviour, so as to place it beyond the pale of civilised and acceptable conduct.[12]

The dark cloud of annihilation has been an ever-present feature of Israel's external environment. Commentators often seem to forget that Arab hatred of Israel long antedated the Six Day War of 1967 and the ensuing 'illegal occupation and settlements.' Blogger Mark Pickles calls it the Nazi elephant in the room: 'The primary and sustaining cause of the Arab-Israeli conflict is genocidal antisemitism; the rest is footnotes. It's as simple as that. And it's as serious as that.'[13]

Despite the short timespan of her (modern) existence and her shameful treatment at the hands of her neighbours and the global community, Israel's achievements – in agriculture, science, technology, medicine, education, housing and the arts – are extraordinary by any standards. These have been made possible by the ingenuity of her people combined with the strength of her armed forces without which the country would not have survived. Yet her position remains precarious. The world has yet to heed the distress call of the blue-and-white canary in the mine. Because of its quasi-psychotic nature, antisemitic anti-Israelism threatens the institutions, lifestyles and lives of all Arabs, Muslims and ultimately the wider world. History teaches that what starts with Jews never ends with Jews. That insight can and should lead to focused effective action to correct this injustice and bring about a rapid realignment of attitudes and policies. Unfortunately, a serious obstacle stands in the way of such a transformation – denial.

Denying the Evidence

Historical research has been helpful in documenting the evolutionary change in Arab and Muslim anti-Jewish attitudes over almost a millennium and a half. It has revealed prolonged periods of warm inter-communal relations that enabled individual Jews and Jewish communities to prosper and contribute enormously to wider society. While the historical experience of Jews at the hands of Muslim rulers cannot be compared to the antisemitic savagery unleashed by European authorities on their Jewish subjects, the record is clear: hostility to Jews was never far from the surface in most parts of the Middle East and North Africa. The culturally inherited negative stereotyping of Jews was not confined to a bigoted, easily identifiable minority but was rife throughout the region. Its destructive effect cannot be wished away by the pretence that it was non-existent.

The evidence is equally compelling that *eliminationist antisemitism,* often directly inspired by Nazi ideology,[14] has long played a significant role in the Arab-Israeli conflict by launching the anti-Zionist war, in obstructing its resolution, and in seeking its perpetuation long into the future. Those who – having studied the evidence – deny or minimise this reality are either disingenuous or naïve. The world's tendency to passivity in the face of continued politicidal and genocidal antisemitism is unconscionable and must cease. Denialism may prove to be the first and possibly most intractable obstacle to mounting an effective counterstrategy.

The controversy unleashed by Goldhagen's work highlights the manner in which the significance of antisemitism – even when it results in mass murder – is marginalised.[15] Goldhagen ruffled feathers in the German historical establishment that had, in the post-war years, constructed a narrative of specifically Nazi rather than general German culpability for the Holocaust. He was accused of unoriginality, arrogance and anti-German bias – none of which criticisms engaged with his central thesis that the German people as a whole had become infected by eliminationist antisemitism. It is alarming that so many distinguished academics were prepared to align themselves with Holocaust deniers and minimisers to resist the notion that virulent societal antisemitism was the prime driver of the mass murder of millions of Jews. A similarly self-serving narrative has been constructed around the Arab-Israeli conflict in which the role of Arab-Muslim antisemitism is minimised or erased.

Though antisemitism is resurgent everywhere, a dangerous complacency blighted the Jewish world itself – until 7 October 2023. Until that date, Jews often expressed the belief that the danger posed by antisemitism had been permanently neutralised by the very fact of Israel's existence. That was (and remains) a myth for three reasons. First, if antisemites succeed in turning Israel into a pariah state, she will be unable to maintain her qualitative military superiority over her enemies with potentially fatal consequences. Second, the Islamist antisemitic cognitive model has fostered, in Iran at least, the ambition to develop an even more deadly genocidal technology than was available to Adolph Hitler. Third, because around half of the world's Jews still live in the diaspora, they present a vulnerable target for determined antisemites everywhere.

Following the events of 2023-24, there is now less Jewish reluctance to recognise the lethality of the antisemitism that remains prevalent throughout the world and, above all, in the Middle East. All the IHRA illustrative examples of antisemitism are reflected in today's Judeophobia, anti-Zionism and anti-Israelism. The rebirth of Israel has been a game-changer in that all Jews now have a haven of last resort and an available means self-defence. But the existential threat to that refuge remains real.

Holocaust educators have been remiss in failing to emphasise this dimension of the modern landscape. The *Shoah* has become sanctified as a one-off historical Jewish tragedy that has little to do with our own times except as a warning of what might recur (or afflict other groups) in some theoretical dystopian future. Europe has a special responsibility to grasp the nettle of antisemitic anti-Israelism yet it is that continent that has contributed most to legitimise it. British journalist David Collier is scathing: 'The demonisation of Jewish people, via a colossal anti-Israel disinformation campaign, has infected every local authority and education establishment in Europe. A continent-wide antisemitic trend just seventy years after the Europeans exterminated six million Jews. Truly sickening.'[16]

Although the counterarguments to the 'antisemitic elephant' hypothesis fail the test of scrutiny (see Chapters 8 and 9), the *reductio ad absurdum* that the conflict is solely attributable to Arab or Muslim antisemitism is equally untenable; there are and always have been many other factors at work, including anti-Western sentiment, pan-Arab and local nationalisms, religious conservatism, and jealousy of Zionist and Israeli economic, technological and military successes. Equally false is the notion – rarely expressed by Jews but endlessly set up as a straw man by anti-Israel activists – that all criticism of Israel is inherently antisemitic.

The incontestable reality is that strong evidence points to antisemitism, stretching back centuries to the early years of Islamic history, as the principal (though not exclusive) driver of the Arab-Israeli conflict from its beginnings after the First World War right up to the present day. Moreover, that same evidence is compatible with the hypothesis that antisemitism remains the main (though not exclusive) barrier to the resolution of the conflict. There is no credible alternative explanation for the self-harming rejectionist behaviour of so many Arab (particularly Palestinian) leaders when faced with territorially generous and politically far-reaching offers of peace and coexistence, based on the mutuality principle, from successive Israeli governments with the full backing of international partners.

Confronting the Elephant: a Prerequisite for Peace

The purpose of this book has been to attempt to throw light on a near-invisible phenomenon: the role that antisemitism – the elephant in the room – has played in initiating and sustaining the Arab and Muslim war against Jews, Zionism and Israel. Once that key driver of the conflict is acknowledged, we can seek ways to neutralise it so that a sustainable peace can be achieved. How can we tame the elephant? Or is the attempt doomed to failure?

The nihilistic view – that antisemitism will always be with us – is unnecessarily defeatist. We may not be able to rid the world, or even just the MENA region, of this longest hatred but we can seek to mitigate its impact. Hence the title of this book: we must develop effective ways of confronting the elephant even if we are unable, as yet, to eject it from the room. A few flickering glimmers of light are cause for encouragement.

The recently signed Abraham Accords demonstrate that wholesale Arab antipathy to Israel can be overcome in propitious circumstances. Perhaps the most gratifying manifestation of this trend is the number of expressions of friendship towards Israelis from social media users throughout the MENA region including citizens of Saudi Arabia, a country that until recently was implacably opposed to Israel's existence and the epicentre of vitriolic antisemitism. For whatever reason, the Kingdom is, it seems, making exceptional if belated efforts to remove the most extreme antisemitic material from school and university textbooks. Perhaps this sudden reversal of the previous anti-Israeli and anti-Jewish bigotry has been prompted by the growing military threat from Iran but it might nevertheless presage the establishment of formal peaceful relations between the Kingdom and the Jewish state.[17]

It is hard to assess the extent to which antisemitic anti-Israelism is moderating in Arab countries, including those that have entered (or are contemplating entering) the Abraham Accords. Recent surveys of public opinion in the first two countries (Egypt and Jordan) to have made peace with Israel are discouraging: a large majority of respondents continue to express strong opposition to diplomatic recognition of the Jewish state.[18] Antisemitic attitudes remain far more prevalent in the Middle East than in any other region and appear to have barely shifted over recent decades. Two events in 2022 were particularly sobering: the hostile behaviour of Arab football fans towards Israelis attending World Cup in Qatar (including the harassment of an Israeli television journalist live on air)[19] and the UN's compliance with the disgraceful Palestinian demand that Israel's Independence Day be annually commemorated as a *Nakba* (disaster).[20]

No magic bullet exists that can pierce the thick hide of the inveterate antisemite. Nor has an antidote been found for the negative cognitive MENA model of Jews Zionism and Israel. That does not relieve us of the responsibility to seek a remedy, however long-delayed its discovery might be. To address the threat posed by this specific version of antisemitism, the first step is to recognise and document it with the aid of the IHRA definition. Also needed is a dispassionate scholarly analysis of its origins, characteristics and threats, as that knowledge will arm us with the necessary information to mount a more effective counterattack.[21] That confrontation, the purpose of which must be to modify the contemporary antisemitic model of Jews, will require the involvement of all the relevant actors – Jews, Israelis, Arabs and the international community. Because the newest variant

9. Rabin, Clinton Arafat sign Oslo Accord on White House lawn 1993. Source: US Federal Government. Public Papers of the Presidents of the United States William J. Clinton: 1993, Book II, Photographic Portfolio

10. Signing of Abraham Accords 2020. Source: Trump White House Archives (public domain)

of antisemitism is comparable to the threat of a pandemic-inducing microbe, it merits an equivalent degree of global attention.

In the previous chapter, I outlined some elements of a strategy for countering the threat. The ultimate *vision* is of a world liberated from the tyranny of antisemitic anti-Zionism and anti-Israelism. The *objectives* arising from that vision include: to investigate the origins and nature of antisemitic anti-Zionism and anti-Israelism; to increase awareness of antisemitism in the conflict by using the IHRA definition as a tool for monitoring, research, accountability and education; to expose the wider global threat posed by antisemitic anti-Zionism and anti-Israelism; to boost support for Israel's basic rights through joint diaspora-Israeli and global initiatives; and to *change the culturally shared cognitive model of Jews and Israelis in the MENA region and worldwide.*

Out of this crowded and ambitious agenda, where to start? Erasing or modifying the underpinning anti-Jewish prejudice must be the goal but that may prove a bridge too far in most of our lifetimes – not because it is impossible (as the denazification programme in Germany demonstrated) but because of the vested interests of UN and other bodies as well as the high global prevalence of antisemitism. The prevailing Arab-Muslim perception of Jews and Israel will prove to be a stubborn one as it has been consciously or unconsciously integrated into the worldview of Israel's enemies as well as that of some of her friends, including a growing minority of Jews and Israelis. Given the longevity of antisemitic Judeophobia, anti-Zionism and anti-Israelism in the MENA region, and its steady colonisation of large sections of international public opinion, it would be naïve to imagine that this psycho-cultural disturbance can be easily reversed. Modest progress may be within reach if we can identify some low hanging fruit.

Three intermediate objectives may be achievable over the short to medium term:

- to launch a media campaign to raise public awareness of the toxic role of antisemitism in the current discourse around the Arab-Israeli conflict and in the international community;
- to publicise the need for justice for the Jewish refugees, the victims of the Jewish *Nakba*, in parallel with a fair settlement for the Palestinian refugees;
- to establish a World Coalition for Israel – a global network of pro-Israel organisations – to take forward a comprehensive strategy designed to roll back the tide of antisemitic anti-Zionism and anti-Israelism in the twenty-first century (see Appendix).

The elephant of antisemitism will not take kindly to attempts to confront it, nor will it budge of its own accord from its commanding position in the control centre of the Arab-Israeli conflict. We will all have to play our part in helping it on its way.

Notes

1   I. Marcus, 'Teaching Terror to Tots: A Study of *Waed, Fatah*'s Magazine for Children ages 6-15', Palestinian Media Watch, 12 December 2022. https://palwatch.org/Storage/Special-Reports/Teaching-Terror-to-Tots-digital.pdf (Last accessed 13 June 2024).
2   I. Marcus, 'How the Palestinian Authority Turns Good People Into Terrorists', Abraham Society (London, UK). Zoom Webinar, 30 December 2022. https://us02web.zoom.us/rec/play/_JQSxFXw_Rp_t1m-HUaVU s8bp9_5F9jhHnwTxPDTcGL7_R4ynIes_anVbcj3kMEfFJFsAxavBkLRKc Ha.c4Zaj7syMJZ_5BE4?continueMode=true&_x_zm_rtaid=Un18ySELS9 2RUzQLgDStRA.1672422777170.8cca8040c3255304757cc1dad9fb2385&_ x_zm_rhtaid=636 (Last accessed 13 June 2024).

3   D. Hirsh, H. Miller, 'Durban Anti-Zionism: Its Sources, Its Impact, and Its Relation to Older Anti-Jewish Ideologies', *Journal of Contemporary Antisemitism*, 5,1, (Spring 2022). https://static1.squarespace.com/static/5fd29a1f51ae5c1b3ea73a07/t/6261af23326b464ded57b935/1650568995923/02_JCA_5-1_Durban+preprint.pdf (Last accessed 13 June 2024), p.24.

4   R. Shepherd, *A State Beyond the Pale*. (London: Orion Books, 2009), p.208.

5   L. Julius, *Uprooted* (London: Vallentine Mitchell, 2018).

6   M. Gilbert, *In Ishmael's House: A History of Jews in Muslim Lands* (Toronto: Yale University Press, 2011).

7   Colin Shindler, 'Jews pledged their love to Stalin's Russia – and he slaughtered them', *Jewish Chronicle*, 12 August 2022 https://www.thejc.com/lets-talk/all/jews-pledged-their-love-to-stalin%27s-russia-and-he-slaughtered-them-5eiMFHFsdYjkBdqs4yfHIR (Last accessed 13 June 2024.

8   E. Karsh, *Palestine Betrayed* (New Haven: Yale University Press, 2011), p. 17.

9   Ibid, p.30.

10 Elder of Ziyon, 'Nazi-level Jew-hate in Jordanian news site op-ed', 30 August 2022. https://elderofziyon.blogspot.com/2022/08/nazi-level-jew-hate-in-jordanian-news.html (Last accessed 13 June 2024).

11 D. Hirsh, 'The Jerusalem Declaration defines the 'community of the good'', *Jewish Chronicle*, 1 April 2021. https://www.thejc.com/comment/opinion/the-jerusalem-declaration-defines-the-community-of-the-good-not-antisemitism-1.513816?fbclid=IwAR3VANTUqc_9YkMotSAEa-AV2XDTJYVC2jCznhE5EoZjE0FFfORUKkIKucY (Last accessed 13 June 2024).

12 R. Wistrich, 'Anti-Zionism and Anti-Semitism', *Jewish Political Studies Review*, 16, 3-4

13 M. Pickles, 'The Arab-Israeli Conflict Made Simple', 1 August 2019. https://markpickles.wordpress.com/2019/08/01/the-arab-israeli-conflict-made-simple/ (Last accessed 13 June 2024).

14 M. Küntzel, 'The 1948 Arab War Against Israel: an Aftershock of World War II?', *Fathom*, June 2023. https://fathomjournal.org/the-1948-arab-war-against-israel-an-aftershock-of-world-war-ii/ (Last accessed 13 June 2024).

15 A. Barkai, 'German Historians Versus Goldhagen', *Yad-Vashem Studies*, 26, 1998, pp. 295-328. https://www.yadvashem.org/articles/academic/german-historians-versus-goldhagen.html (Last accessed 13 June 2024).

16 Tweet from David Collier, @mishtal, 29 September 2019. https://twitter.com/mishtal/status/1045921897681178625 (Last accessed 13 June 2024).

17 Ariel Ben Solomon, 'Saudi social-media influencer: "Hope our nation will sign a peace treaty with Israel"', *Jewish News Syndicate*, 11 August 2022.

https://www.jns.org/saudi-social-media-influencer-hope-our-nation-will-sign-a-peace-treaty-with-israel/ (Last accessed 13 June 2024).

18 Doha Institute for Graduate Studies, The 2022 Arab Opinion Index. Qatar, Doha Institute, 2023. https://www.dohainstitute.org/en/Lists/ACRPS-PDFDocumentLibrary/the-2022-arab-opinion-index-in-brief.pdf (Last accessed 13 June 2024).

19 Maya Gebeily, 'Arabs shun Israeli media at Qatar World Cup, cooling hopes of a thaw', *Reuters*, 21 November 2022. https://www.reuters.com/world/middle-east/arabs-shun-israeli-media-qatar-world-cup-dashing-hopes-warming-2022-11-21/ (Last accessed 13 June 2024).

20 Adi Schwartz, 'Palestinians help Israel when they focus on "Nakba Day"', *Israel Hayom*, 5 December 2022. https://www.israelhayom.com/opinions/palestinians-help-israel-when-they-focus-on-nakba-day/ (Last accessed 13 June 2024).

21 Rich, D., *Everyday Hate: How antisemitism is built into our world – and how you can change it* (London: Biteback Publishing, 2023).

Postscript

I did not want to write this book. Having long viewed the Arab-Israeli conflict as essentially a territorial dispute between two peoples, I was wedded to the comforting belief in its resolvability through territorial compromise. With the passage of time and the acquisition of knowledge, I have come to realise that my optimism was misplaced. For the evidence indicates that the conflict primarily arises not from contested territorial claims, as so many commentators assert, but from a much darker source. I was forced to confront that source as a result of searing personal experience that compelled me to re-evaluate my own prior beliefs about the nature of the conflict, its causes and its prospects for resolution.

In the course of my academic career in Scotland, I found myself on the receiving end of steadily intensifying broadsides from colleagues whenever the subject of Israel was raised. The critics were anxious to learn my views about specific Israeli policies – mainly in relation to settlements and the disputed territories – with which they disagreed. That caused me little difficulty as I disagreed with many of them myself. As a card-carrying member of the dovish Israeli *Peace Now* movement (that I had joined in the 1980s during one of my spells of residence in the country), I was a strong if starry-eyed advocate of withdrawal from most of the remaining territories that Israel had occupied in the course of a series of defensive wars. Naturally I was delighted when Israel withdrew from southern Lebanon in 2000 and Gaza in 2005. Neither of these courageous unilateral moves – that occurred despite the crushing disappointment of the Oslo Accords a few years earlier – led to anything resembling peace. (Fast forward two decades: Lebanon bristles with 150,000 Iranian-supplied Hezbollah missiles aimed at Israeli cities while Hamas-ruled Gaza, long a hotbed of jihadist terrorism from which thousands of rockets were fired at Israeli civilians, became the launching pad for the largest-scale slaughter of Jews on a single day since the Holocaust. Worse, in neither case have Israel's adversaries abandoned their politicidal and genocidal goals).

To return to my campus tale of woe. None of my arguments seemed to impress of my 'progressive' academic colleagues who, by the early twenty-first century, felt emboldened to challenge me on Israel's right to exist as a Jewish state. That troubled me more than their earlier 'criticisms' for obvious reasons. Before long, they threw caution to the winds and subjected me to brazen antisemitic abuse that included the deicide charge. By now, I was apprehensive. One phrase that came to mind was the slippery slope but I became preoccupied with another metaphor: the chicken and the egg. Did their antisemitism arise from their distaste for Israeli behaviour or *vice versa*?

It took a while – and the help of a handful of seasoned observers of the Middle East whose analyses I studied over many years – for the penny to drop. All the smoke and mirrors of the repeated loop of failed negotiations concealed an unpalatable truth: the war would continue – with the approval and often collusion of the international community – unless the Jewish state disappeared. I could find no logical explanation for that apocalyptic and unrealisable demand bar one: those who hate Israel hate Jews and *vice versa*. Suddenly I solved the chicken and egg puzzle. Hatred is hatred, whether of individual Jews or of the Jewish state. That insight was just as applicable to the Victorian cloisters of my Scottish university as to the Middle East. The world's oldest hatred had fixated on a new target. For the entire duration of the Arab-Israeli conflict, antisemites had occupied centre stage and had no intention of vacating their privileged spot. Their 'invisible' presence – hidden in plain sight – constituted the main obstacle to peace between Arabs and Israelis.

How had I missed it? The honest answer is ignorance, combined perhaps with a degree of emotional resistance to a phenomenon that seemed improbable. Like many others, I had always believed that sympathy for the Palestinians was an understandable reaction to a humanitarian tragedy; it had not occurred to me that other motivations might be in the frame. Once I began to study the evidence and to listen to what many Arabs, Iranians and (especially) Palestinians and their supporters were actually saying (and not saying), the elephant in the room became visible.

I should have realised that something was amiss when the slaughter of thousands of Palestinian civilians in Lebanon's civil war in the 1980s was met with barely a murmur of protest (unless Israelis could somehow be blamed), and my suspicions might have been vindicated when similar apathy greeted the expulsion of at least a quarter of a million Palestinians from Kuwait at the end of the first Gulf War in 1991 and the killing of countless more during Syria's brutal repression of its own people a couple of decades later.

But it was not until the Second 'Intifada' – an Arabic word meaning uprising or rebellion (a gross misnomer for the brutal terrorist campaign unleashed on Israelis by PLO chief Yasser Arafat in 2000) – that I discovered how deeply embedded antisemitism had become within Arab culture. I had embarked on a lengthy correspondence with a Palestinian colleague at Birzeit university in Ramallah. We were seeking common ground in an attempt to make sense of the near-daily carnage on both sides when I was taken aback by this question: 'Why do Jews only help other Jews?' I asked what she meant. This was her reply: 'Jewish scripture says that if a Jew sees another Jew lying in a ditch he must help his fellow but if he sees a non-Jew in a ditch he must keep walking.' When I reacted with indignation at this crude antisemitism, she replied, 'Well that's what we are all told about Jews.'

That sentence was my wake-up call. I had naively sought to cling to the assumption that the Palestinians blamed Israelis – *qua* Israelis rather than Jews – for their plight and that the militant pro-Palestinianism of the MENA countries primarily reflected a natural concern for the suffering of the Palestinian people, most of whom were fellow Muslims after all. That theory was terminally punctured by the utter indifference of most Muslim-majority states towards the recent revelations of the Chinese treatment of the Muslim Uighur minority.

As for the vast army of 'pro-Palestinians' in the rest of the world, they have long been equally clear that they have little genuine interest in the welfare of the Palestinians or in exploring possible paths to peace for one reason: their 'Palestinianism' is almost always predicated on their hatred of Israel. Tens of thousands of 'pro-Palestinians' poured onto the streets of world capitals in solidarity with the Hamas perpetrators of the October 2023 pogrom in southern Israel before any significant Israeli military response had even begun.

There is a twisted logic to the behaviour of these Israel-haters who hide behind the mask of pro-Palestinian activism. What these faux-idealists desire above all is to delegitimise and ultimately destroy a state whose mere existence is an affront to all they hold dear and to restore the *status quo ante* in which the despised 'Zionists' will return to their deserved fate of eternal wandering, vulnerability and powerlessness.

The Jewish people, whether in Israel or the diaspora, naturally decline to follow this script, or to contemplate joining their ancient forebears on the rock of Masada by committing mass suicide. Until the world wakes up to this reality, the nightmare of misery and death will continue – for Israelis and Jews, Arabs and Muslims – and risks ultimately engulfing us all.

Appendix

Towards a World Coalition for Israel (WCI) to Counter Antisemitic Anti-Israelism

Provisional List of Invitees

Abraham Global Peace Initiative
Academic Engagement Network
AMCHA Initiative
American Jewish Committee
American Jewish Congress
American-Israel Public Affairs Committee
Anglo-Israel Association
Anti-Defamation League
Antisemitism Policy Trust
Australian Friends of Israel
Australia Israel and Jewish Affairs Council
Begin-Sadat Center for Strategic Studies
Belgian Friends of Israel
BICOM: British Israel Communications and Research Centre
Board of Deputies of British Jews
Bridge Christian Fellowship
CAMERA: Committee for Accuracy in Middle East Reporting and Analysis
Campaign Against Antisemitism
Canary Mission
Centre for Israel and Jewish Affairs
Christian Friends of Israel
Christians United for Israel
COFIS – Confederation of Friends of Israel in Scotland
Combat Antisemitism Movement
Community Security Trust
Conservative Friends of Israel
Endowment for Middle East Truth (EMET)
European Friends of Israel
European Jewish Association

European Jewish Congress
Europe Israel Public Affairs
European Leadership Network
Fathom (online journal)
Fighting Online Antisemitism
Foundation to Combat Antisemitism
Friends of Israel (India)
Friends of Israel Initiative
Glasgow Friends of Israel
Hadassah, Women's Zionist Organization of America, Inc.
Hague Initiative for International Cooperation (thinc.)
Harif: Association of Jews from the MENA
Hasbara Fellowships
Hertfordshire friends of Israel
Holocaust Educational Trust
Honest Reporting
Institute for Black Solidarity with Israel
Institute for the Study of Global Antisemitism and Policy
International Holocaust Remembrance Alliance
International Legal Forum
Ireland Israel Alliance
Israel Academia Monitor
Israel Advocacy Movement
Israeli-American Council
Israel Britain Alliance
Israel on Campus Coalition
Israel Defence and Security Forum
Israel Democracy Institute
Israel Forever Foundation
Israel War Room
Jerusalem Center for Public Affairs
Jewish Institute for Liberal Values
Jewish Institute for National Security of America (JINSA)
Jewish Medical Association
Jewish on Campus
Jewish Virtual Library
Jimena: Jews Indigenous to the Middle East and North Africa
Labour Friends of Israel
Lawfare Project
Liberal Democrat Friends of Israel
London Centre for the Study of Contemporary Antisemitism

Louis D. Brandeis Center
Med Israel for Fred (MIFF) – With Israel for peace (Norway)
Middle East Forum
Middle East Media Research Institute
Middle East Truth
Muslims Against Antisemitism
New Zealand Friends of Israel
National Jewish Assembly (UK)
NGO Monitor
North East Friends of Israel
North London Friends of Israel
Northern Ireland Friends of Israel
North West Friends of Israel
Orthodox Union
Palestinian Media Watch
Peres Center for Peace and Innovation
Philos Project
Pinsker Centre
Reut Group
Scholars for Peace in the Middle East
Shalom Hartman Institute
Simon Wiesenthal Center
South African Friends of Israel
South African Zionist Federation
StandWithUs
Stop Antisemitism
Students Supporting Israel
Sussex Friends of Israel
Tel Aviv Institute
UK Lawyers for Israel
United Nations Watch
United With Israel
We Believe in Israel
Wiener Holocaust Library
World Jewish Congress
World Values Network
Yorkshire Friends of Israel
Zioness (US)
Zionist Federation of Great Britain and Ireland
Zionist Organization of America

Bibliography

Baddiel D, *Jews Don't Count.* (London: TLS Books, 2021).

Blois M, Tucker A, *Israel on Trial: How International Law is Being Misused to Delegitimize the State of Israel* (The Netherlands: thinc.,2018).

Dershowitz A, *The Case for Israel* (Hoboken: John Wiley & Sons, 2003), p.14.

Elder of Ziyon, *Protocols: Exposing Modern Antisemitism* (USA: EoZ Press, 2022).

Gilbert M, *In Ishmael's House: A History of Jews in Muslim Lands* (Toronto: Yale University Press, 2011).

Goldhagen D, *Hitler's Willing Executioners* (London: Abacus, 1997).

Gordis D, *Israel: A Concise History of a Nation Reborn* (New York: HarperCollins, 2016).

Hirsh D, *The Rebirth of Antisemitism in the 21st Century* (Abingdon: Routledge/LCSCA 2024)

Horn D, *People Love Dead Jews* (New York: WW Norton & C0, 2021).

Josephus, *The Jewish War* (London: Penguin Books, 2003).

Julius A, *Trials of the Diaspora* (Oxford: Oxford University Press, 2010).

Julius L, *Uprooted* (London: Vallentine Mitchell, 2018).

Kahneman D, *Thinking, Fast and Slow (New York:* Farrar, Straus and Giroux, 2013**).**

Karsh E, *Palestine Betrayed* (New Haven: Yale University Press, 2011).

Küntzel M, *Jihad and Jew Hatred: Islamism, Nazism and the Roots of 9/11* (Candor NY: Telos Press, 2007).

Küntzel M, *Nazis, Islamic Antisemitism and the Middle East* (Abingdon: Routledge, 2024).

Lacquer W, Rubin B, *The Israel-Arab Reader: A Documentary History of the Middle East Conflict* (New York: Penguin Books, 2008).

Laqueur W, *The Changing Face of Antisemitism.* (New York: Oxford University Press, 2006)

Lewis B, *Semites and Anti-Semites: An Inquiry into Conflict and Prejudice* (New York: WW Norton & Company, 1999).

Lipstadt D, *Antisemitism Here and Now* (London, Scribe Publications, 2019).

Litvak M, Webman E, *From Empathy to Denial: Arab Responses to the Holocaust* (London, Hurst and Company, 2009).

Morris B, *1948. A History of the First Arab-Israeli War* (New Haven and London: Yale University Press, 2008.

Nelson C, *Israel Denial* (Bloomington: Indiana University Press, 2019).

Rich D, *The Left's Jewish Problem* (London: Biteback Publishing, 2018).

Rich D, *Everyday Hate: How antisemitism is built into our world – and how you can change it* (London: Biteback Publishing, 2023).

Ross D, *The Missing Peace: The Inside Story of the Fight for Middle East Peace* (New York: Farrar, Straus and Giroux, 2005).

Schneer J, *The Balfour Declaration: The Origins of the Arab-Israeli Conflict* (London: Bloomsbury, 2010).

Schwartz A, Wilf E, *'The War of Return: How Western Indulgence of the Palestinian Dream has Obstructed the Path to Peace* (New York: All Points Books, 2020).

Shapira A, *Israel: A History* (London: Weidenfeld & Nicolson, 2015).

Shepherd R, *A State Beyond the Pale.* (London: Orion Books, 2009).

Simons J, *Israelophobia: The Newest Version of the Oldest Hatred and What To Do About It* (London: Constable, 2023).

Stellman H, *What Is AntiZionism? (and is it Antisemitic?). A Short Handbook for Activists and Analysts* (Soesterberg: Aspekt Publishers, 2019).

Turnberg L, *Beyond the Balfour Declaration* (London: Biteback Publishing Ltd, 2017).

Wistrich R, *Antisemitism: The Longest Hatred* (New York: Pantheon Books, 1991).

Yemini B-D, *Industry of Lies: Media, Academia, and the Israeli-Arab Conflict* (New York: Institute for the Global Study of Antisemitism and Policy, 2017).

Index